Small Group Communication: A Functional Approach

Michael Burgoon
Judee K. Heston
James McCroskey

West Virginia University

Holt, Rinehart and Winston, Inc.

New York   Chicago   San Francisco   Atlanta   Dallas
Montreal   Toronto   London   Sydney

DEDICATED TO
the late Dr. Verling "Pete" Troldahl.
Thanks.

Acknowledgments

To Dr. Cal Hylton and Dr. William B. Lashbrook, who began as our friends and became our critics on this text. To Paul Schmitt, who began as our editor and became our friend. To Barbara Chapman, Mary Jane Colen, and Carole Pilkington, who began as our secretaries and became overworked. To Morgantown, West Virginia, for providing no distractions from our work. And, finally, to the demise of the notion of process: we now clearly understand the concept of beginning and end.

Copyright © 1974 by Holt, Rinehart and Winston, Inc.
All rights reserved
Library of Congress Cataloging in Publication Data
Burgoon, Michael
Small group communication: a functional approach

   1. Small group. 2. Communication—social aspects. 3. Communication—
   psychological aspects.
I. Heston, Judee K., joint author
II. McCroskey, James C., joint author
III. Title

HM133.B84 1974 301.18'5 74–686
ISBN: 0-03-011061-0
Printed in the United States of America

   90 038 09876543

Preface

This book represents our attempts to create a textbook that can be useful to teachers who want to integrate behavioral science findings in persuasion, conflict resolution, decision making, leadership, and a number of other communication areas into a course in small group communication. Admittedly, the book draws on areas that have not been considered unique to communication in the small group. It is our feeling that one cannot understand small group communication without understanding the broader process of human communication. We have therefore included such materials as general communication models, information on creation of messages, and other findings that affect communication regardless of the setting. Some subjects discussed are as applicable to the dyadic situation or public speaking situation as they are to the small group. Other material discussed is unique to small group communication.

Some writers in small group communication hold assumptions that do not fit our biases or conform to our experience. We do not believe that all small groups function to produce a "group product," cooperate for the good of the whole, or perform in a variety of ways designed to produce a product superior to efforts of individuals. However, most texts on small groups assume that these are the only ways to regard small group communication. It has been our experience that members often come to the small group setting with no intent other than to persuade other group members to think or behave in a prescribed manner; perhaps this is not the way people *should* come to small groups, but it is the way they *do* behave. This approach denies many of the advantages we discuss in Chapter 1 that can accrue to the small group. Therefore, we discuss in detail the general process of persuasion and attempt to relate it to small group communication. Some would argue that the small group is more than just a series of prepared oral messages. While we do not disagree with that position, we do believe the small group is a powerful place to influence, and persuasion deserves more attention than it has been given in small group literature.

We also give general overviews of functions of small groups and describe how they operate. The chapter on small group communication as therapy describes a currently popular type of small group. Frankly, we do not know what the future of therapy groups will be; they have been used and abused frequently and deserve discussion. The chapter will not tell anyone how to run an encounter session nor will it provide much scholarly data about the effects of therapeutic groups. Part of the chapter is personal testimony which we hope the student will enjoy reading. We also hope the student will have some appreciation of the goals of an encounter group even if he does not completely understand its operation or effects. Other chapters are more prescriptive in their suggestions for successful attainment of small group functions.

Conflict resolution and decision making are other important functions of small group communication that are discussed. We attempt to relate the literature from a variety of disciplines in order to come up with models of conflict resolution that deserve testing in the small group situation. Decision making is treated as the exclusive function of small group communication in some books, and we believe that it is an area deserving continued attention. The chapters on decision making present examples of procedures for arriving at decisions and explain some of the variables that lead to good and bad decisions. Frequently, the establishment and maintenance of social relations is considered out of the scholarly domain of writers in speech communication. We obviously believe that social relations not only affect small group communication but improved relations can be a desired output resulting from communication.

We provide an appendix on small group interaction instruments that allows the student to observe communication in a systematic way. It is our hope that the instructor will have the students observe ongoing discourse using these instruments so that the class can produce prescriptive statements about the kinds of interaction that lead to persuasion, conflict resolution, social gratification, and good decision making. We think that a discussion of the appendix and training in the use of the instruments is a good way to begin a course. It is our hope that the interaction measures will be used in and out of class to determine effective communication.

We intended to produce neither a research monograph nor a performance manual. Our conclusions are in large part based on empirical findings, but we are not afraid to speculate or draw conclusions based upon our experience as communicators and teachers. Our hope is that we clearly identify which is which. Much is to be gained by a concern for group discussion as a performance activity and small group communication as an area with substantial theory and research accumulated. A need to bring both perspectives together in a single text motivated this undertaking.

It is our belief that better discussion for a variety of purposes can result from understanding and applying theory and research from communication literature. Moreover, better theory can develop from observation of and participation in communication. To that end, we believe this book serves several audiences.

It is probably fitting that such a text was written by a "small group." Hopefully, it reflects the "assembly effects" that accrue to a group without the weaknesses that sometimes result. To the extent that it does or doesn't we, as a group, are willing to take all praise and/or blame.

Michael Burgoon
Judee K. Heston
James C. McCroskey

Morgantown, West Virginia

Contents

INTRODUCTORY COMMENTS

Someone once said that a camel is a horse designed by a committee. They were probably trying to make the point that small group experiences often end unsatisfactorily. In this chapter, we give you our assumptions about small groups and suggest that we can avoid creating "camels." We believe that small group communication pervades our daily lives. We also believe that the small group is a unique setting in which to study communication. This introductory chapter identifies some characteristics and functions of small group communication. It presents our bias that systematic study of communication in small groups can make us more effective in relating to people and achieving a variety of desired outcomes.

The Small Group as a Unique Communication Situation

"NONE OF US is as smart as all of us." This notion underlies our faith in the ability of small groups to deal with problems. We generally believe that two heads are better than one, so several heads must be best of all. Not only do we rely on groups to solve problems, groups intrude on every aspect of our existence. We begin life in the most primary and potent of groups — the family. Within the family group our personality is shaped, our intellectual and emotional development is influenced, and our cultural awareness is initiated. When we are first nudged out of the security of the family circle, we are confronted with more groups in the form of schools: nursery schools, church schools, kindergarten. Even our friendships develop in groups, with smaller subgroups developing closer relationships. Beyond the school years, our social and business relationships continue to operate frequently in groups. Just think of all the group memberships the typical college student holds in committees, clubs, dormitory houses or fraternities, classes, work groups, church organizations, political causes, family and friendship networks. Our lives are even governed by groups that we are not members of: decision-making bodies such as the legislature and board of regents, clubs and organizations whose recognition and acceptance we seek, and groups that establish society's norms and values. It is clear that we can never escape the impact of groups on the quality of our day-to-day living. It makes sense, then, for us to study how groups operate and how they affect us so that we can improve those to which we belong and reduce the power of those that we do not want to influence us. By moving our subconscious awareness of groups into consciousness, we can increase control of our own role within the spheres of groups that affect us. Communication provides one key to control. The better we understand our own and others' methods of communication, the better we can maintain our own independence and benefit those with whom we associate in groups.

A DEFINITION OF THE SMALL GROUP

Before analyzing the communication that takes place, we need a common understanding of what constitutes a small group. As the definition is explained, it will become clear why we are confining ourselves to *small* groups. One definition of small groups that combines elements of several other definitions is "the face-to-face interaction of two or more persons in such a way that members are able to recall the characteristics of the other members accurately."

Let us look at this definition in more detail. The first key term is *face-to-face*. This means that people must be in proximity to be considered a small group. Republicans in two separate cities would be members of the same large group but not the same small group. The second key term is *interaction*. To be a small group, the members must communicate with one another. Three people standing face to face waiting for a bus would not be a group; if the same three individuals began complaining to each other about the lateness of the bus, they would have the beginnings of a small group. The stipulation of interaction limits this book to small groups because spontaneous, oral communication is integral to small groups. The third key phrase is *two or more persons,* which indicate simply that two people may constitute a group and that there is supposedly no upper limit. However, as groups become excessively large, interaction is reduced and the group eventually fails to meet the criterion that all members interact. For practical purposes, a small group is generally defined as two to twenty-five people. The final key phrase is that *members are able to recall the characteristics of the other members accurately.* This signifies that the members relate to one another in such a way that they become aware of the existence of a group and their identification with it. If the relationships are significant enough to draw the attention of the members, a group may be said to exist. Take, for example, the people waiting for the bus. If they talk long enough to recall the conversation later and remember the other persons accurately, we could legitimately call them a group. If, on succeeding days, they continue to interact while waiting for the bus, we would have further confirmation of the existence of a group.

There are some additional characteristics of small groups that provide further definition of the concept and serve to distinguish the small group as a unique communication environment.

THE UNIQUENESS OF SMALL GROUPS

The first characteristic of the small group that makes it a unique communication context is *frequent interaction*. This distinguishes the small group from a public-speaking situation where usually one person is speaking to an audience that has little opportunity to interact. Similarly, it differentiates the small group from a classroom or work group where communication is restricted and infrequent. If a teacher allows her students to talk (or cannot keep them quiet), then a classroom can also be considered a small group. The key factor is whether or not a high degree of interaction occurs.

A second unique characteristic of small groups is the development of a *group personality*. The group takes on an identity of its own. It can be viewed as a singular, separate entity rather than a conglomeration of the various personalities of its members. Just as a person can be extroverted and optimistic, so can a group become outgoing and optimistic in its view. Like the authoritarian person who is highly conventional, dogmatic, and rigid, a group may be traditional, inflexible, and authority-oriented. The point here is that groups develop their own modes of behavior and orientations just as individuals do.

A third characteristic of small groups is the establishment of *group norms*. Groups develop their own value systems and their own normative behavior. An excellent example comes from a description of a typical street gang: "The Cobras" place a high value on toughness and trouble. Members must be skilled in fighting, insulting, storytelling, "rapping," and most of all hustling (conning, selling dope, stealing). Prestige is gained by being in reform school or having connections with pushers or persons with influence on the gang. The norm for members is to spend most of their time "hanging on the set," gambling, flying pigeons, and drinking wine until some kind of "action" presents itself. It is also normative to do poorly in school, since academic success is irrelevant to group status. All of these behaviors and attitudes are defined and maintained by the group. Such group norms, to a large extent, become individual norms. That is, individuals want to be like the group and so behave in that manner.

Intricately related to group norms is a fourth characteristic: *coping behavior.* Groups develop their own patterns for coping with outside threats and maintaining their existence. In the case of street gangs, fighting, and carving out actual territories are ways of warding off intrusions by outsiders. A formal structure with a president, vice president, prime minister, and war lord exists to solidify the group and direct its dealings with nonmembers. These behaviors, which are designed to preserve the group and reduce the incursion of outside influences, are examples of coping behavior. Group habits also fit into this category. For instance, a group that is in the habit of meeting for only an hour may be coping with outside demands for the members' time or, in cases of groups in high-stress situations, they may be coping with their psychological and physiological limitations caused by anxiety. In either case, longer meetings might lower attendance or increase conflict, which would threaten the group's cohesion. Another aspect of coping behavior is the development of group language. Groups generally develop their own unique jargon and language patterns. Words like "paradigm," "hypothetical construct," and "teleological system" might be heard from a group of social scientists but would be unlikely at a cocktail party of artists. Similarly, "jive," "dude," "lame," and "bust" would be common vocabulary among a group of young blacks, but not the suburban PTA. Different interaction patterns also characterize different groups. One group may be prone to long, involved comments by its members, while another may tend toward short, concise, businesslike statements. Whatever the pattern, the language that develops evolves out of the unique needs and nature of the group and serves to solidify its identity. It is a partial means of coping with the rest of the world.

A fifth distinguishing characteristic of small groups is *role differentiation.* Within a group, individuals tend to specialize and perform certain roles that are interlocking. These roles include those that are necessary for the completion of a task, such as supplying information, asking for opinions, and giving the group direction, and those that are necessary to maintain a satisfactory social and emotional atmosphere, such as encouraging others, creating harmony, and controlling the flow of communication. Different situations dictate which roles are needed. Usually, each person adopts many roles; in fact, each member could conceivably perform all of them. But generally, different people emphasize different roles or clusters of roles: some people are more concerned with getting the job done, while others are more concerned with personal relationships. Such role differentiations also take the form of a division of labor. By specialization on the part of each member, groups are able to tackle problems more efficiently. This division of responsibilities is a special advantage of groups.

A sixth unique characteristic of the small group is *interdependent goals*. Some members have certain goals that overlap with those of the other members. These shared goals become the group's goals and members are expected to subordinate their personal goals to those of the group. For example, suppose you have been assigned to solve a problem in a group in chemistry class. The mutual goals of your group members would be to solve the problem assigned and earn a good grade. To achieve these goals, you might have to suppress your personal desire for separate recognition or superiority over the rest of the group. Because each person's success at achieving the primary goals is dependent on the rest of the group, the goals are interdependent. To cite another example, each member of an encounter group facilitates the common goal of increasing self-awareness. Again, individual achievement of the goal is largely dependent on the rest of the group. Because group members share the same goals, they frequently find themselves in positions of common fate: what is rewarding for one is rewarding for all, and vice versa. This interdependency of individuals influences communication in groups because much of the content centers on these goals or on sustaining satisfactory interpersonal relations to secure them.

The final unique characteristic of small groups is something called the *assembly effect bonus*. This refers to extra productivity that is caused specifically by the nature of groups. A more concise definition of an assembly effect bonus is productivity in excess of the combined product of the same individuals working independently. It is analogous to the extra productivity that results from using an assembly line in a plant rather than having each person do the whole job alone. It is a bonus because the total output of the individual efforts would not equal that of the same people working as a group. The extra productivity results from the division of labor and coordination of effort that takes place in a group. It is also due to the fact that the contribution of one member triggers new ideas and recall of information in the minds of other members. Such ideas and information might not have been spontaneously generated by each person working alone. For example, if a single individual could produce an average of five creative solutions to a problem, a collection of five such individuals working independently would produce an average of twenty-five solutions. By contrast, the same five individuals working in a small group might produce thirty-five solutions. The extra ten solutions produced by the group would be the assembly effect bonus.

The seven characteristics discussed above distinguish the small

group from other communication situations. These unique characteristics may serve both as facilitators and inhibitors of communication
in the small group.

A FUNCTIONAL APPROACH TO SMALL
GROUP COMMUNICATION

Small group communication can be viewed from several perspectives. We have chosen a functional approach. The notion of
"function" should be familiar. The function of a typewriter is typing;
the functions of a refrigerator are storage and cooling; the functions
of a poker game are entertainment, mental stimulation, and, hopefully,
financial gain. In the same way, the functions of small groups are the
purposes they serve. A functional approach to small groups examines
the functions groups serve and how they achieve them. Thus, a group's
functions are its desired outcomes. For example, the desired outcome
or function of a bridge club is primarily social gratification; the major
function of a corporate board of directors is to make decisions. Sometimes a group may have a single function. More often, however,
groups are multifunctional. For example, the board of directors may
also have the function of persuasion, both persuading its own disagreeing members to conform to the majority position and persuading
the rest of the corporation to accept its decision. The board may also
function to satisfy social desires or to resolve conflicts. While groups
are generally multifunctional, one overriding purpose usually domi-
nates. In fact, some of the functions groups fulfill may be unintended
and unnoticed. When the functions of groups are discussed in more
detail in later chapters, this should be kept in mind.

Not all of the outcomes of groups are desirable. When the outcome
of a group is unproductive or counterproductive, it is commonly
labeled as dysfunctional. Thus, if a group produces conflict rather than
conflict resolution, conflict is a dysfunction. Throughout this book,
references will be made to individual behaviors and group outcomes
that are dysfunctional. Whenever small group communication produces negative results, it may be regarded as dysfunctional.

In assessing whether communication is functional one should consider how the elements or people in the small group process are
linked or related to one another.

Two basic types of links exist: control links and feedback links. A
control link exists if one element directly influences the status of another element. A *feedback link* exists if one element transmits information to another about its current state. A good analogy is the
thermostat in a house which both controls and provides feedback to
the heating system. Within a small group, control and feedback links

operate at several levels. Members control and give feedback to each other through communication within the group. One aspect of the group communication process, such as the interpersonal relationships, affects other aspects, such as the task network. Groups as a whole control and provide feedback to other groups or are controlled and receive feedback themselves. Thus, control and feedback are integral elements of small group communication.

One final consideration in the functional analysis of groups is the focus of analysis. Groups can be analyzed according to how they function to meet society's goals, how they function to satisfy the groups' purposes, or how individuals function within them to meet their own individual goals. While the role of groups in society should not be overlooked, this text concentrates on group behaviors to satisfy group and individual purposes. We examine the group inputs that create the group's structure, how the group interacts within that structure to achieve its functions, and how well it meets its goals. The important elements are briefly introduced here and discussed in more detail later.

Inputs (Structural Variables)

The inputs into a small group determine the structure or framework for group communication. They serve as the foundation or confines of the communication that will occur, much as the concrete foundation and wooden framework of a house dictate the form and functions of the final building. Inputs may be broken down into three main categories of variables: individual characteristics, group characteristics, and external factors. These various elements are called variables because they do not remain a constant quantity. Some elements vary independently of the rest, while others are dependent on another variable or several variables for the direction and amount of their change. Because most of the elements are variables, not constants, we cannot predict or explain the outcomes of the group until we understand the *interrelationship* of the relevant elements.

The first category of variables is *individual characteristics*. Each person in a group has many unique characteristics. These characteristics are individual differences among group members in the way they think and behave. We could probably produce an infinite list of individual characteristics, but let us consider just a few of the more important ones. Personality comes to mind first. A group made up entirely of introverts or pessimists would be expected to behave differently from one comprised entirely of extroverts or optimists. Individual beliefs, attitudes, and values are also important. People differ in their perception of truth, in their negative and positive evaluations of people and events, and in their underlying value systems. The amount and nature of these differences inject variety, interest, and sometimes conflict into groups. A third category of variables might be labeled general abilities: intelligence, aptitude, quickness, and verbal facility. We know that the bright student, the glib politician, and the witty professor all have impact. The initial status of an individual in a group is usually determined by his general abilities plus his competence, achievement, and attractiveness. These qualities will influence the choice of a leader and structure the nature of communication among members. Also, intricately related to these variables is the individual's areas of experience: the events of his past and his previous surroundings, including socioeconomic class, geographic locations, family relations, and education will to a large extent affect his ability to relate to other group members. In general, the greater the number of similarities the higher the potential for effective communication.

Another group of variables include individual goals and expectations. Each member has his own private goals and usually develops expectations of how the group will affect attainment of them. Individuals are also likely to have expectations of how rewarding the group will be in comparison to the amount of effort they anticipate expending. A final individual input worth considering is individual personality and tendency to conform. Factors such as age, sex, and several of the inputs mentioned already will determine which members are most susceptible to persuasion or are most likely to conform under group pressure.

The second category of structural variables is *group characteristics*. This category is much smaller. It includes the demographic features of the group upon which predictions can be made prior to any interaction. One such factor is group size. Groups of three people may not function in the same manner as groups of four, which, in turn, may function differently from groups of five or more. A second factor is the type of group. Is the group primarily social, or is it problem-oriented? Are members present voluntarily? Is the group continuous or temporary? Communication can differ according to the type of group. A similar consideration is the implicit and explicit goals of the group. Is the purpose of the group education, self-awareness, problem-solving, action, pleasure or several of these? If the group is task-oriented, the nature of the task is important. The kind of task, its complexity, and any other requirements such as time limitations are all variables that determine the group's structure and influence its outcomes. A final consideration is the frequency and length of interaction. Is the group a several-hours-a-day activity (like a family or class) or more like a monthly business meeting?

The third category of variables is *external factors*. These can be broken down further into externally imposed restrictions and environmental factors. Externally imposed restrictions include any rules or laws governing the group that are determined by a power outside the group. Any time, size, location or content restriction imposed from outside would qualify as an external factor. Designated status or leadership is also an externally applied restriction on the freedom of the group's operations. Environmental factors are elements in the immediate environment of the group which may have impact on its functioning. Temperature, lighting, amount of space, amount of noise and distractions, furnishings, colors, and attractiveness of surroundings all fall into this category.

Recognizing the major individual, group, and external characteristics that serve as inputs is important to understanding why a group behaves as it does. These variables not only identify for us the initial state of the group (i.e., its starting point) but they allow us to make certain predictions about the functioning of the group before it has begun operation. Once the group begins processing these inputs, a second set of factors comes into play: interaction variables.

Group Interaction

Inputs establish the group's communication predispositions, that is, the communication patterns and content most likely to occur. When interaction actually commences, three new classes of variables begin to act upon the initial inputs. They are task, procedural, and interpersonal factors; these three sets of variables affect each other and the communication that results.

Task variables include all factors that are relevant to the completion of the group's task (whether it be solving a complex task or just satisfying a need for conversation). Considerations such as the nature of the task, the method of information exchange, the task roles members assume, and the amount of conflict over ideas affect the channels of communication used, the networks that are established, and the messages that are created. The communication that occurs can, in turn, facilitate or create obstacles to task completion.

The second category is *procedural variables*. They concern the manner in which tasks are handled rather than the exact nature of the tasks. All organizational issues, including patterns of problem solving and decision making are procedural issues. A beginner can glimpse the effect of these factors by observing groups that strictly adhere to *Robert's Rules of Order* and comparing them with those that have no procedures for maintaining order. (The former may become hopelessly bogged down while the latter may be chaotic.) Even in social groups, we frequently decide the timing and order of activities.

A third classification is *interpersonal variables*. This category includes all factors that are relevant to the establishment of interpersonal relations in the group. They concern the way in which group members relate to one another and how they communicate, regardless of their specific tasks. Some key variables that have an impact on the inter-personal relationships are members' credibility, personal attraction, power or status, degree of similarity, conformity pressures, degree of trust among members, level of competition, language usage, and com-munication strategies. All these variables determine the socioemo-tional atmosphere of the group.

The interaction of these three sets of task, procedural and inter-personal variables significantly affect the communication that occurs in the group. The effectiveness or ineffectiveness of the communica-tion, in turn, influences how successfully the group achieves its de-sired outcomes. These outcomes may be regarded as the major func-tions of groups.

Small Group Functions

The five most significant functions or outcomes of small group communication are persuasion, therapy, conflict resolution, social re-lationships, decision making, and problem solving. Since these form the focus of most small group communication, we have devoted a chapter or more to each of these functions.

The group outcomes can be evaluated by comparing them to the goals established by the group. Three common criteria used to assess group outcomes are productivity, group cohesion, and member satis-faction. Quantity, quality, and efficiency are all aspects of productivity. If a group's goal is to exchange a great deal of information or produce a decision in a short period of time, the quantity and efficiency aspects of productivity are relevant criteria. Group cohesion signifies how solidified the group is at the conclusion of an interaction period and how attractive the group remains to its members. This criterion is especially relevant to social and therapeutic groups. The final criterion is member satisfaction, or how well the group satisfies each individu-al's needs, goals, and expectations. The success of a persuasive cam-paign or the resolution of a conflict, or both, may provide high member satisfaction. Groups that fail to meet these criteria may be re-garded as dysfunctional.

The ability of the group to satisfactorily fulfill its functions is de-pendent on its adaptability to the constraints of its individual, group, and external characteristics, and the balance of feedback and control in the communication that occurs during group interaction. Too little or too much feedback or control, among members may result in un-satisfactory task, procedural, or interpersonal relationships within the group, leading to dysfunctional outcomes. To understand better the role that communication plays in achieving group functions, the gen-

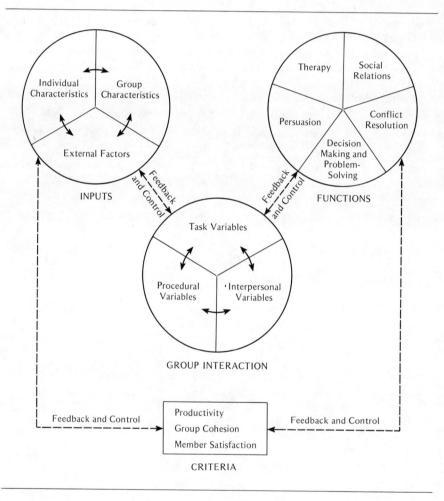

Figure 1.1. Small Group Communication: A Functional Approach

eral process of communication needs further explication. Some views of communication stress control while others place a high value on the reciprocal effects of human interaction. The next chapter examines several views of the general process of human communication.

SUGGESTED READINGS

Cartwright, D. and **Zander, A.** (eds.) *Group Dynamics.* 3d ed. New York: Harper & Row, Publishers, 1968.

Cathcart, R. S. and **Samovar, L. A.** *Small Group Communication: A Reader.* Dubuque, Iowa: William C. Brown Company, Publishers, 1970.

Mills, T. M. *The Sociology of Small Groups.* Englewood Cliffs, New Jersey: Prentice-Hall, Inc., 1967.

Olmsted, M. S. *The Small Group.* New York: Random House, Inc., 1959.

Rosenfeld, L. B. *Human Interaction in the Small Group Setting.* Columbus, Ohio: Charles E. Merrill Publishing Company, 1973.

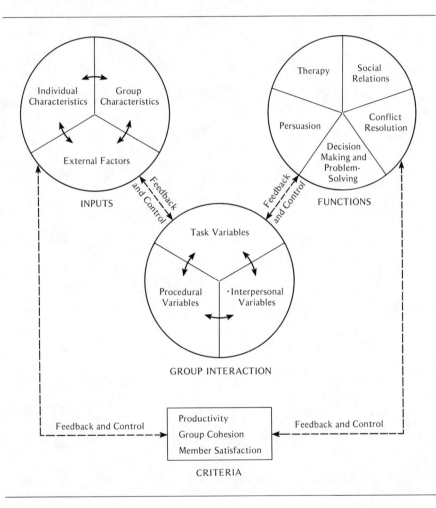

INPUTS

Individual Characteristics   Group Characteristics

External Factors

Therapy   Social Relations

Persuasion

Conflict Resolution

Decision Making and Problem-Solving

FUNCTIONS

Feedback and Control

Feedback and Control

Task Variables

Procedural Variables   ·Interpersonal Variables

GROUP INTERACTION

Feedback and Control

Feedback and Control

Productivity
Group Cohesion
Member Satisfaction

CRITERIA

Variables in Human Communication

THE PRECEDING chapter was an extensive examination of the nature of groups and the functions of communication in small groups. Although, there are characteristics unique to small groups, there are also many communication variables that operate across all communication situations. Therefore, in this chapter we are going to discuss some assumptions and factors that affect human communication in general. We believe that for people to operate effectively within the small group situation, they must increase their awareness of the complexity of the entire process of communication. We explore in this chapter some assumptions people make about the communication process. These assumptions affect the way people interact with others whether in a dyad, a small group, or a public speaking situation. Several models of the communication process are presented that reveal differing assumptions. These models are intended to develop a clearer understanding of the general process of communication by examining various aspects of human communication. The final model depicting small group communication incorporates various aspects of the other models. We close this chapter with a discussion of the importance of two variables that have received limited attention in the small group literature: nonverbal communication and trust. We feel that nonverbal behaviors affect all of the functions in important ways, and a person who wishes to be an effective communicator should be aware of this area. All the things we said in the previous chapter about the benefits of small groups as communication settings are negated if interpersonal trust is not established. In fact, none of the functions of conflict resolution, persuasion, therapy, decision-making, or social relations can be satisfactorily achieved without the development of trust. Therefore, we choose to discuss these functions earily in the text so that the student can keep these important areas in mind as he reads the rest of the text.

Basic Assumptions About Human Communication

People view human communication in different ways. The results of these different views are somewhat analogous to looking at the same scene through variously colored glasses. The basic assumptions that we hold when we view human communication are our variously colored glasses. Although we are looking at the same thing in each case, our choice of assumptions will determine to a major extent what we see.

Linear Assumption. The oldest, and probably the most commonly held, assumption about human communication is that causes and effects occur in a linear manner. When we use this assumption, we think of a communication interaction as being composed of a a source and a receiver. We see the source engaging in certain communication behaviors, and we observe that these behaviors have certain effects on the receiver. This has sometimes been referred to as a "hypodermic needle" model of human communication. This model assumes that certain inputs regularly result in certain outputs. For example, if the source uses more evidence to support positions that are taken, the receiver will be more likely to agree with them. This way of viewing human communication has some validity. Some inputs do, indeed, regularly result in predictable outputs. However, if we restrict ourselves to this view of human communication, we tend to overlook many important elements.

Process Assumption. If we examine the communication in which we engage every day, we will quickly note that people shift from sources to receivers during interaction. Tom may begin as the source and say something to Mike. At this point, of course, Mike is a receiver. If Mike responds by saying something back to Tom, the source-receiver roles are reversed. Any continuous interaction, therefore, may be viewed as a process with shifting source-receiver roles. Viewing human communication as a process, therefore, does not assume that independent source-causes regularly result in independent receiver-effects. Rather, viewing human communication as a process assumes that the effects two people have on one another through communication are interactive (Berlo, 1960). Viewing human communication in this way permits us to examine the adaptation of one person to another during communication.

Transactional Assumption. When we view human communication as a transaction, we assume that people engaging in the interaction have reciprocal effects on one another (Watzlawick, Beavin, and Jackson, 1967). This assumption is relatively similar to the process assumption, but there is one important distinction. Using the process assumption, it is possible to perceive one person maintaining a constant effort to produce a certain, predetermined response in a receiver. Viewing human communication from the transactional assumption point of view denies this possibility. The assumption that human communication is transactional necessitates viewing all communicators' motivations as variable and dependent upon the interaction of other communicators.

All three ways of looking at human communication provide unique insights. None of the three is either right or wrong. Some variables in human communication have direct, predictable effects. Some variables operate in parts of a process but not in others. Some variables have reciprocal effects and causes within human communication. It is important that we keep all of these assumptions in mind as we examine the many variables affecting human communication.

Models of Human Communication

This section is devoted to three models of human communication. Each model is designed to provide insight into how human communication works. A model is simply an approximation of reality. Since human communication is dynamic rather than static, our models cannot be completely representative of the reality of human communication. Rather, they will merely provide us with an approximation of how we may view human communication.

A Basic Linear-Process Model. Figure 2.1 presents the McCroskey (1968) model of human communication. This model is essentially a linear one but does take into account some possibility of a process view. The model includes a source, a receiver, and a connecting channel that includes a message. These four elements have long been

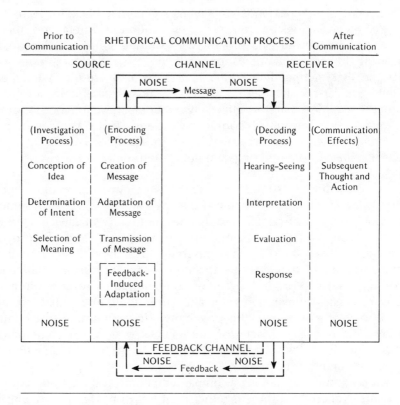

Figure 2.1. The McCroskey Model*

considered the most important ones in human communication. We will consider further each of these elements later in the chapter.

Several other parts of the McCroskey model need to be considered at this point. First of all, the model notes that people who are sources are not always engaged in communication. The broken line that divides the source in half signifies this distinction. In the left half are listed some of the things that people do prior to engaging in communication. One of these things is the selection of the meaning that they wish to communicate to a receiver. A source begins communicating by "encoding" (producing ·some kind of message). Meaning is an elusive thing that only exists in the minds of people. When we engage in human communication, we cannot simply transmit meaning to another person, unless we are both experts at ESP. Rather, we must approximate our meaning with some kind of code. We commonly think of one of these codes when we think of communication

* (See Figure 2.2) Reprinted from *An Introduction to Rhetorical Communication* by James C. McCroskey, Englewood Cliffs, N.J.: Prentice-Hall, Inc., © 1968, with permission from the publisher.

—words. However, there are many nonword codes that we employ as well, such as our vocal expression, our posture, our gestures, and our other nonverbal behaviors. However we may code our meaning, the code we choose represents messages that are transmitted to our receiver. The receiver begins the communication process by "decoding" messages. "Decoding" means taking message codes and extracting meaning in our own mind. As the McCroskey model notes, the receiver also engages in behaviors that are not part of the communication process and is hence divided by a broken line.

The linear assumption about human communication is evident in this model; a source encodes a message, thus serving as a cause, and a receiver decodes the message, thus being affected. The process assumption is also evident in this model which takes into account the receiver's response, feedback, to the source's original message. In the context of the model, feedback is an effect on a receiver that is observed by the source. The observation of a response permits the source to adapt subsequent messages to alter effects in the receiver.

One final element in the McCroskey model should be noted, noise. Noise is conceived in the model as any element that interferes with or distorts message encoding or decoding. It may be noise in the literal sense, such as distracting sounds that impinge on the channels, but, more commonly, noise is a figurative term for such things as attitudes, personality characteristics, culture, communication skills, and all other criteria that make human beings unique from other species and from one another.

An Interpersonal Communication Model.　Figure 2.2 presents an interpersonal model of human communication (McCroskey, Larson, and Knapp, 1971). This model permits one to view human communication with either the process assumption or the transactional assumption. A key element in this model is the indication that people serve as both sources and receivers in the same interpersonal communication encounter, with the source and receiver roles alternating. The model reflects the process assumption in that the flow of communication forms a never-ending circle. There is no clear starting or ending point. If we enter the model with person A serving as a source, we may follow the flow of communication through the receiver's (person B) decoding and response to the effect of communication. As is indicated in the model, the effect of communication is normally the formation of ideas and the selection of behaviors. One of the behaviors that may be selected is the continuation of communication; in this case, person B would change from a receiver into a source and continue the communication process.

An examination of this model may also help us to understand more clearly the transactional assumption about human communication.

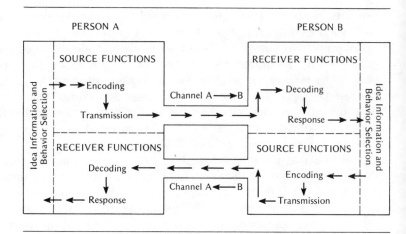

Figure 2.2. The McCroskey-Larson-Knapp Interpersonal
Communication Model *

While both the linear and process assumptions, if we may speak analogically for a moment, assume that two plus two equals four, the transactional view of human communication recognizes that two plus two may equal five, or even five hundred. In essence, the transactional assumption postulates that the whole of human communication may be greater than the sum of its constituent parts. Both the linear and process assumptions consider it possible for people involved in a given communication encounter to remain unaffected. The transactional assumption of human communication, however, commits us to the position that there is no such thing as "no effect." This view holds that communication results inherently in change in the communicators. In terms of the model presented in Figure 2.2, if person B engages in decoding and response, he has been affected. Whatever effect or effects have occurred may vary. The effect may be the one intended by person A, or it may be completely unrelated to person A's intention. For example, person A may have been trying to get person B to understand how to program a computer. One of the effects that might occur as a result of this communication encounter could be that person B develops very negative attitudes toward computers. The transactional view of human communication considers such effects to be at least as interesting as effects that are intentional.

While the models presented in Figures 2.1 and 2.2 permit substantially different views of human communication, all the elements that

* Reprinted from *An Introduction to Interpersonal Communication* by James C. McCroskey, Carl E. Larson, and Mark L. Knapp, Englewood Cliffs, N.J.: Prentice-Hall, Inc., © 1971, with permission from the publisher.

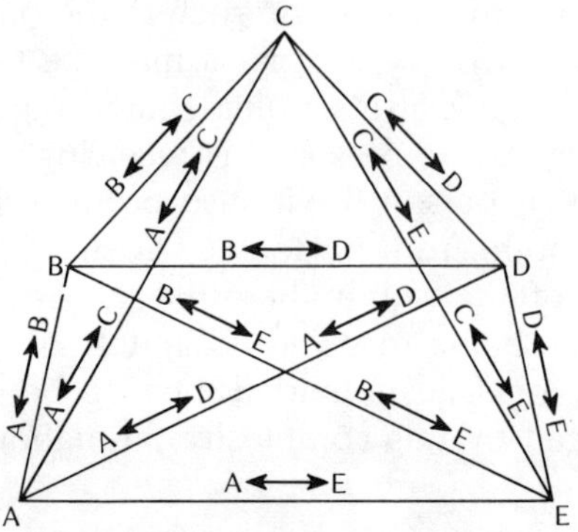

**Figure 2.3. A Model of Small Group Communication
Among Five People**

are observable in Figure 2.1 are present in the human communication encounter represented by Figure 2.2. The main distinction between the two models lies in the fact that the interpersonal model is more representative of the human variables in human communication. Specific attention should be directed to the existence of two channels in this model. In one, messages move from person A to person B, and in the other, messages move from person B to person A. In terms of our first model, channel A←B is a feedback channel. However, from the vantage point of person B, channel A→B is the feedback channel. Stated simply, all messages transmitted by person A are feedback for person B, and vice versa.

A Model of Group Communication.   Figure 2.3 presents a very simple model of communication within a small group of five people. Many elements present in the two previous models cannot be included in a model designed to represent small group interaction because of the extreme complexity of the process. Consequently, we must keep in mind, as we examine our small group communication model, that small group communication is also interpersonal communication, and the insights provided by our interpersonal models should be retained as we examine small group communication.

The model in Figure 2.3 includes five people. The connecting arrows represent the channels of communication among the five. We notice a major increase in the number of existing channels when we increase the number of people involved in a human communication encounter from two to five. For this reason, if for no other, we must recognize that communication in a small group is a much more complex process than interpersonal communication between only two people. In a face-to-face group, such as the one represented by Figure 2.3, whenever person A encodes a message to be transmitted to person B, the message is also simultaneously transmitted to persons C, D, and E. Similarly, while person B is receiving person A's message, it is highly likely that person B will also be receiving verbal or nonverbal messages, or both, from persons C, D, and E. Such an abundance of messages will often result in the primary messages in small group communication not being received accurately or decoded in the way the source of the messages intended them to be. We will consider problems introduced by this complexity throughout the remainder of the book.

Major Variables in Human Communication

In the preceding section we indicated that the four major variables in human communication have long been considered to be the source, the receiver, the channels, and the messages. In this section we will consider each of these in a bit more depth.

The Source Variable. It is certainly risky to try to attribute various levels of importance to the four major variables in human communication. However, the source variable has received the most attention from communication researchers, and this may be an indication of the comparative importance that communication scholars attribute to this variable. The present authors also consider the source variable to be one of the most important variables in human communication because of its pervasive influence on the others.

In human communication, the source is the person or persons who encode and transmit messages. It should be stressed that a source may be either a single person or a collective group. In many cases, organizations, as a collective entity, transmit messages to the public. However, within the context of small group communication, the overwhelming percentage of sources of communication are single individuals.

In human communication, the attributes of the source are often as important, or more important, than what the source says. Receivers do not decode sources' messages in a vacuum. For example, if a war hero speaks out against military expenditures, we could anticipate that it would have a different impact on receivers than if a teenage street demonstrator were to say the same things. Receivers' attitudes toward sources, therefore, are a major variable in human communication. We will consider further the problem of a source's credibility in the next chapter.

The Receiver Variable. The receiver is the person who receives and decodes messages in human communication. Although both sources and receivers are affected by their involvement in human communication, we are normally more interested in the effects on receivers, since human communication usually occurs as a result of someone's motivation (a source) to influence the thinking or behavior of another person or persons (receivers). Since receivers are human beings, there are major differences in the ways that receivers decode and respond to messages. Many of the people variables that affect the way receivers respond in human communication will be considered in the next chapter.

Channel Variables. The channel is a concept that is defined in at least two distinct ways. First, when we think of the mass media, we think of them as tools that serve as channels of communication. Newspapers, radio, and television convey messages from sources to receivers, and in this sense serve as channels. Our concern in this book, however, will not be with this kind of channel. The second concept of channel we might mention here is sensory channels. Each of the human senses provides a means by which people may receive messages. We can see, hear, feel, etc. Most, but not all, of the messages transmitted and received in human communication in a small group setting employ the auditory and visual senses. In the models discussed in the previous section, each channel indicated actually represents a multiplicity of channels which, in turn, represent the various senses. However, we may think of these channels in a singular sense between any two people, with the flow of messages moving in both directions between the two people.

Message Variables. As we have indicated previously, messages are codes representing meaning in the mind of the person transmitting the messages. Messages may be either verbal or nonverbal. Verbal messages employ linguistic codes. This type of message will be discussed in considerably more depth in Chapter 4. Nonverbal codes do not involve language as we normally conceive of it. When we think of human communication, we often think in terms of language. Actually, however, there is good reason to believe that more human communication occurs at a nonverbal level than through the use of language itself. Because of the importance of nonverbal communication, we will consider some of the nonverbal message elements in more depth in the following section.

Nonverbal Messages in Human Communication

Space. People tend to use space differently in various types of communication transactions (Hall, 1959). For example, in North American culture, in general, people tend to stand between six and eighteen inches apart when they engage in intimate conversation. For more normal conversation among friends, the interpersonal distance tends to vary from three to four and one-half feet. It should be stressed that these interpersonal distances, while typical in North American culture in general are not typical in other cultures. For example, Southern Europeans and South Americans tend to stand much closer together when engaging in normal conversation than do typical North Americans. Furthermore, both the sex of the communicators and the race of the communicators have an impact on what is considered "normal" interpersonal distance. For example, in an interview setting, both males and females tend to sit about two and one-half feet from a female interviewer. Females prefer to be about three feet away from male interviewers, and males prefer to be almost four feet away from male interviewers. These distances are estimates based on research reported by Rosegrant, who also found that the race of communicators has an impact on distance. Rosegrant (1972) observed that her black interviewees chose to sit between two and one-half and three feet from either black or white interviewers. However, her white interviewees chose to sit about two feet from white interviewers whereas they chose to sit almost three and one-half feet from black interviewers.

One might reasonably ask whether such distances have any importance. There is considerable research to indicate that they do if the norms are violated. People who move too close to us tend to be perceived as pushy or overly aggressive. People who stay too far away from us are likely to be perceived as unfriendly or looking down on us. For example, in black-white relations, the distances noted above are sharply discrepant. It is quite probable, therefore, that both blacks and whites unconsciously cause people of the other race to misperceive them through their use of space in communication.

In the small group setting, where people choose to sit tends to have an impact on the interaction in the group. For example, at a rectangular table, those who sit at the "head" or "foot" of the table tend to assume more of the leadership of the group than those people sitting on the sides of the table. They also tend to dominate the participation in the group. The use of space, therefore, is a powerful nonverbal communicator.

Time. The way a person uses time communicates a good deal about the person to other people (Hall, 1959). We use timing in our everyday conversation to control the interaction of other people. For example, when we have completed a thought and are looking for a response from another person, we tend to stop talking and pause. This signals the other person that we have finished, and it is appropriate for him to talk.

Waiting time also communicates. In North American culture in general to keep someone waiting for more than five minutes normally causes some negative feelings. Consequently, if someone appears at a conference thirty minutes late, this nonverbal communication may completely dominate the other conferees' responses to the late individual's participation.

When we choose to communicate also communicates. A meeting that is called at 4:45, when quitting time is 5:00, is likely to be perceived as either an extremely important event or as an unusually annoying inconvenience. It would seldom be perceived as "normal." This would clearly have an impact on the interaction in the meeting and the perceptions of the people involved.

Eye Behavior. In face-to-face communication, human beings make extensive use of their eyes to communicate. In North American culture, direct eye contact is generally taken to indicate interest and attention. It is also sometimes thought to indicate honesty, although it is quite an unreliable indication of character. We also use our eye behavior to control interaction. If we do not wish to be interrupted, we will often glance away from the person to whom we are talking until we complete our thought. When we glance back to the person, it is a signal that it is the other individual's turn to speak. Once again, we must stress the impact of culture on nonverbal behavior. In parts of Africa, for example, direct eye contact as we know it, is studiously avoided since the cultural norm dictates that direct eye contact expresses a lack of respect for the person who is being looked at.

Touch. One of the least used nonverbal messages in North American culture is touch. Touch has come to have many negative, particularly sexual, connotations. Whereas, in many parts of the world hand-holding by males while engaged in normal conversation is a regular occurrence, such touching behavior is almost unheard of in North American culture in general. Since touch has taken on so many negative overtones, it has become an even more potent nonverbal message. Used sparingly, touch can signal considerable interest, attention, and warmth, as well as sincerity. If overused, however, it will generally lead to a negative reaction from receivers.

Gesture. It has been estimated that there are over 700,000 possible physical signs that can be transmitted by gesture (Birdwhistell,

1970). It is reasonably safe to say that none of us is in a position to control our physical behavior to the extent that we can be completely aware of what we are communicating by gesture during interaction with other people. Leaning toward a person generally communicates interest and attention, while leaning away from the person, or assuming an overly relaxed position while listening to the person, generally communicates disdain. We are all aware of the impact of a smile or a frown, which are both gestural messages. Even the way we sit can communicate. If we cross one leg over the other, so that the crossed leg points away from the person to whom we are talking, we may communicate a feeling of exclusion to that person. Crossing our leg the opposite direction tends to communicate a feeling of inclusion (Scheflen, 1966).

Paralanguage. The term "paralanguage" has been used to refer to all the elements present in the human voice during communication except the words themselves. Paralanguage includes elements such as inflection, tone, volume, voice quality, and so forth. All these characteristics of our voices communicate things about us to other people. It has been found, for example, that without ever seeing a person, most people can fairly accurately determine the individual's sex, race, size, age, education level, region of origin within the United States, social status, and even emotional state from cues in the voice alone (Knapp, 1972). But possibly, what is even more important, consistent stereotypes have developed that relate to voices. For example, the female with a breathy voice is generally considered prettier and more feminine than females without a breathy voice; and males with a high-pitched voice are generally perceived as more feminine and weaker than their baritone friends. There are many other similar stereotypes that seem to be in operation. The important point is not that a breathy-voiced girl is pretty, but rather that people tend to have this perception whether it is correct or not. Few people are fully aware of what they are communicating to other people through their particular voice quality and voice use, but the impact in a communication transaction can be overwhelming.

Our purpose here has been merely to provide a brief introduction to the nature of nonverbal messages in human communication. We cannot, in this short treatise, adequately explore this very important area of human communication. The reader who is interested in learning more about this important facet of human communication should read Mark L. Knapp's (1972) excellent book, *Nonverbal Communication in Human Interaction.*

Interpersonal Trust—The Crucial Variable

Throughout this chapter, we have considered a wide variety of variables that affect human communication. We have attempted to define these variables and provide a relatively brief explanation of them. There is one variable that we have not yet considered, one that is probably more important than all of the others combined, interpersonal trust. Interpersonal trust is a relational concept. It refers to the way one person relates to another person in communication. In the absence of trust, very little communication will occur. When trust is present, almost anything is possible.

Trust and Risk Taking

In most human communication transactions, some risk is involved for a person who chooses to communicate with another person (Rogers, 1961). It is usually possible for an individual to tell more about himself or herself than he or she really wants the other person to know. We all know people with whom we feel comfortable talking about our real feelings and our needs and desires. We also know other people with whom we would not even consider talking about such things. The difference in these two groups of people lies in our level of trust. The level of trust present is directly correlated with the willingness of people to encode and transmit messages to one another. If I feel that you will use what I say against me, I am very unlikely to say very much that is of any importance. I will not take the risk. Consequently, if we do not establish a basis of trust for our communication, we will probably never learn much about one another at deeper than a surface level. Our interpersonal or small group communication will most likely fail to result in the outcomes that will be discussed in the remaining chapters of this book.

Trust and Acceptance of Group Communication

The degree of trust established among people in a group is highly related to whether or not the results of group communication ever lead to anything. If a person is a member of a group that the person does not trust, it is most likely that whatever conclusion the group reaches will be perceived by that person as "their conclusion" rather than "our conclusion." When this occurs, it is most unlikely that the individual will engage in any behavior that is necessary to implement the group's conclusion. If enough people within a group feel this lack of trust, no amount of communication and no amount of apparent agreement can lead to a direct group product. Without trust, therefore, human communication in a small group is meaningless.

People within a small group must be amenable to being influenced, as well as influencing others. Unless people change their thinking to some extent during small group interaction, the interaction is quite pointless. Other kinds of variables besides trust that affect people's willingness to accept other people's views are the subjects of the following three chapters.

SUGGESTED READINGS

Burgoon, M. *Approaching Speech/Communication.* New York: Holt, Rinehart and Winston, Inc., 1974.

Knapp, M. L. *Nonverbal Communication in Human Interaction.* New York: Holt, Rinehart and Winston, Inc., 1972.

McCroskey, J. C., Larson, C. E., and **Knapp, M. L.** *An Introduction to Interpersonal Communication.* Englewood Cliffs, New Jersey: Prentice-Hall, Inc., 1971.

Rogers, C. *On Becoming a Person.* Boston: Houghton Mifflin Company, 1961.

Watzlawick, P., Beavin, J. H., and **Jackson, D.** *Pragmatics of Human Communication.* New York: W. W. Norton & Company, Inc., 1967.

Wenburg, J. R. and **Wilmot, W. W.** *The Personal Communication Process.* New York: John Wiley & Sons, Inc., 1973.

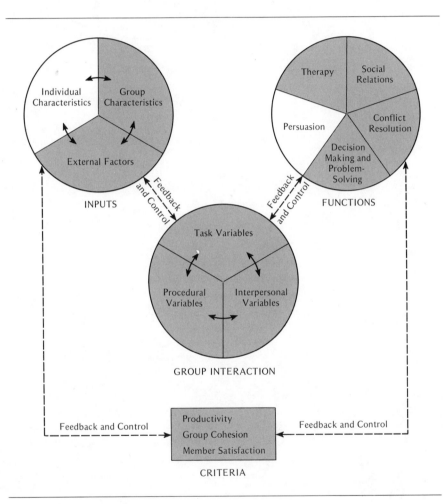

Small Group
Communication
to Persuade:
People Variables

A GROUP OF HOUSEWIVES pickets a local grocery store — food prices drop. The Campus Crusade convinces a new student to join their cause. A committee of concerned students persuades local officials to investigate student ghettos and prosecute landlords of substandard housing. A father succumbs to the pressure of his family and quits smoking. A class convinces its instructor to cancel the final exam. All these examples demonstrate one of the major functions or outcomes of small group communication — persuasion.

Persuasion is involved in much of our communication, whether in or out of groups. In fact, some authorities argue that all communication is persuasion. While we do not hold such an extreme view, we recognize that a significant proportion of our communication is devoted to persuasion. And much of that persuasion either takes place in groups or is an output of groups. Since persuasion is so important, we have chosen to spend two chapters discussing the major inputs and process variables in a group that influence the persuasion taking place. This chapter looks at people variables (individual characteristics) that affect the process. The next chapter analyzes the message strategies that lead to effective persuasion.

PERSUASION IN THE GROUP

Before proceeding to people variables, we need to clarify exactly what is meant by persuasion in this book. We have a preference for the definition offered by Bettinghaus (1968): a persuasive communication situation is one that involves "a conscious attempt by one individual to change the behavior of another individual or group of individuals through the transmission of some message." (p. 13) We will expand this definition to include groups as the sources of persuasive attempts and to allow nonverbal communication to be included as messages. Thus, persuasion involves an individual or group intentionally attempting to influence other individuals or groups through the vehicle of verbal and nonverbal messages.

Persuasion occurs at two levels in a group. The first is *internal* persuasion; that is, individual members persuading the group and vice versa. The second level might be called *external*. Groups frequently attempt to persuade others outside their groups. In other words, groups engage in persuasive campaigns. An example of both levels is a government lobby group. First, the membership must be persuaded to support one specific policy. Then the lobby engages in a persuasive campaign to gain adoption of the plan by the appropriate agency. Thus, in groups we are concerned with both the individual's persuasiveness and the group's persuasiveness. Individuals may overtly or covertly try to persuade a group. In turn, groups as a whole may persuade their members or people outside the groups.

One recognized phenomenon in groups is the pressure toward conformity and unanimity. Group norms and group personalities develop in this way. The continued survival and success of a group is frequently dependent on a high level of agreement among group members. To insure uniformity of values, attitudes, beliefs, and behaviors, members who deviate are pressured to conform. Initially, when a member begins to deviate, a high degree of communication is directed toward him to persuade him to return to the group norms. If the influence attempts fail, communication with the deviate is reduced and he is eventually isolated and ignored by the group. The isolation of deviant factions is usually not a desirable development; it may hurt group cohesion, productivity, and member satisfaction. This makes successful persuasion an important tool of the group. Either the group must succeed in convincing its disagreeing members to accept group positions, or the deviating members must succeed in persuading the group to accept their point of view.

This chapter considers characteristics that affect how well individuals may persuade others and how easily they may be persuaded by the group. We want to make one thing clear to the reader before continuing this chapter. The assembly effect, referred to in the first chapter, is a powerful reason for concern with small group communication. If groups can make better decisions or be more productive, or both, than individuals, then there is good reason to work in groups. However, it should be noted that the assembly effect is only a *potential of a group* and that the people variables discussed in this chapter can hinder as well as help the realization of that potential. People with certain personality syndromes can actually be dysfunctional to small group communication. Too much attraction or similarity among group members may reduce the input of new ideas that lead to better decisions. One individual who has too much influence can similarly reduce the potential assembly effect. We urge the reader to evaluate each of these people variables with these perspectives in mind.

PERSONALITY VARIABLES

Personality types vary in their persuasiveness (i.e., how well they persuade others) and their persuasability (i.e., how easily they are persuaded by others). We know a great deal more about differences in personalities than about the impact of these personality differences on persuasion in a group. Certain personality variables have been singled out by authorities as likely to affect the persuasion process. Others, we can only speculate on. We have selected for attention those that we feel may play a significant role.

Machiavellianism

One of the most intriguing personality types is the high Machiavellian. The label originates with the name of a famous sixteenth-century Italian writer, Niccolo Machiavelli, whose motto might have been "the ends justify the means." As expressed by Christie and Geis (1970):

> Since the publication of The Prince in 1532, the name of its author has come to designate the use of guile, deceit, and opportunism in interpersonal relations. Traditionally, the "Machiavellian" is someone who views and manipulates others for his own purposes. (p. 1)

Not only is the high Mach willing to manipulate others, he is more successful at it and enjoys it. Some of the presumed characteristics that contribute to this ability to control others are a relative lack of emotional involvement in interpersonal relationships, a lack of concern for conventional morality (i.e., an amoral point of view), an absence of serious mental problems, a rational view of others, and a low commitment to ideologies (i.e., a pragmatic approach emphasizing immediate goals rather than long range ideological goals). Furthermore, the high Mach is likely to distrust others, has little faith in human nature, admits to high hostility, and is anomic (Wrightsman and Cook, 1965). In comparison to a low Mach, the high Mach rates those he works with as less interesting, less assertive, less generous, less productive, less cooperative, less sympathetic, less intelligent, and more guileless. In other words, he sees others as relatively undesirable co-workers and as susceptible to manipulation.

How do all these characteristics affect the high Mach's behavior in a group? First, the high Mach is unlikely to be influenced by other group members and is quite successful at persuading others. Second, he has a low regard for others, treats them as objects, and is uninterested in their feelings. He, himself, is less emotionally involved in the group, is very task oriented, and takes the initiative. Conversely, the low Mach is very vulnerable to the influence of others, follows rather than leads, and is more emotionally involved, at times even becoming sidetracked by feelings that are irrelevant to the task. In other words, the low Mach is more personally and socially oriented and more easily manipulated (Christie and Geis, 1970). What this boils down to is that the high Machs are most likely to determine the outcomes of group activities. This has been found to be true in a variety of situations. High Machs win more often in group games (Christie and Geis, 1970) and have even, somehow, manipulated classrooms to gain higher grades (Burgoon, 1971a).

Anomia-Alienation

A closely related personality type is the anomic or alienated individual. The anomic person is one who has failed to adopt society's norms and values. He is characterized by feelings of powerlessness, meaninglessness and social isolation (Dean, 1961). He is typically anxious, apathetic, and potentially suicidal. The extreme form of anomia is alienation, which is most often characterized by hostility. Many of the characteristics of the high Mach also show up in the anomic or alienated individual, but to a lesser degree: he has little faith in human nature, exhibits suspicion of others, feels hostile, and may engage in verbal hostility.

We know less about how the anomic or alienated person behaves in a group than we do about high Mach behavior in a group. We do know that such people perceive that they are denied communication by others (Giffin, 1970) and that they are less willing to communicate with peers, parents, or superiors (Heston and Andersen, 1972). They also regard others as objects or nonpersons (Heston, 1972). From these characteristics, we may infer that the anomic or alienated individual would probably not try like the high Mach to manipulate others, but would be less emotionally involved, more task oriented, and tend toward withdrawal in a group. Their distrust of others would hint at them being less susceptible to persuasion.

While at first glance you might not expect to run into this type of person frequently, there is a good deal of evidence that anomia and alienation are widespread, cutting across all age groups and social classes (cf. Clinard, 1964; Friedenberg, 1959; Shore and Massimo, 1969). All of which suggests that you may well have to contend with this kind of individual frequently. In fact, you may easily find some of his traits within yourself.

Dogmatism

A third major personality trait that may affect a group is dogmatism. The dogmatic personality is rigid and closeminded; his commitment to ideology causes him to be inflexible and intolerant of others. The term "authoritarian" derives from the high respect he gives to authority; he is, in fact, dominated by authority. Dogmatic people are typically characterized by feelings of anxiety and insecurity (Rokeach, 1960).

Based on these characteristics, McCroskey, Larson and Knapp (1969) have suggested some possible communication behaviors of the relatively dogmatic person. First, he is more likely to respond to persuasive messages on the basis of irrelevant or internal drives than for reasons of logical consistency. In other words, his habits, beliefs, power needs, ego, feelings of anxiety, and so forth will strongly influence his decisions. For instance, if such a person believes that women are inferior to men in intelligence, an abundance of evidence to the contrary will probably have little effect. Similarly, the farmer who is convinced that Daylight Savings Time is a Communist plot is unlikely to believe or accept logical arguments about not losing any actual time or sunshine. A second predicted behavior of a high dogmatic would be to see wide discrepancies between his views and the expressed positions of those who disagree with him. A staunch conservative might label anything moderately liberal as socialist, while the ardent liberal might label anything slightly conservative as a step toward Nazism. Although the dogmatic person is generally not very easy to persuade, the exception would be when someone in a position of authority is the source of the persuasive attempt. Because he relies heavily on absolute authority, the high dogmatic seeks the opinions of someone in authority to bolster his own beliefs and is susceptible to his point of view. Thus, if you want to persuade a closed person, you need to convince him that you hold a position of authority or that you accept the legitimacy of authority. You will also have more success if you attempt to change his peripheral beliefs rather than his central beliefs (Wright and Harvey, 1965). Another worthwhile note is that small group interaction may work to reduce levels of dogmatism. In Milwaukee's Project Understanding, as a result of a lecture and discussion workshops, Catholic, college-educated parents under age 35 became significantly less dogmatic in their attitudes and values that had been generating prejudice among children (Robinson and Spaights, 1969). This implies that group persuasion may be relatively more effective than individual persuasion in changing the views of high dogmatics.

Anxiety and Tolerance for Ambiguity

We have already discussed two personality types that are characterized by general anxiety: the anomic-alienated person and the high dogmatic. Generalized anxiety is not confined to these types of individuals; a great many people may have chronically high levels of anxiety without being anomic or dogmatic. This trait is generally referred to as chronic anxiety. Such people are commonly tense, nervous, worried, and discontented. The effect of anxiety makes these people generally less persuasible (Millman, 1965).

Complementing chronic anxiety is situational anxiety. For some people, anxiety is situation specific, that is, it only occurs under certain conditions. One major type of situational anxiety is communication apprehension. This communication-bound anxiety is also known as stage fright. Communication apprehensives have such a fear of speaking to others that their emotional state hinders their communication. This speech-related anxiety may take two forms: reticence or exhibitionism (McCroskey, 1968). Exhibitionism refers to excessive, nonpurposeful communication. The exhibitionist's talkativeness may be mistaken for confidence and an outgoing personality. But the person who overdoes it may actually be trying to mask his anxiety.

The more common form of communication apprehension is reticence. The reticent individual is unusually quiet, tends to avoid interaction, is threatened by face-to-face contact, and intimidated by superiors (Phillips, 1968). It would be reasonable to conclude that such people are less likely to attempt to influence others and more likely to be susceptible to persuasion. And it has been found that people who have situational anxiety are, in fact, more persuasible (Millman, 1965). The explanation seems to be that by accepting the position of others they reduce their anxiety.

A person's anxiety level contributes to another characteristic that is relevant to groups: tolerance for ambiguity. Individuals with high anxiety have very low tolerance for ambiguity or uncertainty. Their intolerance for ambiguity is evidenced by their perception of situations and proposals as being either good or bad, right or wrong. They become rigid and feel threatened when the "correct" choice among alternatives is not immediately apparent (Budner, 1962). For example, the person with low tolerance for ambiguity would see the issue of amnesty for draft dodgers as having two alternatives: to give them complete amnesty or prohibit their return to the U.S. on penalty of imprisonment. The possibility of some "middle ground" alternatives, with no "absolutely right" solution would be disturbing.

In a small group, a variety of factors may introduce ambiguity into the situation. The group may be dealing with a problem for which there is no obvious solution; the group's status structure (to be discussed shortly) may be ambiguous; the feelings, opinions, and actions of certain members may be unclear to others; the group's task itself may be unclear to the members. Any of these sources of ambiguity may be frustrating to individuals with a low tolerance level, causing them to be resistant to persuasive attempts. Thus, the extent to which the group allows or encourages ambiguity may hamper or increase its effectiveness in persuasion.

Introversion-Extroversion

Another personality trait is a person's level of introversion or extroversion. The extrovert is outgoing, gregarious, and oriented toward external factors. The introvert seems shy and introspective, more concerned with his inner feelings and thoughts than those of the people around him. The typical communication pattern of the extrovert is highly verbal, and he seems to be at ease while speaking. In contrast, the introvert is quiet and possibly even reticent.

This would lead us to expect the extrovert to lead a group, while the introvert would follow. And this, in turn, should lead to the conclusion that the extrovert attempts more often to persuade, while the introvert is more easily persuaded. Research on group leaders provides indirect substantiation: those who send and receive the most communication tend to be the leaders (Collins and Guetzkow, 1964).

Self-esteem

An additional attribute that may influence individual behavior in a group is self-esteem. People with low self-esteem devalue their own abilities and are lacking in confidence. They may have a negative self-image, feelings of unattractiveness or failure, and low self-respect. The high self-esteem person, by comparison, is confident in his own abilities and has a positive self-image.

Self-esteem influences a group in the following manner: individuals with low regard for themselves are more vulnerable to persuasion than those who regard themselves highly. The student who repeatedly receives low grades is more likely to follow the recommendations of his more successful peers in a class discussion than to volunteer his own opinions. The employee who has been reprimanded by his boss will be more easily influenced by those who have been praised by the employer. People who consistently confront discouraging life experiences, such as poverty, failure, or rejection by people whom they value highly will generally feel that their own ideas are not worthwhile and will, therefore, be likely to adopt the ideas of those who have succeeded where they could not. Even a temporary reduction in self-esteem will increase persuasibility. By criticizing a person who respects you or lowering his self-esteem in some other fashion, you can increase his vulnerability to your influence, but beware the side effects. His respect for you may also vanish.

Persuasibility and Conformity

We have already discussed several personality attributes that contribute or are suspected to contribute to a person's persuasibility. We have pointed to the low Mach, the communication apprehensive, the situationally anxious, the introvert, and the person with low self-esteem as likely to be easily persuaded. Conversely, the high Mach, the anomic and alienated, the chronically anxious, the high dogmatic (except when faced with an authority figure), the extrovert, the person who is intolerant of ambiguity, and the person with high self-esteem have been described as more resistant to persuasion.

Some additional characteristics may also determine persuasibility. Individuals with higher intelligence have been found to be less persuasible. Older people are likewise less open to persuasion. Women, on the other hand, have been labeled as more persuasible. This latter conclusion should be regarded as tenuous, however, since there are flaws in the research that has led to it.

All of these factors contribute in varying degrees to a group member's general tendency to conform to the group's position. There is a great deal of evidence to indicate that personality characteristics predispose an individual to accept the opinions of others when there is conflict (Crutchfield, 1955). Of course, other factors are also important: the amount of conflict or uncertainty the person is experiencing within himself, how much group support and evidence he has in relation to the opposition, how important the group is to him and how much pressure it is exerting. It is important to realize that conformity plays a major role in the persuasion of individual group members when reaching a group consensus.

ATTRACTION, SIMILARITY, AND CREDIBILITY

A second major category of individual variables affecting persuasion in a group includes the highly interrelated variables of attraction, similarity, and credibility. They are interrelated because the effect of each is partly dependent on the other two. For the sake of clarity we will talk about them separately, but it should be realized that the division is rather arbitrary.

Attraction

All of us at times have found ourselves drawn to the person with the magnetic personality. John F. Kennedy's popularity was often attributed in part to his personal magnetism or charisma. This personal attractiveness can be used effectively to influence others, particularly in a group. The fact that people who evolve as leaders in a group are generally among the most popular and liked testifies to the power of interpersonal attraction.

Research has attempted to decipher which elements contribute to high attraction. Apparently, there are at least three relevant factors (McCroskey and McCain, 1972). One is a *social* or liking factor: we are attracted to people we personally like and feel could be our friends. Another is a *physical* attraction factor: we are attracted to people whose dress and physical appearance we find pleasing. The last factor discovered so far is a *task* or respect factor: attraction is dependent on how easy or worthwhile it is to work with a person. The combination of high social, physical, and task attraction can increase a person's influence in a group. Similarly, the fact that the individuals in a group are attractive along the same dimensions may boost the group's persuasiveness.

Whether or not attraction develops among group members is dependent on several considerations. Three important ones are the frequency of interaction, the amount of personal reward, and the similarity of group members. The more often people interact with each other, the more likely they are to be attracted to one another. Friendships often develop simply because people are together frequently. Attraction also develops when one person rewards another. When we anticipate or receive praise, positive reactions, and other rewards from someone, we become more attracted to that person (Griffit, 1968; Byrne and Griffit, 1966; Landy and Aronson, 1968). The third variable, similarity, deserves more extended consideration.

Similarity

The similarity of group members is just as important in its effect on attraction. Not only are we more attracted to people like ourselves, we are more influenced by them (Rogers and Shoemaker, 1971). The similarities may be based on age, sex, appearance, beliefs, attitudes, socioeconomic status, education, past experiences, or a number of other factors. Slight dissimilarity between two people fosters the most growth and the most potential for influence, which results in the best relationship. The reasoning behind this is that if two people are exactly alike, they will have no disagreement and nothing to learn from each other. However, if they are highly dissimilar, they are less likely to have some common ground for communication. As a result, there may be less understanding and more chance for distrust of the unfamiliar.

Just as individual influence is affected by the similarity of the parties involved, so the influence of a group is enhanced by its similarity to the people it is trying to persuade. This suggests a persuasion strategy for both the individual and the group that consists of emphasizing their similarities to the people or groups to be persuaded. This is a traditional technique of the public speaker, who tries to establish "common ground" with his audience before proceeding to the issues of concern.

Credibility

Credibility in simple terms refers to a person's or group's believ-ability. Another frequently used term is ethos. The person with high ethos or credibility is the one we respect and whose word we accept. His credibility is based on our perception and impressions, not something inherent in him. A variety of attributes contributes to our perception of high credibility (McCroskey, Jensen and Valencia, 1973). The most significant dimension is usually a person's *competence,* which depends on whether or not we view him as expert, intelligent, informed, intellectual, logical, and so forth. A second dimension is his *character:* is he honest, sympathetic, kind, good, responsible, and virtuous? A third dimension is *sociability.* Factors such as cheerfulness, friendliness, sociability, and good-naturedness determine our view of a person's sociability. *Composure,* a fourth dimension is based on whether a person seems poised, relaxed, calm, and composed. A fifth dimension is *extroversion.* If a person is bold, verbal, aggressive, outgoing, and energetic, we perceive him as extroverted. A sixth dimension might best be called *character/sociability* because it seems to be a blend of the two. It includes attributes such as cooperativeness, refinement, niceness, pleasantness, justness, and admirability. One additional dimension that is frequently mentioned is trustworthiness. The importance of trust in a group is discussed elsewhere; it is mentioned here simply to point out that it relates to credibility. The varying levels of all these elements contribute to our judgment of a person's credibility.

The person with high credibility generally produces a fair amount of attitude change (Haiman, 1949), although a variety of factors may intervene to depress this effect. But it is still a wise strategy for the individual or group to try to create favorable credibility so that the chances for effective persuasion are improved.

As mentioned earlier, attraction, similarity, and credibility interact. The person who is attractive tends to be perceived as more credible and to succeed frequently at persuasion (Widgery and Webster, 1969; Mills and Aronson, 1965). Attraction in turn affects similarity. People who are attracted to each other perceive each other as more similar (Inglis, 1965) and are likely to develop more similar attitudes (Brewer, 1968), which suggests that they persuade each other. Once similarity is established, it evidently works toward heightening attraction in a group: group members find a voluntary group more attractive when they feel their opinions are similar to those of the leaders (Rogers, 1968). This latter finding reintroduces notions of credibility, since high credibility is a prerequisite to attainment of leadership positions. We may draw the conclusion that all three variables are inextricably intertwined and in combination affect persuasiveness.

Another related variable that is instrumental in persuasiveness and may partially dictate a person's credibility rating is status or power.

STATUS AND POWER RELATIONSHIPS

Within a group, status and power relationships inevitably evolve. Since status is in itself a source of power and since power conveys status, the two are treated synonymously.

Power may be derived externally or internally, that is, from outside or inside the group. Sources of external power include factors such as previous success and reputation, age, high socioeconomic status, educational level, professional position, and designation as the leader. This means that the person who has built a strong reputation, who is older, who is professional or highly educated, or who has been appointed as leader of the group will wield power in a group. A person may also gain power within the group by appearing highly credible, by developing interpersonal attraction, by controlling resources, or by somehow controlling rewards and punishments. Power developed within the group is usually regarded as more legitimate than externally bestowed power. The student appointed leader by a faculty member will have more difficulty maintaining power in a group than the student who, through his own abilities, develops a power base within the group.

Power is important in a group because power means influence.

Based on an abundance of research, Collins and Guetzkow (1964) have extracted several propositions about the effects of power on groups:

1. High power people exert influence without making overt behavioral attempts to influence.
2. High power-status people initiate a greater total number of communications.
3. High power people initiate more communication classified specifically as influence attempts.
4. High power persons will be successful in a larger percentage of influence attempts than low power persons.
5. High power people are less affected by the efforts of others to influence them.
6. High power members tend to form cliques.
7. Low power people behave deferentially toward high power people.
8. Low power people are suspicious of high power agents who can arbitrarily award or withhold important resources.
9. Low power people are threatened if ambiguity exists in their relationship with high power agents.
10. Low power people are less deferential and less threatened when supported by their peers.

What does all this mean? It means that people with more power will participate more fully, influence others more often, and gain support from other high power people by forming coalitions. However, their influence may be lessened if they are arbitrary, if they make other members feel threatened, or if low power members can gain support from their peers. Since low power people generally defer to high power people and seek their approval, there is less likelihood of strong movements or insurrection by low power members.

The power of the group to influence people outside the group is analogous to the individual's power within the group. Groups must also establish legitimate power and be cautious in their exercise of it. To the extent that others perceive it to have power, a group should be successful in its influence attempts.

ATTITUDES, BELIEFS, AND VALUES

A chapter on individual factors contributing to persuasion would be incomplete without some mention of attitudes, beliefs, and values. The goal of persuasion is to change or reinforce attitudes, beliefs, values, and ultimately, behavior. Attitudes are a person's "predispositions" to behave in a negative or positive way toward something; they are a person's favorable or unfavorable evaluations. Beliefs, on the other hand, refer to whether a person feels something is true or false; they are probability statements about the likelihood of something being true. Values are similar to attitudes but are broader in scope. They are a person's underlying concepts of good and bad. Because behavior is assumed to be based on a person's attitudes, beliefs, and values it is essential to know the initial positions of a person if we are to predict the success of persuasion.

Once these initial attitudes, beliefs, and values have been identified, the question confronting the individual or group is how extreme should a position be in order to persuade others. The principle of similarity discussed earlier would predict that an argument highly discrepant from the persuadee's position would be rejected. A body of theories on attitude change results in conflicting recommendations.

One theory, known as the involvement or social judgment theory (Sherif, Sherif and Nebergall, 1965), would concur with the principle of similarity. According to this theory, our judgments fall into three categories: a latitude of acceptance, a latitude of noncommitment, and a latitude of rejection. The latitude or range of acceptable, neutral, and unacceptable positions depends on how involved we are with an issue. The more involved we are, the smaller the range of acceptable positions. Thus, young men during the Vietnam War era found the issue of the draft highly involving, which means they probably accepted a narrow range of arguments. Based on this theory, the individual or group attempting persuasion would be advised to argue for positions not too discrepant from those of the persuadee, that is, positions falling within the persuadee's latitude of acceptance or noncommitment.

Three other related theories, however, might recommend taking more extreme positions. These theories all deal with cognitive consistency or balance. In simplest terms, they argue that when two or more attitudes, or beliefs, or values, or all of these are incongruent or inconsistent, mental tension develops that motivates the individual to change one or more of them to achieve a balanced state (Festinger, 1957; Heider, 1946; Osgood and Tannenbaum, 1955). The attitudes, beliefs, and values may relate to sources as well as issues. For example, if a person likes another group member, but opposes the position he favors, his attitude toward the person is incongruent with his attitude toward the issue. According to these theories, the larger the discrepancy, the greater the change that will occur to resolve the dissonance, or disturbing state. The best strategy to get the most change would be, therefore, to take positions distant from those of the persuadee.

Since these various theories are somewhat contradictory in their recommendations, what should you do to be an effective persuader? Probably, the best advice is to follow a campaign strategy where small changes at a time are attempted, in order to avoid rejection for being too discrepant. At the same time, advocated positions should be dissimilar enough to create cognitive imbalance so that the person is motivated to change. If the advocated position is too similar to the persuadee's, it may seem to be the same as his position, which would leave him in a balanced, static state, rather than pushing him into a dissonant, dynamic one. This strategy of planning a campaign of moderately discrepant arguments combines the elements of all four theories that we feel are the most useful.

It should be noted that also implicit in these theories are recommendations for strengthening existing views and making people resistant to change. Frequently in a group, maintenance of present views, rather than change, *is* the goal. Similarly, our group efforts to persuade outsiders may be geared to strengthening them against counterpersuasion. Under such circumstances, the theories discussed above suggest that we should heighten involvement, reinforce views that help maintain cognitive balance, and work to change elements that are causing dissonance. More specific recommendations for persuasive message strategies will be made in the next chapter.

SUMMARY AND APPLICATION

So far, this chapter has attempted to isolate the various people-related factors that affect persuasion within and by a group. The question still to be answered is how to apply all of this to group persuasion. At this point, we would like to partially answer that question in the process of summarizing these variables. Our recommendations must be regarded as tentative because, in most cases, the research is inadequate to make firm statements.

Before looking at the specific variables, we would like to underline the observation that groups are highly complex systems. If you gear a persuasion attempt to one individual's unique characteristics you may find yourself violating the needs of another. It is probably a nearly impossible task when planning a persuasive campaign to balance effectively all the individual differences. Moreover, the task increases in difficulty when you consider the complexity of the audience outside the group. But, analyzing your audience will give you a higher potential for success than being totally unaware of their characteristics.

With that in mind, let us examine more closely the people-related variables. We talked first about Machiavellians. If you are a Machiavellian, your chances for success at persuading others is already high. If in a group, you are attempting to minimize the influence of a high Mach, one of the few things you can do is emphasize the task, while reducing irrelevant emotional involvement which serves to distract other members and give the high Mach more opportunity to succeed. You should also recognize that he will be little influenced by others and that he has a low regard for them. Consequently, excessive effort to establish credibility with him or to persuade him may be wasted.

Similar statements might be made about the anomic or alienated individual since he distrusts others and regards them as nonpersons. Unless trust can be established with such people, they may have very low involvement in the group. To the extent that the group helps the anomic overcome his feelings of meaninglessness, powerlessness, and social isolation, they may find him susceptible to group persuasion and active.

The dogmatic personality will also be resistant to persuasion unless it comes from a source that he perceives to be an authority. To overcome his inflexibility, you must increase your own credibility by demonstrating that you are an authority. As pointed out earlier, group interaction itself may also help to soften the rigidity of the high dogmatic.

The anxiety level of individuals affects their persuasibility. People with high chronic anxiety are less persuasible, while people with high situational anxiety are more persuasible. Moreover, chronically anxious people tend to be intolerant of ambiguity. It may be possible to reduce their anxiety and increase their persuasibility by reducing sources of ambiguity, such as unclear tasks or status hierarchies and inadequate feedback on their opinions and behaviors. Individuals with communication-bound anxiety may become less anxious if the group provides an accepting, encouraging atmosphere. Other forms of situational anxiety (such as those induced by fear appeals) may be taken advantage of in increasing the success of persuasion.

Expectations of the behaviors of introverts and extroverts are not clear-cut. It is possible that a persuasive campaign directed toward the introverts may be more successful than one directed toward the extroverts. Similarly, people with low self-esteem are more vulnerable targets than people with high self-esteem. This suggests the possibility of intentionally criticizing a person to lower his self-esteem so that he is more susceptible to opinions, but ethical considerations argue against this strategy.

In addition to the already mentioned personality variables, people with lower intelligence, younger individuals, and possibly women may be more persuasible. Based on these and other factors, some individuals will be highly likely to conform to group pressure. Persuasion within the group is likely to be more effective if it is more representative of a group consensus than an individual effort. Group pressures toward conformity and uniformity are powerful forces in producing change and resistance to change.

Besides personality factors, there are the interrelated variables of attraction, similarity, and credibility. Individuals or groups who can develop their attractiveness to others through methods such as frequent interaction, rewarding and praising others, and emphasizing their similarities to others are more influential. Individuals or groups who desire to be persuasive should also work to establish high credibility, although not to the extent of being highly dissimilar to the receivers. The combination of attraction, similarity, high credibility, and other factors lead to high power. Whether externally or internally derived, high status-power people are more successful at persuasion as long as they are not excessively arbitrary or create ambiguity for low power persons.

Finally, to be successful at persuasion, the interested individual and group must take into account the attitudes, beliefs, and values of the receivers. Specific recommendations for dealing with these factors will be discussed in the next chapter.

SUGGESTED READINGS

Cartwright, D. and **Zander, A.,** eds. *Group Dynamics.* 3d ed. New York: Harper & Row, Publishers, 1968: 139–297.

Christie, R. and **Geis, F. L.** *Studies in Machiavellianism.* New York: Academic Press, Inc., 1970.

Clinard, M. B. *Anomic and Deviant Behavior: A Discussion and Critique.* New York: The Free Press, 1964.

Collins, B. E. and **Guetzkow, H.** *A Social Psychology of Group Process for Decision Making.* New York: John Wiley & Sons, Inc., 1964.

Rogers, E. M. and **Shoemaker, F. F.** *Communication of Innovations: A Cross-Cultural Approach.* New York: The Free Press, 1971.

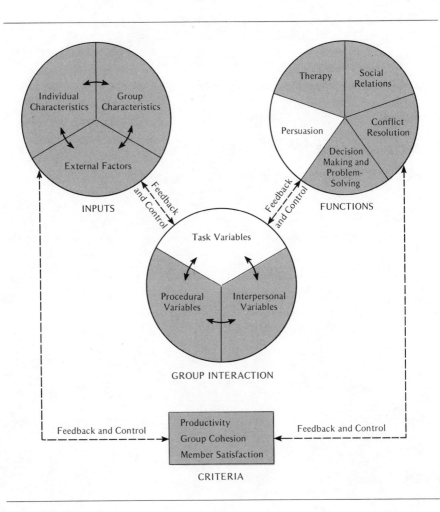

INPUTS

Individual Characteristics

Group Characteristics

External Factors

Feedback and Control

FUNCTIONS

Therapy

Social Relations

Persuasion

Conflict Resolution

Decision Making and Problem-Solving

Feedback and Control

GROUP INTERACTION

Task Variables

Procedural Variables

Interpersonal Variables

Feedback and Control

Feedback and Control

Productivity

Group Cohesion

Member Satisfaction

CRITERIA

Small Group Communication to Persuade: Message Variables

"Then you should say what you mean," the March Hare went on.

"I do," Alice hastily replied; "at least — at least I mean what I say — that's the same thing you know."

"Not the same thing a bit!" said the Hatter, "Why you might just as well say that 'I see what I eat' is the same as 'I eat what I see'!"

from Lewis Carroll
Alice's Adventures in Wonderland

IN THE preceding chapter, we discussed the many factors that affect people when they are trying to persuade people in the group situation. In this chapter, we continue to take the view that any one group member can bring as an *input* to the group communication situation the intent to persuade. Although a large part of the literature discussed in this chapter is also applicable to and derived from situations other than the small group setting, we think that it is wise to equip people to be as persuasive as possible with other members of a group. There are many real life situations in which one member of the group enters the situation with the desire to control the *process* and the desired *outcome* is for the group to comply with his wishes. Therefore, we believe that a person can prepare himself better for the function of persuasion in a group situation by planning and structuring his communication so that it is likely to result in compliance by other group members.

All of us are familiar with the injunction "it is not *what* you say but *how* you say it that matters." While this statement has a grain of truth in it, it is misleading for those who wish to exert influence in small groups. A great deal of this text is concerned with the "how" variables of group communication. How can I create situations that will make group members more effective in persuasive communication? How can I analyze myself, fellow group members, and the situation to persuade and inform? While all these "how" questions are important in obtaining effective group communication, we still need to know how *what* we say affects other group members. This chapter describes and summarizes ways to structure messages that are likely to produce social influence.

The Elements of Persuasive Messages

Perhaps a good way to begin our attempt to understand how persuasion operates in the small group would be to look for elements that are common to most, if not all, persuasive messages. Toulmin (1959) discusses three elements that seem to be present in most influence attempts: a claim, a warrant, and data. These elements tell us what idea or course of action a group member wants accepted and provide reasons for the acceptance.

A *claim* tells us what a source wants group members to believe or do. When a communicator makes an assertion, he is asking someone else to accept a claim. He may make a policy claim, which specifies a course of action and calls for its adoption. For example, in planning a course, one group member might make a claim of "policy" by saying that there should be no tests in introductory courses. The communicator might also make a claim of "fact"; for example he might say, "Some introductory courses have instituted a discussion: paper format (i.e., no tests)." Finally, a communicator might make a claim that expresses his judgment concerning the goodness, morality, merit, or "value" of a person, object, or event: Students learn more in courses that require creative thinking than they do in courses where they memorize by rote. Obviously, the kind of claim a communicator makes in persuasive discourse influences the kind of supporting material he must offer the group if his influence attempt is to succeed.

A *warrant* is a general belief or attitude which justifies acceptance of the claim. If a communicator suggests to the university student government that an executive board is more effective than an officer and committee format because an executive board provides a check on the president and is more efficient (a warrant), then we have at least a skeletal persuasive unit. If we agree with the source's view that the executive board is more efficient, we have a reason to accept the claim. While the above example expresses only a relationship among phenomena, warrants may implicitly or explicitly use values to be persuasive. For example, past student body presidents may have told governing organizations that executive board formats are bad because the president is often unaware of the board members' actions. The warrant (whether actually stated or not) to the claim is that an executive board format is bad. If we share this attitude toward executive boards and concur with the source that inefficiency occurs when the president does not have complete authority, we will probably be persuaded that an executive board format is bad. A word of caution seems appropriate at this point: many persuasive attempts fail because of inappropriate linkages between warrants and claims. While one group member might accept the claim that the executive board format should not be instituted, a warrant suggesting a link between the board format and the inefficiency of the university power structure may seem so ludicrous that it might result in counter-persuasion.

Data are specific beliefs and attitudes about the existence of objects or events. McCroskey (1968) has suggested three distinct types of data: first-, second-, and third-order data. First-order data are beliefs shared by the speaker and the other group members. If a communicator knows the group believes that memorizing facts is not a learning experience, he may use as first-order data examples of the harmful effects of memorization on creativity. Second-order data are beliefs of the source that are not necessarily shared by the rest of the group. Every persuasive attempt probably contains second-order data (source assertion) which is dependent on how credible the source is to his audience. Usually the invocation of source credibility is implied rather than stated. An example of second-order data would be:

1. I believe the pass-fail grading system is bad.
2. As a professor I am a credible source (unstated warrant).
3. Therefore, the pass-fail system is bad.

Thus, if my credibility is high enough, the implied warrant will make this statement first-order data (the group will come to share my belief) and it can be used in further argument. However, if my credibility is low, the source assertion will probably have little or no effect.

When a member and the group do not share similar attitudes or when the member is low in credibility, he must resort to third-order data. This type of data is called *evidence* and is attributed to someone external to the immediate communication transaction occurring within the group.

1. Classes will soon adopt a discussion: paper format (claim).
2. I am a truthful person (warrant).
3. A group of educators recently published an article which said that the lecture: test format was not conducive to creativity (third-order data).

The effective establishment of source-group agreement (or first-order data in McCroskey's model) by using third-order data is contingent on several variables. First, the group must believe the communicator is telling the truth about what others say, and second, the outside source must be believable and relevant to the issue. If the source is not trustworthy or the group dislikes or disbelieves the outside source, or both, little persuasion is likely to occur. Finally, the claim made by a communicator may be so unacceptable to the group that no matter how high the speaker's or outside source's credibility, persuasion will not occur.

While it is useful to understand these common message elements in persuasive discourse, only understanding these variables will not explain how to construct effective messages when the intent of small group communication is persuasion. There are several message variables that may or may not be present in any specific message element.

The rest of the chapter discusses questions that are relevant to using these persuasive message elements. How do we effectively use third-order data (evidence)? Do we present data to the group on both sides of a controversial claim? How can we structure support for our claims? How can we insure that our claims are resistant to persuasive attempts by other people in the group? How much fear do we use to persuade others? How intense do we make our persuasive appeals? Consideration of these questions is important to the person who wishes to be influential in his communicative activities.

Evidence

Most traditional theories of persuasion suggest that evidence or what we have referred to as third-order data is important in effecting attitude change. However, the appropriate order of data for a communicator to use may vary across communication situations. A large part of the research generated by persuasion scholars has not taken this into account and has produced conflicting results. Some studies find that evidence has little or no impact on persuasion, while others indicate that the inclusion of evidence is very important in facilitating persuasion.

The following generalizations should be considered when preparing persuasive communication (McCroskey, 1969):

1. Evidence is only effective if the other members of the group were not previously aware of it. If the group already knows about the evidence, they have probably already accepted or rejected the data and a mere restatement of it is unlikely to enhance the persuasive message. If in the example above, the group is already aware of the educator's findings on course formats, mentioning the findings if they had already accepted the data would have little persuasive impact; however, if the receiver had already rejected the findings, it is possible that including the data would make him even more resistant to the claim.

2. The credibility of the communicator is probably more important than evidence in persuasive communication. If a communicator is perceived as competent and trustworthy, he probably has no need to include evidence from people external to the small group discussion. In the cited example, if I believe the communicator is credible and he tells me that the lecture: test format stifles creativity, I will probably believe him. Citing the educator's study in this case will not increase his persuasiveness as I am already prepared to believe him.

3. Evidence must be presented "well" if it is to be persuasive. If the evidence is not delivered well, it may not be understood by the receiver. Also, a poor delivery might reduce the credibility of the speaker, which would result in less overall persuasion.

Two additional considerations should be mentioned about the use of evidence in persuasive messages. Although there is no adequate theoretical explanation for the findings, it seems that the three generalizations given above are most relevant to messages attempting to induce immediate attitude change. Evidence seems to increase the persuasiveness of both high and low credible sources when a delayed measure of attitude change is obtained. Therefore, the use of evidence may be extremely important if attitude change over any length of time is desired. This is especially important when the group is an ongoing unit who will work together for a while. Also, evidence may make the members of the group more resistant to counter-influence by another member or different group. So, if we know people in the group are going to hear persuasive communication that argues against our claim over a length of time, we would be wise to include evidence, regardless of how credible we are perceived to be.

Little research is available that distinguishes between "good" and "bad" evidence. However, as previously suggested, evidence relevant to the claim should be more effective especially when linked by a warrant. Therefore, every attempt should be made to cite relevant evidence from highly credible sources.

Message-Sidedness

Since most claims a communicator might introduce in group discussion have arguments available on both sides, it is important for the message source to know when to cite opposing arguments. A two-sided message sets forth the communicator's claim but also acknowledges opposing arguments. The research generally supports the following conclusions:

1. If the audience is initially in agreement with your claim, a one-sided message can further bolster their support for your position; if the receivers are initially opposed to your claim, a two-sided message is more effective (Hovland, Lumsdaine, and Sheffield, 1949).
2. Two-sided messages tend to be more effective with people with more formal education, regardless of their initial attitude. It is reasoned that people with more education will probably think of objections to the claim on their own and be generally suspicious of an argument which does not concede opposing arguments.
3. If the group members have already been exposed to the opposing arguments, a two-sided message is more persuasive. If our intended receivers heard the claim that the test: lecture format gave instructors insight on their students' abilities and the group members were aware of evidence disputing that claim, the source must at least give an indication that he is aware of the opposing side or the receiver is likely to perceive him as incompetent for not knowing about the data and/or untrustworthy for not mentioning it. Either or both of these perceptions by the receiver of the source would reduce the persuasive impact of the source.

Given this research evidence, it seems clear that the best advice to give most group discussants is to use the two-sided message strategy. There are several considerations which support this suggestion. First, as a society, we are becoming more educated and it is likely that the reader of this book will probably spend a majority of his time communicating in groups composed of relatively well-educated people. Second, the media present such a barrage of information on most issues of social import that it is highly unlikely that any small group would not have at least one member who is aware of some of the opposing arguments on most persuasive topics. Finally, one does not always have adequate information to determine whether group members initially agree with or oppose one's stand; therefore, a two-sided message is probably less risky in most small group situations.

We end this section with a customary word of caution and a paradox that is difficult to resolve. There is evidence that there is a potential "backlash" effect in certain· situations with the two-sided message. While it is extremely wise to cover the opposing arguments that members of the group are aware of, mentioning more arguments than the receiver initially had knowledge of can lead to attitude change in the *opposite direction of the claim advocated by the communicator* (Weston, 1967). Therefore, one is faced with the difficult task of assessing what other people in the group know and making sure one acknowledges only those arguments and little else in the way of unfamiliar opposing information.

Message Strategies to Induce Resistance to Persuasion

Although the previous discourse has centered on how to prepare messages to change people's attitudes, much persuasive communication seeks to reinforce currently held convictions and to make them more resistant to change. A great deal of research has been done on message strategies that are designed to inhibit change; it is complementary to the research on message-sidedness that is discussed above.

McGuire (1964) has formulated a theory based on a biological analogy to explain inducing resistance to persuasion. He claims that just as a person is immunized by exposing him to weakened doses of a disease, so a communicator can immunize people against future persuasive appeals. McGuire's procedure requires messages that will stimulate defenses but not destroy them. There are two separate message strategies designed to immunize people against persuasive messages: (1) supportive message pretreatments (i.e., evidence that either further supports or induces individuals to gain information that further supports their present beliefs), and (2) refutational pretreatments (i.e., statements attacking beliefs counter to the group members' beliefs). Perhaps an example would clarify the differences between these strategies. Suppose a book salesman wants to insure that a book adoption committee is not persuaded by another salesman to switch textbooks. If he wants to use the supportive message strategy, he emphasizes positive things about a book (e.g., perhaps the reputation of the authors and contributors, the low price, the fact that the professors are familiar with the text). Of course, if the salesman knows why the committee originally adopted the text, he can emphasize new arguments to bolster and strengthen the group's beliefs. If he wants to use the refutational strategy, he attempts to attack the competition's arguments about their text or points out weaknesses in what the competitor might say about the text he is attempting to sell.

Research generally attests to the superiority of the refutational strategy over the supportive messages. However, there is some evidence to suggest that combining refutational and supportive message strategies is superior to using either, alone. In our previous example, the salesman reaffirms positive aspects of his text, then refutes potential arguments a competitor might advance.

Surprisingly, few people have written about the similarity between the results of message-sidedness research and of inducing resistance to persuasion studies. The supportive strategy of bolstering a belief and thus making a person resistant to persuasion is very similar to changing a person with a one-sided message. Whether trying to change an attitude or inhibit change, this strategy is minimally effective. The combining of refutational and supportive messages in the resistance to persuasion studies is similar to using a two-sided message to change attitudes. In summary, there seems to be a great deal of similarity between the kinds of messages that are effective in changing beliefs and in making them resistant to subsequent persuasive appeals. The effective group discussant should be aware that it is important to make sure that the group is persuaded and remains that way.

The Structure of Persuasive Messages

Although teachers of public speaking and group discussion would have us believe that the degree of organization in a persuasive appeal is a significant predictor of its effectiveness, there is little evidence to support this claim. It has been found (McCroskey and Mehrley, 1969) that severe disorganization reduces the persuasiveness of a message but less dramatic disorganization has little effect. These findings are counter to what we might intuitively expect and deserve more explanation. All of the studies were concerned with the "logical" organization of messages. Messages were organized with patterns of claims and supporting statements that were judged to be coherent and logically valid. Disorganized messages had this pattern altered by changing sentences and paragraphs in some manner. There seemed to be little effect produced by this disorganization.

There are several plausible explanations for this. People obviously have the ability to organize communication that comes to them in a "logically" disorganized fashion. Marshal McLuhan claims that the electronic media have created an environment that forces us to organize events rapidly and recognize patterns. The book and printed word influence us to think in a linear, "organized" manner while the contemporary media place a premium on assimilating and understanding events as they occur. Given the large amount of time each of us spends with the new media, this explanation seems particularly sound.

There is another explanation that comes from our experience in the classroom (on both sides of the podium). Most of the research discussed in this text has been conducted on college students. The college lecture and discussion classes are probably prime examples of "disorganized" messages. We rarely find ourselves, nor can we remember many of our professors delivering lectures in what would be called a logically organized manner. Therefore, it is possible that organizational abilities are a learned ability of the college student; perhaps it is even mandatory for survival in the university system. Organization of messages *might* be more important when communicating in noncollege groups. Finally, one can speculate that organization is less important in interpersonal and small group communication situations where questions and feedback often change or disrupt logical patterns, or both. This fact should be of primary interest to the readers of this text.

So far, the discussion of structure has been concerned only with the logical organization of persuasive messages. There are also structural variables that psychologically affect group members and make them more or less receptive to the persuasive appeal. Should one present the good arguments first or last? Is it best to cite a source before or after presenting evidence? Is it effective to tell the group that one is going to attempt to persuade them? Is it more effective to present solutions or the problem first? What is the best way to begin an attack on a person's present beliefs? Should one tell the group the conclusions one specifically wants accepted or should one just imply them? These questions are important considerations that have an impact on the psychological disposition of the group and are our next topic for discussion.

Where Do the Supporting Arguments Lead?   If you take the previous advice and use a two-sided message, you must decide where to use the arguments that support your claim. Let us assume that I want to persuade a group that families should not have more than two children. There is no way that I can believe that people are unaware of opposing arguments so I decide to employ a two-sided message. Should I discuss first the reasons supporting planned parenthood, then follow with arguments against the claim and finish by refuting those arguments? Or would I be more persuasive if I discussed and refuted the arguments against planned parenthood prior to discussing the positive aspects of population control? Although there is a limited amount of research in this area (Miller and Campbell, 1959) we can tentatively conclude that the former method is more persuasive (i.e., present the positive arguments, then discuss and refute the opposing arguments). In fact, even when opposing arguments are not refuted subsequent to discussion, mentioning positive arguments first is more persuasive. It is believed that when people hear supporting arguments first, they become persuaded by those arguments and are therefore closer to the position of the source when the source attacks the opposition. If the communicator initially attacks the opposition, it may be perceived by the group that they and their beliefs are being attacked, and it is possible that they will react very defensively and resist any arguments the source produces to support his claim. Moreover, if a person reviews the opposition first, he may actually strengthen the receiver's initial attitude by discussing the opposing arguments with which the receiver may already agree. Therefore, we would advise the source to be careful not to completely disrupt the group process by emphasizing negative statements early in the group discussion.

When Do You Cite the Source of Evidence?   If a source external to the immediate group communication transaction (third-order data/

evidence) is being used, it must be decided when to tell the group the identity or qualifications, or both, of the external source. It seems to depend on the credibility of the source of the evidence. Greenberg and Miller (1966) found that when the evidence source is high in credibility, it does not matter whether we identify him before or after presenting his evidence statement. However, when the receiver perceives the source of evidence to be low in credibility, it is better to cite the evidence source *after* giving the evidence. In fact, when the source is cited after the evidence is given, a high credible source of evidence is no more persuasive than a low credible source. Thus, since we do not always know how a group will perceive an evidence source, the communicator interested in the greatest persuasive effect should give his evidence prior to identifying the evidence source. One can easily see the validity of this advice when speaking in a group whose members have differing perceptions of an evidence source.

Do You Reveal Your Intent to Persuade?   Whether one is wise to forewarn a group that one is attempting to persuade them is a complex question. If a group is known to be strongly opposed to the claim one is supporting, forewarning the group that one is going to attempt to change their attitudes is not effective (Allyn and Festinger, 1962). Thus, one would probably be ill-advised to state initially a persuasive intent if one were speaking to PTA members on the favorable aspects of living together as opposed to marriage. However, this conclusion warrants some qualification; if all members of the group like one another, the potential persuader will be more effective if he openly admits his intent to persuade than if he does not. If the group dislikes the source, admitting his persuasive goals is no more effective than remaining silent about his intent (Mills and Aronson, 1965). A respected supervisor in an organization might well inform his employees about his desire to persuade them not to go on strike, but one who is unsure of how well he is liked by the group would be advised to leave his persuasive intent unstated. Another situation that is tangential to the question of strategy is "overheard communication." Walster and Festinger (1962) found that when a person is led to believe he has accidentally overheard a communication transaction, he tends to be persuaded by that message. All of us can probably think of times when we have been influenced by communication we "should not" have heard. In this case, *thinking* a person has no intent to persuade us is effective in changing our attitudes. Many times a group member can turn to another person in the group for a "private" comment and influence the entire group with the overheard conversation. This tends to work only when the receivers are involved or interested in the topic and initially favorable to the communicator's position; in other words, this strategy bolsters existing attitudes.

Do You Present Problems or Solutions First?   Suppose I wanted to convince the members of a class that there are grading problems that can be solved by grading on the curve. I could structure my message to present first the problems of grading and then propose grading on a curve as the solution. Another alternative would be to discuss initially the merits of grading on the curve and then explain problems one faces in assigning grades. The problem-to-solution pattern has been found by Cohen (1957) significantly more effective in producing attitude change both immediately after presentation of the message and over a length of time. This has been explained by suggesting that the problem-to-solution-type message is more interesting and the solution is more clearly understood when the group is aware of a problem or need prior to hearing a solution. Moreover, when the solution is presented first, the group members do not necessarily understand its relevance because a need has not been developed. Possibly, people pay little attention to the solution-to-problem pattern and are therefore unpersuaded by the argument. The important thing is to establish a need in the mind of the group members and then provide them with a way to solve that need.

How Do You Begin to Attack a Person's Beliefs?   In most persuasive communication situations, one finds that the members of the group one is attempting to persuade agree with some of one's beliefs and disagree with others. When does one discuss the point of common agreement? Some people claim that the best strategy is to discuss points that all agree on first, then move to items of disagreement. Presumably, discussing common views captures the group's attention and heightens their evaluation of the source, which carries over to the disputed claims and makes the receivers more receptive to the persuasive appeal. Encyclopedia salesmen pretending to do "market research" often use this strategy with great success. They structure a series of questions that potential customers are likely to agree with, e.g., "Would you use these books if they were in your home? If we made you a gift of these books, would you tell your friends about them?" and finally, "Would you pay a 'small' service charge for the rest of your natural life?" The salesman hopes to establish a pattern leading to final acceptance. Unfortunately, from many points of view, this strategy is quite successful, attesting to the generalizability of the previously mentioned research.

How Clear Should Conclusions Be?   Cronkhite (1969) provides a statement that clearly summarizes our knowledge to date about conclusions, when he claims that most audiences respond most favorably when conclusions are explicit and appeal for a specific action. Most research indicates that if a communicator explicitly states conclusions there is more attitude change than when the group is allowed to decide for themselves which actions or beliefs the communicator is advocating. People with a more clinical approach to communication would not agree with these conclusions; they would contend that allowing a person to participate in the communication by drawing his own conclusions leads to more lasting attitude change. (We discuss this approach in more detail in Chapter 6.) Of course, one of the dangers of this approach is that there is a distinct possibility that the group members will not arrive at the same conclusions as the ones the communicator wanted them to accept. Thus, when persuasion (as opposed to other functions of communication such as information exchange, conflict resolution, or therapy) is the goal of the communication transaction in group discussion, one is advised to be explicit in one's conclusions and specific in one's claims.

All these variables seem to have a great impact on the psychological receptivity of the group and thus dramatically affect the persuasion process. The communicator should consider the questions raised in this section when structuring messages designed to influence other members of the group.

Fear Appeals

One has only to watch advertisements about seat belts or the dangers of cigarette smoking, listen to politicians warn about the threat of impending doom if their proposals are not accepted, or hear a freshman student give a speech on any issue from gun control to student rights to realize that a large amount of persuasive communication tries to arouse receivers by appealing to fear. Given the pervasiveness of fear appeals in our everyday communication experiences, it is hardly surprising that a great deal of research has been conducted to specify the effects of fear arousal in persuasive messages.

A fear appeal indicates the harmful consequences that will befall the group (or someone significant to them) if they do not adopt the course of action suggested by the communicator. A strong fear appeal dramatically expresses the aversive consequences (e.g., films of severely diseased gums and decayed teeth to encourage people to brush their teeth regularly). A moderate fear appeal would show less dramatically that lack of proper hygiene leads to dental problems, while a low fear appeal might only mention the link between lack of proper brushing and tooth decay. Obviously, a potentially persuasive communicator needs to know which type of fear appeal is most effective in producing change in the group members.

The findings are disturbingly conflicting: some studies find that a strong fear appeal is best, while others argue convincingly that a moderate fear appeal is most persuasive. When this kind of confusion results from research efforts, people must look for other factors that influence receivers' judgments. Such an investigation was carried out and the results indicate that the following variables influence how people react to fear appeals in a persuasive message (Miller, 1963):

1. The credibility of the communicator influences how receivers react to fear appeals. A highly credible source is more persuasive using high rather than moderate fear appeals; however, a low credible source is less persuasive with the high than the moderate fear appeal.
2. When the fear appeal is directed toward a "valued other" (e.g., the anti-smoking commercial showing a young son smoking his first cigarette in an attempt to get the father to give up cigarettes), the strong fear appeal is more persuasive than a mild fear appeal. When the fear appeal is directed toward others we care about, it is hard to discount the appeal by rationalizing that one is only harming himself by not accepting the communicator's claim.
3. Evidence supporting the fear appeal influences the persuasiveness of the message. A strong appeal *with evidence* is more effective than a strong appeal *without evidence* or mild fear appeals, with or without evidence. However, the effect of the fear appeal seems to be short-lived. After only two weeks, the effect of the strong versus mild fear appeal vanished and only the people who received messages containing evidence retained their changed attitudes. In other words, people who received either the strong or mild fear appeal *with evidence* remained persuaded while those receiving both types of fear appeals *without evidence* quickly reverted to the positions they held prior to receiving the persuasive message.

In summary, strong fear appeals are effective when the communicator is high in credibility, when they are directed toward valued others, or in the long run when they are supported by evidence. However, one should not carry these findings to an absurd extent. If a message is too frightening or vivid, it may cause the group to repress thoughts that anything so horrible could occur. Such an event probably took place in the 1964 Presidential election when an anti-Goldwater commercial showed a small girl, then a nuclear explosion, with the implication that the election of Goldwater would bring this tragedy upon us; this controversial commerical probably appeared so unreal that it lacked persuasive impact. However, fear appeals used with reason are an effective strategy for the persuasive communicator.

Language Intensity

Closely related to using fear as a persuasive technique is the use of intense language to promote attitude change. Language intensity can be conceptualized as the degree to which a claim deviates from a neutral position. For example, the claim that "grading on the curve is a *terrible* method" indicates a more intense claim than "grading on the curve is an *inadequate* method." Bowers (1964) suggests two different means one can use to vary the level of language intensity in a message. The first method is the insertion of "qualifiers." One type of qualifier indicates the probability of an action or event occurring: saying that the abolition of capital punishment will "certainly" lead to more violent crime is likely to be perceived as more intense then if one inserted the word "perhaps." Another type of qualifier indicates extremity: saying that one "dislikes" a course of action is a less intense statement than indicating that one "despises" an outcome. The second way to increase intensity is by the use of metaphors, especially metaphorical statements alluding to sex or death (e.g., college education is a systematic "rape" of the mind; the "demise" of free speech). The question for the communicator, then, is how to structure messages of appropriate intensity to be as persuasive as possible.

Few prescriptive statements can be made about how intensely one should argue. McEwen and Greenberg (1970) found that people exposed to highly intense persuasive messages rated the communicators as generally more credible and believed the highly intense persuasive messages were more clear and of higher quality; however, they were not more persuasive. Others have found that low intensity messages produced more attitude change. There are several explanations for this "backlash" effect of messages employing language of high intensity. One explanation would suggest that when one argues in a highly intense manner, one is probably taking a position that is very discrepant from that of other group members: when the message is very discrepant from the audience position, they tend to "contrast" what the speaker is saying with what they believe and psychologically refute his arguments as they hear them and thus remain unchanged. However, if the language is only moderate or low in intensity, people can probably see similarities between their beliefs and those of the communicator and "assimilate" his claims more easily into their structure of beliefs. If one has reason to believe that people are extremely ego-involved in the topic (i.e., their present beliefs are very important to them), one should anticipate a contrast effect and little or no attitude change if one uses highly intense language. If the topic is less involving or important to the receiver, the source can use more intensely worded claims to achieve persuasion.

Research on opinionated language is generally supportive of the above conclusions. Opinionated language conveys two separate types of information: (1) the claim of the source, and (2) his attitude toward those who agree or disagree with the claim. An opinionated rejection statement derogates those who disagree (e.g., only a Fascist would oppose gun control laws), while an opinionated acceptance statement praises those in agreement with the claim (e.g., any person who dislikes violent crime would support gun control laws). A nonopinionated statement only gives the claim (e.g., I favor gun control laws). Miller and Lobe (1967) found that opinionated rejection statements seem more intense than nonopinionated statements and are effective for high credible sources: for low credible sources, nonopinionated language is more persuasive. When the audience is very ego-involved in the issue, nonopinionated language is more effective than the more intense opinionated rejection statements; when the audience is neutral on the issue, opinionated rejection statements are more persuasive than nonopinionated statements (Mehrley and McCroskey, 1970). These findings conform to "assimilation-contrast" explanations and we can tentatively make certain suggestions in summary:

1. When a communicator knows a receiver has high regard for him, he can be relatively intense in stating his claim and succeed in persuading.
2. If it is known that the topic is very important or ego-involving, or both, to the receiver, a communicator is advised to state his claim in a less intense manner.

Since so little is known about the effects of intense language, it is difficult to offer many conclusions. The reader has no doubt noticed that nothing has been said about opinionated acceptance statements; this is quite simply because no one has systematically studied these messages. Many believe intuitively that we must state our position intensely if we are to be persuasive; the value of this section, perhaps, is to point out that this is not always true and to urge the potential persuader to exercise reason and caution when deciding how intensely to word his claim.

Summary and Conclusions

There seem to be at least two variables that affect most of the strategies we have discussed here. First, the amount of credibility the communicator has in the eyes of the group appears to be very important in determining the kind of message that is likely to be most effective. The amount of regard other group members hold for the communicator is partially responsible for the answers to many questions we posed. Second, the initial attitude of the group members on the issue affects how they react to persuasive appeals. Thus, the communicator should make every effort to determine how his target audience feels *both* about him and about the issue at hand prior to attempting attitude change; this information will make success much more probable.

In this chapter, we have considered several issues that are important to the communicator who wishes to exert influence in small group discussion. In the process we have undoubtedly raised more questions than we have been successful in answering. However, we have tried to review available research conscientiously and select the studies that were carefully done and appeared to provide valid results. Translating the technical research of scholars into practical suggestions for the communicator is not always an easy task. We have tried to balance our desire to make our work practical and useful to the student of human communication with our fears that, since many of our conclusions must remain tentative until more knowledge is available, we might suggest strategies that would decrease the students' interpersonal effectiveness. We urge the student to be aware at least of the complexity of the communication process and test our suggestions to determine the ones that are most effective in the groups he works in.

Obviously, no one can go into a group discussion with a complete persuasive plan worked out in advance. One's plans are often changed by the inputs and questions of others; feedback and new information are brought in and no one can adequately predict the process of communication that a small group will adopt. However, many of the findings in this chapter have proved effective in more formal communication situations (public speech, mass communication, and written efforts). So we believe that when a person desires the compliance of other group members, he would be wise to consider carefully the suggestions in this chapter.

A group member can cite evidence and sources at appropriate times. Both sides of issues can be brought to the group's attention; in fact, we have seen many people fail in group discussion because they refuse to do this. Fear can be as effectively used in a group as it can in other situations. Of course, people can select the proper language to influence others. If people follow some of our suggestions on message construction, they might not only be persuasive but help contribute to higher quality group discussion and decisions. In fact, if all members used these legitimate means of persuasion intelligently, the group might truly come to the best decision without coercing anyone.

A final statement about persuasion in the small group seems appropriate at this point. The comments we have made about constructing persuasive messages can apply to both the individual persuader *within* a small group and the group as a persuader of *others*. Often a small group will have to persuade other people to accept its conclusions or behave in a prescribed manner. There is no doubt that the material in this chapter can be useful to the group that wishes to influence others. However, there are some potential dangers for a person who comes to the group with the sole intent of getting the rest of the group to comply. Much of what we have said about the assembly effect bonuses that accrue to the group as the result of spontaneous interaction is negated if one person merely presents a series of oral messages designed to gain compliance. The person who uses the techniques advised in these two chapters on persuasion is cautioned to be aware of the constraints he places on the group; the final decision will be no better than his original plan, if he does successfully persuade the group. Sometimes this is desirable and at others it is not. However, we know that groups must deal with members who desire to persuade, and perhaps this information that will make some people better persuaders will allow others to resist persuasive attempts when they do not conform to the superordinate goals of the group.

SUGGESTED READINGS

Bettinghaus, E. P. *Message Preparation: The Nature of Proof.* Indianapolis: The Bobbs-Merrill Co., Inc., 1966.

Cronkhite, G. *Persuasion—Speech and Behavioral Change.* Indianapolis: The Bobbs-Merrill Co., Inc., 1969.

Kiesler, C. A., Collins, B. E, and **Miller, N.** *Attitude Change—A Critical Analysis of Theoretical Approaches.* New York: John Wiley & Sons, Inc., 1969.

McGuire, W. J. "The Nature of Attitudes and Attitude Change," in *Handbook of Social Psychology,* Vol. III. edited by G. Lindzey and E. Aronson. Reading, Mass.: Addison-Wesley Publishing Company, Inc., 1969: 136–314.

Miller, G. R. "Studies on the Use of Fear Appeals: A Summary and Analysis." *Central States Speech Journal,* 14 (1963): 117–25.

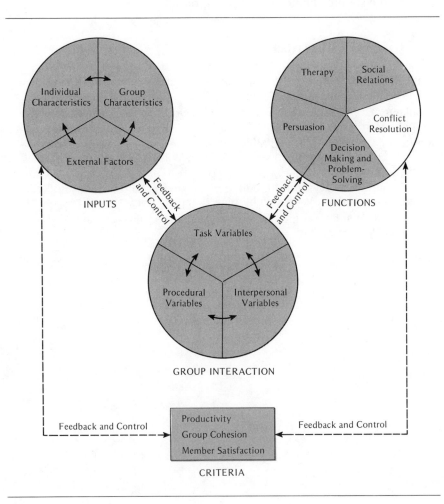

Small Group
Communication
to Resolve Conflict

MANY CONTEMPORARY writers and teachers of courses in small group communication suggest that *competition* and *conflict* are synonymous. Concomitant with this view, prescriptive behaviors are suggested which enable the group to create a climate of cooperation, eliminate competitive behaviors, and at all costs avoid conflict. Some writers have made what we consider an improper, albeit implicit, link between competitive behavior and undesirable personality syndromes such as "closed-mindedness"; the cooperative person is, of course, assumed to be open and receptive. We do not believe we are being unduly cavalier in suggesting that this view of small group communication is less than useful. Competition can be healthy and conflict beneficial. General prescriptive statements condemning competition or conflict while praising cooperation will not stand the test of careful scrutiny. One must look at the results of competition or conflict, or both, on the group prior to making evaluative decisions.

Competition should not be classified as a form of conflict, although it may be an important source of conflict. Competition is the seeking of scarce resources according to established rules that limit the kinds of behaviors each competitor can employ to surpass the others.[1] The object is to obtain the desired, scarce resource but not to destroy the opponent. We would define conflict as behavior that seriously disrupts a situation and makes groups dysfunctional or threatens their continued existence as a unit. Most game situations are competitive, with winning as an objective, and are played according to rules; conflict arises when the rules break down and assaults or violence occur. Debate in the United Nations may be called competitive communication with the purpose being to win, but this does not approach conflict that is characterized by war. In this case, while we might opt for more cooperation among nation-states of the world, the fact is that the very act of competitive debate may be cathartic and prevent real conflict.

The Difference between Competition and Conflict

There is a great wealth of research to show that cooperation *within* a small group results in more productivity and member satisfaction. We have opted to describe in a later chapter how one can participate more effectively in small group communication by adopting a cooperative strategy. People tend to be happier working with cooperative people and often the end result is a better decision or a higher quality product.

However, let us point out at least some of the situations in which competition can be healthy. If a group places the goal of cooperation at-all-costs in a superordinate position over all other goals, mediocre decisions can result. When a faculty makes curriculum decisions on a basis that puts member satisfaction above the needs of the department, the result is likely to be a very "safe" but weak program. We can cooperate and end up with a camel when we wanted a horse. Cooperation or at least the rubric of cooperation can be used to protect the status quo and prevent innovative change. A person with very strong views should not be prevented from expressing them and competing for the "scarce resource" called a group decision. Cooperation should not be an end in itself; rather, it should be a tool, when appropriate, to reach desired ends.

Competition can also be unhealthy and unrealistic in small group communication. People often compete for scarce resources that are in reality not scarce. For example, when a group member competes with another for the attention or admiration of a leader, he may be making

---

[1] Mack, R. W. and Snyder, R. C. "The Analysis of Social Conflict—Toward an Overview and Synthesis," *Journal of Conflict Resolution*, 1 (1957), 212–248 have a similar typology of types of conflict. This article is strongly recommended as additional reading.

some false assumptions. First, many circumstances are not "zero-sum" situations. In a zero-sum situation the gains by one person must result in losses to another, so that the sum of all peoples' gains equals zero. For example, a poker game with five continuing players is a zero-sum game. If you add the winnings and losses of all players, the sum is zero. A leader could be happy with all group members; he does not have to behave as if the only way to get ahead is at the expense of someone else. A nonzero-sum approach would suggest that all would benefit by cooperating because cooperative behavior would lead to better decisions and a more pleasant experience. People who believe that competition per se is preferable to cooperation can be just as dangerous as those who avoid taking a strong position because it might appear that they are being uncooperative. The goal, then, is to be competitive when you think it will benefit the group and cooperate when it will not. In fact, if we define cooperation as subordinating personal interest to the group interest, communication which might at face value seem competitive may, in the long run, be cooperative. It depends on whether the goal is one of self-interest or of obtaining the best product or decision.

TYPES OF CONFLICT

It is important to differentiate between different kinds of potential conflict in the small group. The first obvious distinction is *intrapersonal* versus *interpersonal* conflict. Intrapersonal conflict is within a person and can be caused by discrepancies between how a person is forced to behave and what he believes to be correct behavior (Miller and Burgoon, 1973). It can also result when values, beliefs, and attitudes do not "fit" together and one value or attitude conflicts with another. People who experience too much intrapersonal conflict can literally destroy themselves and turn to escapes such as alcohol or drugs in the process. Another, perhaps less personally destructive avenue, is simply withdrawing from certain behaviors and situations. The main focus of this chapter and entire text is interpersonal relationships and we will deal with intrapersonal conflict only as it affects communication behavior in the small group.

The second distinction is between *real* and *artificial* conflict. Real conflict results when goals or behaviors are incompatible because of struggle for resources, power, or position when a zero-sum situation actually exists. An artificial conflict would resemble the previously mentioned example involving a group member who believed he could only gain prestige with the group leader by lowering the credibility of another group member. Kerr (1954) draws a distinction between *induced* conflict and real conflict. Often a leader will strengthen his hold on his followers by creating an "enemy" or external threat so that the group will be very cohesive in dealing with the conflict between groups. Therefore, the conflict is induced for purposes other than the apparent ones.

Institutional conflict follows rules and procedures. The whole process of negotiating an end to the Indochina war was a case of settling institutional conflicts. Rules and norms of conduct, at least to some degree, governed the war as well as the conflict-resolution phase at its termination. However, to the extent that we accept the anti-war demonstrations as spontaneous and disorganized, they would be classified as noninstitutional conflict. The notion of institutionalized-noninstitutionalized conflict is probably not a dichotomous concept. While the violence at Kent State University was a paradigm case of noninstitutionalized conflict, subsequent student strikes at other universities were probably more organized and could be called more institutional. The degree of disorganization and spontaneity determines how we use this category system.

Violent versus *nonviolent* conflict is the distinction between force and rhetoric and probably needs little further elaboration. Both can be effective means of bringing about change; our biases of course deem the former alternative considerably less desirable.

Most conflict in the small group is *face-to-face* as opposed to *mediated*. People in larger organizations have management, labor unions, and professional organizations to resolve conflict. Members of a small group often have immediate conflict which has to be directly dealt with by interpersonal communication. Therefore, the conflict is much more personal and subjective. Large organizations can have legal aides settle their conflicts in the impersonal, objective atmosphere of a courtroom, while group members can rarely be that detached from the conflict.

A final distinction among types of conflict concerns *principles* and *pragmatics*. Many times conflicts arise while choosing the values with which to operate. For example, a group may have considerable conflict over the principle of student participation in all phases of the university decision-making process. There could be considerable conflict over the principle of student involvement; however, even if the principle were agreed to, several types of pragmatic conflict could occur. First, there could be considerable disagreement over what could be done to implement the principle. Students might argue that token committee membership was not a satisfactory course of action; faculty might argue against voting membership while still supporting the principle of student involvement. Second, accepting a principle and an implementation plan might cause conflict with other accepted values or practices, or both. For instance, allowing students to participate in personnel decisions might be agreed on but the "higher" value of faculty being judged by peers might be a source of major conflict. Clearly, conflicts over principle and pragmatism indicate a need to recognize the overlapping nature of the potential conflicts resulting from value questions. Another source of potential conflict in this area arises from different interpersonal orientations. Some people are willing to let a group become inactive or disband, or both, before compromising a principle, even if the action in a specific case might be desirable. On the other extreme are people who opt for expedience and deny the importance of operating from principle. People like this usually find themselves making decisions on the basis of immediate situations. Others cannot operate this way, and when these two kinds of people find themselves in a small group communication situation, the probability of conflict is high.

CONFLICT SITUATIONS

We are going to describe three different situations that are likely to produce conflicts within individuals or within or between groups. All of these situations, described by Brown (1965), involve decisions and variables necessary to make those decisions potential conflict producers.

Approach-Approach. This decision point produces conflict when two decisions would yield different but attractive results and only one can be chosen. A group discussing whether to vacation in Miami Beach or spend their money on a boat would be in an approach-approach conflict. Similarly, management many times places labor union members in an approach-approach situation by giving a set amount of money and allowing the members to decide whether it should be spent on benefits or increased wages. There are three separate variables that affect the amount of conflict present at the decision point. The first of these is the *value* of the alternatives. If the value of two or more alternatives is approximately equal, then more conflict is likely to occur; this is a notion of relative value. If the absolute values of the alternatives are high, more conflict will result than if they are low. For example, buying a boat or vacationing in Europe might have high *absolute* values because of their desirability. Driving to a nearby lake for a weekend might be less desirable and therefore have a lower absolute value. To find relative values, one compares alternatives. A comparison of the boat to vacationing in Europe might yield equal relative values (both are attractive). Comparing either of these to the trip to the lake would not produce equality. The second variable concerns the *probability* of occurrence of the desired outcomes. The closer the probabilities are to being equal, the higher the potential for conflict. The third variable concerns the *number* of alternatives available to choose from.

Generally, the more alternatives, the higher the potential for conflict. Let us give an example of how this decision situation could lead to both intrapersonal and interpersonal conflict. If a single individual thought that the value of a vacation and a boat were high (he liked both alternatives), he would probably have a great deal of intrapersonal conflict. If he also thought that the probability of being able to take the vacation or find an acceptable boat with the available money were high and equally likely, his conflict would be intensified. If he decided a third alternative, such as saving the money and going to Europe next year, was attractive and feasible, his conflict would be even greater. If the person was operating in a group discussion, he might decide just to withdraw and go along with whatever was decided, figuring any decision was fine. In other words, the group could reduce the conflict by making the decision for him. However, if two members of a group wanted one thing and two others wanted the other, conflict would surely be present. Both alternatives might be attractive; simply withdrawing would not solve the problem.

The approach-approach conflict is probably the easiest conflict to resolve of the three discussed. If one is faced with desirable alternatives only, less hostility is likely to be present, and a means for compromise is easier to discover. As we have said, a person can withdraw or accept another plan without harm to himself or the group. Additionally, research indicates that after approach-approach decisions are made it is easy to direct communication toward bolstering the decision.[2]

Approach-Avoidance. When a group is faced with making *one* decision that has desirable and undesirable outcomes that occur simultaneously, they are in an approach-avoidance conflict. The decision to live in a large city and enjoy all the entertainment it has to offer is confounded by worries about increased cost of living, crime, etc. To the extent that the positive aspects are equal to the negative aspects (value and probability of occurrence), conflict is present. Withdrawing or not participating in communication is not a solution in this conflict situation. Not making a decision is in fact making one, for no decision gives up all the positive aspects.

This kind of conflict often occurs in questions of principle and pragmatics. When the positive aspects of upholding the principle are offset by the specific problems of a decision, conflict must result. For example, a group may want to uphold the principle of democracy in

[2] The entire literature on theories of cognitive dissonance is supportive of this. For a detailed discussion, see Miller, G. R. and Burgoon, M. *New Techniques of Persuasion*, New York: Harper & Row, Publishers, 1973.

decision-making (approach) but be unwilling to spend the extra time in committee meetings that such a management style dictates (avoidance). A decision, obviously, must be made. If through communication, one side can be shown to outweigh the other, a beginning can be made to resolve the conflict. For example, a person who wants to keep control of a group may convince them that the gains made from democracy would not equal the increased effort required to implement it. However, if the group cannot be convinced of the lack of equality in terms of the positive and negative aspects or the probability of their occurrence, a phenomenon called *ambivalence* is the likely result. A person who is ambivalent at best about a group decision will probably be unwilling to do much to support that decision and will probably be less satisfied with his group membership. If this ambivalence continues over time and other decisions are made, withdrawal is probable.

Avoidance-Avoidance.   We hope that you are not presently in an avoidance-avoidance conflict situation with this book. If you are reading it and disliking it, but continue for fear of flunking the course, this is an avoidance-avoidance situation. In other words, it exists when a group or individual is forced to make a decision that is undesirable to avoid another undesirable outcome. For example, a decision to go to prison to avoid the draft might be undesirable, but so is the alternative of serving in the military. A rat caught in a box where shock threatens at both ends will furiously try to escape the box. A person caught in the draft-prison situation may also choose to escape. The financial committee who must either terminate employees or reduce current salaries is similarly caught. It's the classic "damned if you do, damned if you don't" paradox.

If you are given circumstances where the alternatives are bad and you have to make a decision, the best advice is to work at preventing the reoccurrence of this type of situation. People are rarely satisfied with *any* decision that comes out of an avoidance-avoidance situation. Personal relationships suffer, the task is far less well done, and membership in the group is unstable. People quit jobs or seek new groups when they are continually forced to make decisions like this.

CONTRIBUTORS TO CONFLICT IN THE SMALL GROUP

As we have already stated, the number of alternatives under discussion, the relative and absolute value of the alternatives, and the probability of desired or undesired results occurring all combine to intensify or reduce conflict in group life. There are also other factors that contribute to conflict worth mentioning in this section.

Number of Members. Actually, little substantive research is available on the effects of group size on the amount or type of conflict present. However, if one accepts our earlier assumption that increasing the number of decision alternatives increases the potential conflict, a direct analogy with the number of people involved can be drawn. A larger number of people should be expected to have different desired outcomes, operate from different principles, and be willing to accept different implementations. Therefore increasing group size up to a point should increase conflicts. Then, at some point, the size of the group must decrease the chance for individual communication and lead to feelings of less involvement in the final outcome. When groups become too large and lose many of the qualities of small groups we discussed in Chapter 1, it is probably improper to discuss them under the rubric of small group communication; it would be more fitting to view them as organizations.

Amount and Kind of Information. There is little doubt that the amount and kind of information affect the level of conflict in a small group. Ignorance and error are often contributors to conflict; many conflict situations could be avoided by simply making information available to all group members. At other times too much information breeds conflict because it increases the number of alternatives. However, some people believe the old maxim that "information is power" and treat it as a scarce commodity that must be hoarded. In another chapter, we have considered the effects of information processing in various communication networks on decision-making and member satisfaction (see pages 170–171). One can see by reviewing this material that certain networks promote conflict.

The simplest way to reduce conflict might be to control the amount and kind of information available to group members. According to Burgoon (1971b), if the group had information clearly leading to only one alternative, the decision would be relatively simple. However, one is rarely able to control external sources of information on contemporary issues; if it were possible it would probably lead to low quality decisions and certainly stifle creativity.

Subgroup and Clique Formation. People who possess different information or hold differing beliefs, values, and attitudes often form subgroups or cliques that are cohesive units *within* a single group. When there are struggles for leadership and power, cliques often hold together on issues quite disparate from those that originally brought them together. A subgroup who originally formed to resist one decision may continue to operate as a bloc long after the need has ended.

As groups grow in size, clique formation is likely because a spokesman may be more able to get the clique's position expressed. Given this tendency, clique formation can intensify conflict. People with differing views can align with a subgroup and polarize the conflict. For example, people who do not have strong beliefs can still support a subgroup because of personal liking, past experience with the members or a number of other reasons and it becomes "us" versus "them." We personally have been members of a group who would vote 8 to 7 against adjournment.

Zero History versus Ongoing Groups. Newcomb (1958) claims that increased communication leads to increased similarity. Therefore, we should expect more conflict in "zero-history" groups whose members have not spent time communicating with one another. As people gain more predictability about the behaviors of others, they are more able to make adjustments to the idiosyncratic behaviors of others and avoid conflict; this is likely to occur when groups have an ongoing series of interactions. The first communication events of most groups are characterized by uncertainty and tension; as these feelings are reduced over a period of time, the potential for conflict is also decreased.

Some Selected Personality Syndromes. People who are chronically *hostile, anxious,* or *aggressive* can be a continual source of conflict. There are other personality variables that also affect communication relationships within a group. Highly *dogmatic* or *closed-minded* people are a potential problem as they often frustrate other group members who are advocating different positions.

The personality syndrome of tolerance for ambiguity has received some attention in the small group situation (Burgoon, 1971b). Budner (1962) found people with high tolerance for ambiguity are more likely to prefer group as opposed to individual tasks, choose occupations that demand more group decision-making, and prefer to work in groups that have to make decisions based on conflicting information. People with low tolerance for ambiguity prefer to work alone and all desire to work in situations in which they do not have to make difficult decisions (Burgoon, 1971b). Therefore, we must conclude that all people do not view conflict as undesirable; in fact some people enjoy it and like to complete tasks which require conflict resolution. Others find such tasks undesirable and withdraw from even slight amounts of conflict.

FUNCTIONS OF CONFLICT

Conflict is dysfunctional in situations in which it (1) prohibits the group from completing required tasks, (2) is personally destructive of group members, (3) results in lower quality decisions or products, or (4) threatens the survival of the group as an ongoing entity.

However, conflict serves several functions which can be healthy for the group. Conflict, as we have said, can at times make the group more cohesive and give the members a sense of identity. People can learn to deal with conflict and become better communicators under other kinds of stress-producing situations. Group norms can be the result of dealing with conflict. Once a group has successfully resolved conflict in one situation, it is more likely to be able to establish norms for *avoiding* future dysfunctional conflict. When conflict results in better quality decisions as opposed to mediocre ones based on compromise, conflict has been functional.

A difficult decision has to be made in establishing the balance between functional and dysfunctional conflict. It is a subjective judgment that must be left to the group members involved. They must judge when conflict is impairing the positive aspects of small group communication.

CONFLICT RESOLUTION

All our suggestions in earlier chapters on *persuasion* and *consensus* are relevant to those interested in resolving dysfunctional conflict. We believe the current popular saying that "just because you have silenced a man does not mean you have converted him." Persuasion, when legitimate and effective, is a desirable mode of conflict resolution. Our interest in effective decision-making in this text is similarly concerned with providing models that will help a group avoid disruptive conflict.

There are other means such as negotiation, arbitration (whether voluntary or not), legislation, command authority, and violence or force that lead to resolution of conflict. The decision concerning the best means of conflict resolution is dictated by each individual situation. Labor-management negotiations often reach a stage where informal consensus is impossible and binding arbitration mandatory. Nations have throughout history found no way to avoid violence in settling disputes. People create governments and accept legislation as a means of controlling conflict. Public debate of conflicting ideas has long been a part of conflict resolution.

Groups can do many things to resolve conflict. A group who keeps in mind the *superordinate goals* of the group over individual self-interests will find ways to compromise when necessary. Obviously the creation of a climate of *trust* makes conflict management easier. Many times conflict becomes so dysfunctional that a diversion of the group activity toward less controversial items or topics helps. We have experienced many situations in which ending a meeting for the time-being was effective in reducing conflict. At other times issues are "tabled" or *referred to subgroups* for more thinking and action to reduce conflict. If the conflict is the result of unsatisfied *individual needs*, the group can make efforts to reward group members by conferring status or recognizing achievement.

The wise group will learn about the people involved and accept the suggestion that the *best resolution of dysfunctional conflict is to avoid it*. That, of course, requires an astute analysis of the group's situation.

SUGGESTED READINGS

Gerlach, L. P. and **Hine, V. H.** *People, Power, Change: Movements of Social Transformation.* Indianapolis: The Bobbs-Merrill Co., Inc., 1970.

Jandt, F. E., ed. *Conflict Resolution Through Communication.* New York: Harper & Row, Publishers, 1973.

Jacobson, W. D. *Power and Interpersonal Relationships.* Belmont, California: Wadsworth Publishing Co., Inc. 1972.

Mack, R. W. and **Snyder, R. C.** "The Analysis of Social Conflict—Toward an Overview and Synthesis." *Journal of Conflict Resolution.* 1 (1957): 212–48.

Nye, R. D. *Conflict Among Humans.* New York: Springer Publishing Co., Inc., 1973.

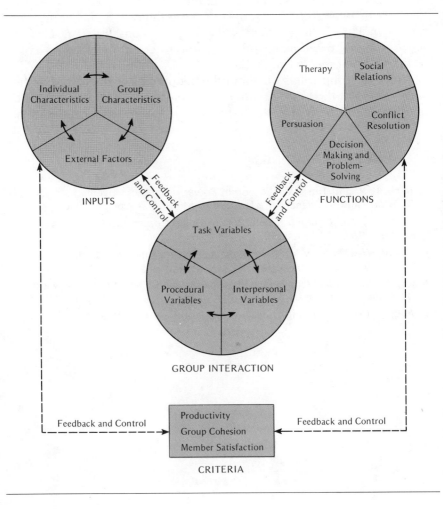

The
Small Group
Communication
Situation
as Therapeutic

IN RECENT YEARS, people have been turning to group situations for therapeutic reasons. The small group can be an excellent place for people to learn more about how their behaviors affect themselves and other people. So far, much of this book has taken a view of small group communication that implies certain assumptions about the nature of group inputs, processes, and outcomes. In Chapters 3 and 4, we assumed that part of the group's inputs were characteristics of the individual, power and authority of certain members, and intent to manipulate other members of the group to accept the beliefs, values, and attitudes of an individual. We also discussed how an individual might tailor his messages to ensure the most compliance from other group members.

The preceding chapter on conflict resolution also assumes that individuals can come to a situation with certain beliefs and have the group work in accordance with them. Although the persuasion situation differs from conflict resolution in many ways, there are similarities in assumptions. Both assume that individuals come to the group with fixed inputs such as attitudes or hostility. They also come with desired outcomes. In the compliance situation the goal is usually to have group members accept a predetermined position or accept some predetermined behavior. The conflict resolution paradigm has the goal of reducing tension, whether it means change by one group member or all. It accepts compliance, persuasion, coercion, or compromise as means to the conflict resolution end. The process of communication within the group is important only to the extent that it facilitates group outcomes; people in the group are considered many times as fixed and as sort of unchangeable.

People like Carl Rogers (1953) would differ with the view of small group communication presented in the last three chapters. The approach that has been labeled *transactional* has different assumptions, according to Rogers. The task of the small group is to help a person achieve, through special relationships with other group members, good communication with himself. Once good communication with one's self is achieved, it is assumed that a person can communicate more freely and effectively with other people. As Rogers (1953) claims: "Good communication, free communication, with or between men, is always therapeutic."

So, therapeutic groups have several goals that need to be discussed. The first assumption is that members come to the group wanting to learn about themselves and change their behaviors. While the preceding chapters assume that personality variables such as anomia, Machiavellianism, and so forth are inputs that people bring to the group and that affect the group process, the transactional approach assumes that the group process can affect the personality of the members. Perhaps, an example of the differences would help.

Group Function: Persuasion

Group Problem: A Group Member Is Highly Closed-Minded
Suggestion:

Since James is so closed-minded, you must do the following if you want him to change: Establish your competence on this issue. Highly dogmatic people change more when they believe you are credible. Structure your message that you want him to accept so that it is not initially too discrepant with his own position or he will shut you out. If you do this he will be more likely to accept your view.

Group Function: Therapeutic

Group Problem: A Group Member is Highly Closed-Minded
Suggestion:

Let us try to relate to John and tell him how we feel about his behavior. Maybe he doesn't know how we are perceiving him. If we try to talk with him and get him to share his feelings with us, perhaps he will see how he has been behaving and change in the future. Or maybe he isn't as closed-minded as we think and we will change our attitudes about him.

These two examples represent very different orientation and functions of groups. The first assumes James is an input and must be *dealt with* to achieve a desired outcome. The second example assumes that the group function is to help other members and that understanding group process facilitates that goal. So we can begin to construct a model of group behavior when the goal is therapeutic communication.

Another function of a therapeutic group is the development of interpersonal trust among members. An earlier chapter discussed some ways that trust affects the group communication process. Since most members who enter a therapy group do so expecting to change or be changed, the development of trust is mandatory. As Rogers (1953) claims, "the risk of being changed is one of the most frightening prospects most of us can face." If people are to change and learn from their own communication behavior, a climate of trust must be formed in the group. Gibb (1964) from his own work in groups claims:

> A person learns to grow through his increasing acceptance of himself and others. Serving as the primary blocks to such acceptance are the defensive feelings of fear and distrust that arise from the prevailing defensive climates in most cultures. In order to participate consciously in his own growth, a person must learn to create for himself, in his dyadic and group relationships, defensive-reductive climates that will continue to reduce his own fear and distrusts. (p. 279)

The small group can intentionally commit behaviors to increase a person's trust of others. To the extent that group members show empathy and genuine interest in others, a climate of trust is likely. Gibb (1964) gives further suggestions for communication behavior to build trusting relationships:

1. Communication that is descriptive and not evaluative produces trust.
2. Communication behavior oriented toward problem solving rather than control of other people is more likely to produce trust.
3. Spontaneous communication is more trusted than strategic communication.
4. People who behave empathically are more trusted.

Learning about One's Self   Helping Others Learn

Desired Outcomes

One can see the differences between this orientation toward small group communication and the compliance model presented earlier. The emphasis here is on empathic, spontaneous communication that builds trust and therefore helps the individuals in the group, whereas the persuasion model designates conformity as an outcome.

Obviously, the functions of trust development and reduction of defensive communication in the small group go hand-in-hand. Defensive behavior can result in withdrawal from the group, disruption of the group, or participation in aggressive behaviors and interpersonal attacks. Taking the Gibb model above, the following suggestions can be made to the group who wishes to avoid defensive behavior.

1. Avoid criticizing other group members who express different views. A tone of voice or verbal content that is perceived as critical will probably produce defensive behavior.

2. Communication that is perceived as an attempt to control others will probably result in negative reactions. We have all been in groups or other situations in which we felt "manipulated" and were resentful. We have personally gone to other stores and paid higher prices for goods to avoid "a high pressure salesman." We withdraw.

3. People who bring "hidden agenda" to a group breed distrust. One of us had the experience of taking his first job with a group leader who espoused the philosophy of group participation, claimed to be open to the wishes of the group, and asked for trust. However, I perceived that he always manipulated the group to make them believe they had made the decision when, in fact, we had done exactly what he wanted. I felt he played games and withheld information so he could "win." I distrusted him and simultaneously withdrew from the group and became hostile toward the leader and other members of the group who allowed themselves to be manipulated. I left the job as soon as I could and do not trust the man to this day. It is a moot point whether this man was a manipulator and bred distrust or whether I reacted defensively. The group did little to help me and felt that the best thing that could happen was for me to withdraw.

4. If the group is to have a genuine relationship of trust, it must learn to cope with deviance and signs of defensive behaviors by providing a supportive climate. The group mentioned above considered themselves very trusting and supportive. Many outsiders who knew this group felt the members were only supportive of those who agreed with them and shared their life-style. Therefore, these people outside the group distrusted them and refused to join the group. This, of course, prevented the group from growing, even though there was considerable trust among members who

were alike. Because I was so personally affected by this experience, I have followed this group ever since I left. They show little
evidence of growth and, in fact, have surrounded themselves with
others who are highly similar. I still distrust them and they still
dislike me and that is kind of unfortunate.

5. An appearance of lack of concern for the feelings of other members is likely to produce defensiveness.
6. An attitude of superiority arouses defensive behavior. A group
that tries to make people feel equal will probably have less defensive behavior. Soliciting opinions and making people feel worthwhile is a goal of therapeutic communication.
7. The more dogmatic or closed-minded people are in their beliefs
about "truth," the more likely others are to react defensively (especially those who disagree).

As interpersonal trust is increased in the small group, certain behaviors of group members should also change. First, there is increased
acceptance of legitimate persuasion attempts by others. Therefore, in
many individuals the behaviors we suggest to build trust will also result
in more persuasion and conflict resolution and are complementary to
the behaviors suggested in previous chapters. Increased trust also leads
to less suspicion of the motives of others. If a true atmosphere of trust
exists, there will be more tolerance of deviance by other group members. This is not to be confused with forcing deviants from the group
and "trusting" everyone who remains.

There is need for more stability in a group when one member is not
trusted. The emphasis should be on finding the source of distrust and
eliminating it. When several members of a group trust one another, it
is easier to discuss sources of concern and look for problem solutions.
The trusting group should also be more concerned with control over
group interaction, i.e., establishing free and open communication, than
control of individual group members, e.g., muzzling a deviant. Giffin
(1967) suggests that although personality measures are difficult to
change, if trust increases, the following personality changes can be ex-

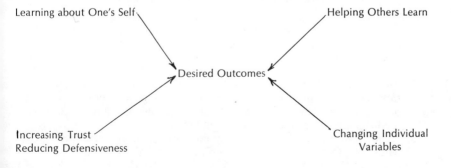

Learning about One's Self → Desired Outcomes ← Helping Others Learn

Increasing Trust
Reducing Defensiveness → Desired Outcomes ← Changing Individual
Variables

pected: (1) self-image is improved and (2) when conflict occurs, less anxiety is felt.

So, now we can add to our model of therapeutic communication.

THE ENCOUNTER GROUP AND WHAT IT DOES

Groups designed to provide therapeutic communication are known by a number of names: encounter group, t groups, sensitivity training groups, or laboratory groups. For simplicity's sake, we will refer to these groups as encounter groups for the remainder of the chapter. Those who developed the first encounter groups (Bradford, Gibb, and Benne, 1964) claim "that individuals are being compelled to change by inexorable pressures from natural sciences and related technologies with little, if any, preparation for handling changes with sensitivity and effectiveness, in themselves and their relationships." Like us, they believe that modern society demands participation in an ever increasing number of small group situations. The encounter group people rejected, as we have not, the form of training that transmits information about leadership and forms of manipulation. They felt that laboratory situations could be created where group communication, process, and structure could be studied to produce more knowledgeable people.

The encounter group people see the small group as a link between the individual and the society in which he lives:

> Can people learn to use groups for individual rehabilitation *and* for reconstruction of the social environment? And can groups be developed which are simultaneously alive to the needs of their members and to the needs of the social environment for reconstruction and improvement? The founders of the laboratory answered "yes." (Bradford, Gibb, and Benne, 1964, p. 5)

So, in summary, the goals of the encounter group are to provide an atmosphere in which the individual can develop as a person and be more effective in a variety of social situations. The following are expected communication outcomes in an encounter group (Bradford, Gibb, and Benne, 1964, p. 17):

1. One desired outcome in the encounter group is increased awareness of and sensitivity to emotional reactions in himself and others. A person should become aware of the complexity of emotional reactions in humans.
2. Another hoped-for-outcome is a greater ability to perceive and learn from the consequences of one's actions through attention to feelings, one's own and others'. Emphasis is placed on using behavioral cues and feedback in understanding one's own behaviors.
3. Some of the most important learning occurs in an encounter group when people discover discrepancies between their values and behaviors

and when other group members give nonjudgmental support in helping people resolve these discrepancies.

4. Many times encounter groups help people bridge the gap between theory and practice in communication behavior. People often know in theory how to communicate but have trouble putting this knowledge into practice. Many encounter situations strive to create situations that allow the participants to link personal values, goals, and intentions to actions consistent with their personal needs and appropriate to the social situation.

5. Much of our ineffectiveness in human communication results from the lack of consistency between our intentions and our behavior. Therefore, often our insights into ourselves and our analysis of group situations run far ahead of our performance skills. In other words, we know how we would like to behave but just do not have the skill to accomplish it. The encounter group attempts to support skill development to achieve our intentions.

Of course, it is the desire of most participants in encounter groups to take some of the insights and behaviors "back home." That is, people want to be able to use what they learn in the group for the variety of communication situations in which they participate on a day-to-day basis. A final objective is to enable the person to "learn how to learn" about himself and others. It directs his efforts toward achieving a positive self-identity so that he can be an optimal participant in the groups in which he finds himself.

Who Participates in Encounter Groups? The encounter group has attracted several different kinds of participants. One type is social workers, therapists, and educators who want to develop skills in interpersonal relationships so they can help "clients" in their own jobs. Another frequently participating category is the professional supervisor or administrator who wants to develop leadership skills. Sometimes entire companies or organizations participate in encounter groups in the hopes of improving relationships throughout their respective institutions. Many college students have become interested in participating in encounter sessions as a part of their educational development and growth. An important contribution has been made in bringing cross-cultural groups together, e.g., people of differing racial and ethnic backgrounds, to promote understanding and conflict resolution. Bradford, Gibb, and Benne (1964) have claimed "a laboratory experience, short as it is, may do more to bring about realistic understanding of similarities and differences among groups than a year or more spent in formal campus or work situations." While we are not ready to hail the encounter group as the panacea for all human communication problems and give it as strong a position as its supporters do, we are in agreement that encounter groups have been widely used in a variety of situations and many people who have participated in these kinds of group experiences testify to their worth. Let us now turn to a short description of an actual encounter group so that you can judge better for yourself the merits of this small group communication system.

A BRIEF HISTORY OF AN ENCOUNTER SESSION

Encounter groups are usually staffed by a "leader," referred to as a trainer. The group we are going to discuss was composed of male college students with an age range of 18–45. The median age was 26. Four of the students were full-time supervisors in local industrial organizations, one was a commissioned officer in the armed forces, and seven of the participants were full-time students. The trainer was one of the authors of this text. This group decided to participate in a "marathon" encounter consisting of six hours on Friday, eighteen hours on Saturday, and twelve hours on Sunday. We will use the classification system suggested by Bennis and Shepard (1956) along with examples from the encounter session.

Subphase 1: Dependence-Submission. The trainer entered the laboratory and announced the meeting times for the group sessions, stated that the purpose of the group was for all of us to learn more about our own and others' communication behavior, and said that he refused to be the group "leader" or further structure the situation for the members. Dan, a middle manager at a local company, immediately took charge and the introduction ritual common to all encounter groups began. Theodore, a foreign student, claimed that he had a great deal of background in the social sciences and preferred to take notes and "observe" the group. In many encounter groups, people with experience in management or the social sciences immediately try to fill the leadership vacuum left by the trainer's initial abdication; our group was no exception. Most of the members went through communication behavior reminiscent of most social situations in which strangers are just getting acquainted. A great deal of the content of the communication centered on problems external to the encounter group. This subphase lasted approximately one hour.

Subphase 2: Counterdependence. After the first hour of small talk by the members and complete silence by the trainer, hostility by certain group members became obvious. Ray and Gerry, who had both been quiet, expressed distrust of the trainer. Since this group was a course for credit, Ray immediately suggested that he didn't trust the trainer and wanted to know how he was being evaluated. Gerry said the group was a waste of time and the trainer should do something. Charles, a friend of the trainer, was obviously upset and verbally attacked the two counterdependents (those against the trainer). Michael, the military officer, was apparently uncomfortable and suggested choosing a chairman and selecting a list of topics to be discussed. Someone countered that this was not a current events course and that the trainer should do something. Two cliques emerged; one supported the trainer and the other attacked him. Theodore wrote and the trainer watched. This lasted for three and one-half hours and is common to many encounter groups. In fact, the amazing thing about these groups is that the same pattern emerges in almost all of them regardless of geographical location, participants, or trainers.

Subphase 3: Resolution. The conflict over the role of the trainer was resolved when Dan and Michael assumed leadership roles. Members became intensely involved in discussing the communication behavior that had gone on in the group. Ray and Gerry continued to press trainer challenges at appropriate times without success. This lasted one and one-half hours. Resolution of the conflict over structure and function of the group is common, and temporary leadership is often assumed.

Subphase 4: Enchantment-Flight. The group met after an eight-hour sleep break and a new type of interaction obtained. Individuals talked in pairs and there was a feeling of well-being among members. There was a general discussion of group history and the activity was praised. A number of people spoke for the first time and participation was spread equally for the first time. The trainer spoke occasionally and seemed to be accepted as a group member. There was a lot of humor and planning of things to keep the group together in the future. We all felt good and Theodore kept writing. This type of session has been called a "honeymoon" period by some. We talked for three hours and took an early lunch. Many pairs wandered off to eat.

Subphase 5: Disenchantment-Fight. After lunch we had a very intense session. The question of group structure and content was raised again. Ray wanted to know his grade. John became visibly upset and claimed the group was invading his privacy. Charles surprisingly switched camps and attacked the trainer; the trainer retreated. Dan and Michael tried to assume their previous leadership roles and were rejected by the group. Tension was high and there was a general denial of the worth of the group experience. All these things are consistent with the descriptions of Bennis and Shepard. However, the phase that followed was a surprise to the trainer. Each individual was subsequently attacked by the group. There was a pattern of very abusive verbal aggressions by a number of members. When Charles was attacked, he indicated his unwillingness to talk any more and never really rejoined the group. Some were attacked for taking leadership roles (Dan and Michael) while others were attacked for not participating. Ray suffered mightily for his attitudes about grades. Theodore was blasted for his superiority complex and his arrogance in just withdrawing and taking notes; and I was glad. Gerry ended this session by revealing that part of his behavior the previous evening had been due to the fact that he had felt it necessary to have a couple of drinks because he was intimidated by the thought of attending the group session. The group was stunned but reacted in a nonevaluative but supportive manner; clearly the attack session was over.

Subphase 6: Consensual Validation. After dinner on Saturday night, there was a general discussion of member roles. The communication was generally about the "here and now" things happening in the group. The group accepted its structure and function, and members seemed to communicate freely about their behaviors and feelings. This session lasted five hours.

Subphase 7: Enchantment-Flight. We had another honeymoon session that lasted two hours. Shorter sessions of enchantment seemed to follow conflict and resolution sessions.

Subphase 8: A Crisis. Although Bennis and Shepard do not mention this, we had our crisis. Another encounter group was meeting in an adjoining room and we discussed how much "better and happier" we were than they. Suddenly, on Sunday they visited us. We all tightened up, feeling very much a member of our own group and hostile toward them. We refused to talk about what was happening and were tense. It was a very real demonstration that a group personality had evolved. We had developed a "we-they" attitude toward the world. We broke for lunch and Don, who had been wearing a white shirt and tie, came back with a turtleneck and medallion (fashionable then). We didn't even mention it. There was a general discussion and affirmation of the worth of the experience. We felt we had learned a lot about our own behaviors and those of others; we knew we were a group.

Our feeling of groupness did not immediately end. We met with the other encounter group a number of times and we sat on one side of the room and they on the other. We learned to get along with them to some degree but always preferred our "own." And so our story of one encounter group ends.

Comments and Reservations. Few can quarrel with the goals of the encounter group; however, we would be remiss in our professional duties if we did not point out that encounter groups have many critics. Some encounter groups have resorted to "bizarre" techniques and questionable practices. There have been nude encounter groups, groups where sexual contact became a primary activity, and sessions which have resulted in violence. While these are not the kinds of groups we are primarily interested in, there are recurring problems common to encounter groups that should be mentioned.

Encounter groups have existed primarily for the training of "normal" people, as opposed to people who have conditions that warrant clinical attention. However, there is always the risk that someone with a serious problem will self-select into a group and the experience can do serious, long-run harm. Also, trainers who do not have the professional competence to run a group can cause great harm. The trainer should be an aware person with training in communication and the social sciences, and it is his duty to ensure that the group situation does not harm its members. Some people cannot take the kinds of feedback they receive in the group and should be protected.

An additional problem lies in generalizing the encounter group experience to the real world. Some people leave the encounter group and suffer "re-entry" problems when other people do not respond in the way the group did. We live in a world in which open and honest feedback is not always wanted or desired. Many people we have known report greater difficulty in accepting and adjusting to social situations after an encounter experience than before. Although the personal testimony we gave about the group experience is positive from our point of view, perhaps it is best to leave you with a thought by psychologist Kurt Back (1973).

> ... We have to go beyond individual witnesses, however, to find whether the risk is worth the gain for most people, whether we can identify the people who are amenable to encounter groups and how society can control the diverse group leaders ...

ROLE PLAYING AND PSYCHODRAMA IN THE SMALL GROUP

Small groups can be used in therapeutic situations to provide an arena for people to perform activities that enable them to change attitudes or behaviors, solve problems with other people, or help solve clinical problems. This group situation uses two main techniques to promote change in people that we will discuss for the remainder of this chapter: psychodrama and role-playing.

Psychodrama. Let us first consider psychodrama, a therapeutic technique developed in large-part by J. L. Moreno (1957). Basically, psychodrama is a strategy that allows people to make favorable changes in self-attitudes:

> Psychodrama consists of two roots—drama means action; and psycho means mind. It is really mind in action. In a way we can say that a psycho-dramatic session is like life in its highest potential. Life, as you are living it, with the one difference that all the inner forces you have are coming out. The psychodrama is, therefore, a vehicle by means of which life itself is lived under the most favorable and most intensive kind of circumstances (Moreno, 1957, p. 281).

The therapeutic group can use and participate in psychodrama sessions to help a member or the entire group develop different attitudes and feelings toward the self. One often-repeated story from Moreno's early work describes how a psychodrama helped a woman adjust to her husband's death. The husband had passed away while she was out of town. She was depressed and the therapist thought she was feeling guilty about her absence and the guilt was causing the problem. To combat the depression a psychodrama was devised to enact the husband's death with the wife as a participant. In an elaborate situation, a member assumed the role of the husband and acted out the coronary attack. A "doctor" pronounced the husband's death, and funeral and burial scenes were performed.

By participating in the psychodrama, the woman was able to bring back the concept of herself as a loving, caring wife. It brought back the meaning of death and the social ritual of mourning for a loved one in which she had not been able to participate. Although this may seem ridiculous and contrived to an analytical observer, it helped a woman who was having serious personal problems.

Moreno (1957) has also used psychodramatic techniques in marriage counseling. In one session, he allowed a husband who was involved with another woman to act out his meetings and feelings with the other woman in a group session. The wife, in another group, acted out her feelings of revenge and divulged that she had slept with her minister, a schoolteacher, a doctor, the gardener, a mentally defective boy, and a farmer in quick succession. It is felt that revealing these thoughts can be cathartic and make the patient aware of his problems so that solutions can be worked out. Sometimes the technique works and sometimes it does not.

Conceptually, though, group psychodrama concentrates on four processes to help people change their self-attitudes. First, it allows freedom of expression (spontaneity) which is often denied to the participant. The enactment allows them to act out things that in real life might be too risky for them. Psychodrama can also be a very involving activity and have much more impact than the mere relating of problems to another person. Often the actions we commit are much more revealing to ourselves and others than the things we are willing to say.

In addition, there is the principle of realization. The participant is able to meet parts of himself and others in his life from a variety of perspectives. He can see how he is behaving and how others might be reacting.

Role Playing.   Although the preceding discussion of psychodrama concerns a specialized form of role playing, we will limit our discussion in this section to the use of role playing as a vehicle to change attitudes and behaviors about things other than the self. The following role playing scene is a good example for our discussion:

Imagine yourself as a patient waiting anxiously in a doctor's office. The doctor enters, a grave expression on his face, and seats himself behind his desk. He speaks:

'Well, last time you were here you asked for the whole truth, so I'm going to give it to you. This X-ray (pointing to it) shows there is a small malignant mass on your right lung. Moreover, results of the sputum test confirm this diagnosis.'

'What you're saying, doctor, is that I have lung cancer, right?'

'Unfortunately, the tests leave no doubt about the diagnosis.'

'What next?'

'Immediate surgery is necessary. I've arranged for you to report to the hospital tomorrow morning. Plan on spending at least six weeks there, because chest surgery requires a long convalescence.'

'I dread asking this question, but how are my chances?'

'I wish I could be totally encouraging; however, frankness dictates that I tell you there is only a moderate chance for a successful outcome from surgery for this condition.'

'Is there anything I can do to improve my chances?'

'We've discussed this before, but I'd like you to refresh my memory on your smoking habits.'

'I suppose you'd call me a fairly heavy smoker. I've been smoking almost two packs daily for the last four years.'

'It is urgent for you to stop smoking immediately, since every cigarette aggravates your condition. Moreover, I know you're quite anxious about the news I've just given you, and this itself will make it harder to stop. Therefore, we should spend some time right now discussing the difficulties you expect to encounter in quitting smoking.'

'Well, first . . .' (Miller and Burgoon, 1973, pp. 45-46).*

This dialogue is patterned after the one used by many researchers to determine if active involvement in emotional scenes would cause changes in role players. As with psychodrama, people are asked to behave "as if" they are in a certain situation. All the role players were moderate to heavy smokers so the situation was probably fairly "real" to them.

Janis and Mann (1965) found that role playing could be a powerful

---

* Copyright © 1973 by Gerald R. Miller and Michael Burgoon. By permission of Harper & Row, Publishers, Inc.

force in modifying attitudes. They found that the following happened to people who engaged in the previously described role playing:

1. They became significantly more convinced that smoking causes lung cancer.
2. They expressed significantly more fear of being personally harmed by smoking.
3. They indicated their willingness to modify their smoking behavior.
4. They indicated an intent to quit smoking immediately.
5. Two weeks later, they reported a significant decrease in the number of cigarettes they smoked daily.

These effects also seem to be long-lasting. Interviews were conducted after eight and after eighteen months and the role players reported a significantly lower daily consumption of cigarettes. All of these comparisons were made to a group of people who had been told the dangers of smoking, but had not role played. This testimony underscores the potential impact of even brief role playing experience. Role playing has been used in a variety of situations. Some communities have instituted programs in which policemen and young people come together and play each other's roles. Management groups have role played blue collar workers to gain understanding. Blacks and whites have worn masks of the other race and played the respective roles in the hopes of obtaining understanding and resolving conflict. We know role playing can involve people and influence them to change attitudes and behaviors; it is an important device for the group to consider.

SUMMARY

The techniques described in this chapter are, to say the least, controversial. The encounter group movement has many followers who give convincing personal testimony about the merits of this form of group behavior; others violently oppose the encounter group and claim that they are dangerous, nonsensical, or a waste of time, or both. We, frankly, do not know how to answer either camp. Obviously, more systematic research needs to be completed to establish what is effective and what is not. Also, we have no idea why certain regularities emerge in these group sessions, but the predictability is often uncanny. Therefore, we reject an out-of-hand indictment of the encounter group, while urging caution interspersed with empirical research and development of theoretical perspectives before loudly praising the encounter movement.

Psychodrama and role playing have appeared to be effective in a variety of situations. There are also theoretical speculations and research by professionals attesting to the efficacy of this small group device. However, we think any form of therapy is potentially a problem if carried to extremes. Like the small boy who was given a hammer and suddenly found that everything needed pounding, the therapeutic group can ensure that you will have a problem when you leave even if you didn't have one when you came in. We urge you to beware of the healer of the healthy.

SUGGESTED READINGS

Back, K. W. "The Group Can Comfort But It Can't Cure." *Psychology Today* 6, No. 7 (1973): 28–35.

Bradford, L. P., Gibb, J. R., and **Benne, K. D.,** eds. *T-Group Theory and Laboratory Method—Innovation in Re-Education.* New York: John Wiley & Sons, Inc., 1964.

Budd, R. W. "Encounter Groups: An Approach to Human Communication," in *Approaches to Human Communication* edited by R. W. Budd and B. D. Ruben, Rochelle Park, New Jersey: Hayden Book Company, Inc., 1972: 75–96.

Miller, G. R. and **Burgoon, M.** *New Techniques of Persuasion.* New York: Harper & Row, Publishers, 1973. See Chapter III.

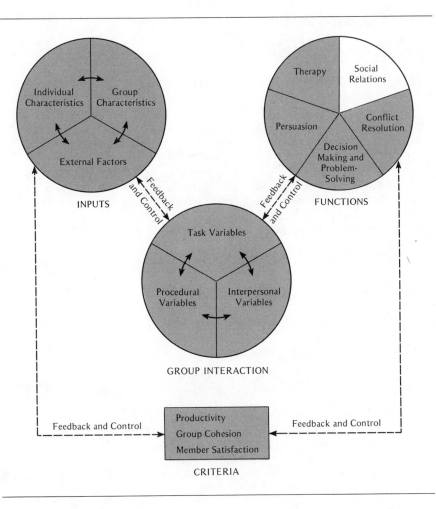

Small Group
Communication
and Social Relations

A VERY POPULAR SONG a few years ago expressed very positive sentiments about "people who need people." Possibly one of the reasons for the song's popularity was a recognition by most people that "people who need people" is a category including everyone. The days of the completely self-sufficient individual, if they ever existed, are long past. People learn from people. People work with people. People enjoy other people. Most of the learning, work, and social enjoyment occurs when people form small groups and communicate about their shared needs and desires. One of the most important outcomes of these communication encounters is either the improvement or the deterioration of social relationships among the people in the groups. That is the focus of this chapter.

The Concept of Homophily

Homophily is probably one of the most significant concepts in human communication theory. "Homophily" means essentially interpersonal similarity, and the opposite, "heterophily," means interpersonal dissimilarity (Rogers and Shoemaker, 1971). No two people, of course, are ever exactly the same as one another. However, the degree to which they are dissimilar can vary widely. There are two important types of similarity. The first of these is similarity of invariant or relatively invariant characteristics. These are characteristics of the individual that are not subject to change at all or can only change over an extended period of time. Characteristics such as age, sex, race, religious affiliation, culture, educational level, personality, and the like are included in this category. The second type of similarity concerns resemblance in attitudes, knowledge, and beliefs, and is highly subject to change as a result of communication. It is generally classified as attitudinal similarity. We say that two people are homophilous if they have a high degree of both characteristic and attitudinal similarity. To the extent that two people differ on either characteristic or attitudinal similarity variables, we say that they are heterophilous.

In the context of small group communication, this concept must be expanded to include more than just two people, since most small groups involve more than two people. Consequently, within a given small group, person A may be highly homophilous with persons B and E but highly heterophilous with persons C and D. We must also think of the concept of homophily in terms of the individual and the group as a collective entity. The individual may have great similarities to the collective group or, of course, be highly dissimilar to the group. Three important principles of human communication are directly related to the concept of homophily, and are sometimes collectively referred to as the "principle of homophily." Let us consider each of them in turn.

1. *Communication Patterns Are Normally Homophilous.* There is a strong tendency for people to communicate with people who are most like themselves on both characteristic and attitudinal dimensions. Farmers communicate mostly with farmers. Undergraduate students communicate mostly with undergraduate students. Faculty members communicate mostly with other faculty members. Small groups, normally, are formed by people who are homophilous, because people tend to avoid association with either individuals or groups that they perceive to be heterophilous. This is not to say that people never engage in small group communication with heterophilous individuals or even heterophilous groups. In many cases, it is necessary. However, the normal human tendency is to avoid heterophilous groups and seek more homophilous ones for association and communication.

2. *More Effective Communication Occurs Among People Who Are Homophilous.* Not only do people seek to communicate with other people like themselves, but they are also more effective in communicating with such people. Farmers generally communicate best with other farmers, undergraduate students normally communicate best with other undergraduate students, and faculty members normally

communicate best with other faculty members. The reason for this is that the more alike two or more people are, the more likely they are to share meanings. They are apt to share not only a common language but also similar meanings for the words in that language. They are likely to be motivated by the same or similar things. Their goals, their information about a given topic, and their values are likely to be similar. Taken to the extreme, if two people are identical (an obvious impossibility, even among identical twins), there is no need for communication because the two people will have identical ideas and behavioral patterns. As we deviate slightly from this ideal homophilous state, we can see that communication is highly likely to be effective because of the scant need to alter thoughts or behaviors, and because any alteration that is needed will tend not to deviate substantially from a person's original thoughts and behaviors.

3. *Effective Communication between People Leads to Greater Homophily in Attitudinal Similarity.* The more two people communicate effectively with one another, the more impact they have on one another's thoughts and behaviors. Since person A seldom tries to influence person B to think differently from person A, effective communication usually results in further shared orientations toward the world.

The above three statements, taken together, form a circle. People who are alike tend to communicate with one another, people who are alike tend to communicate effectively with one another, and people who communicate effectively with one another become more alike. The reverse of these three statements points to the core of human communication problems. People that are *not* alike tend *not* to communicate with one another. When communication occurs between people that are not alike, it tends to be ineffective. Ineffective communication tends to make people more unlike one another.

The implications of the concept of homophily in small group communication are extensive. Let us consider first the most common type of small group. This group is formed because the people are relatively homophilous and are either desirous of or feel that they will benefit from joining together to communicate. The communication within the small group is likely to be highly effective and the people will increase their identification with one another and with the group as a whole. If small groups are voluntarily formed, therefore, we should predict that they will communicate effectively and develop strong interpersonal and group ties that will continue to facilitate communication over an extended period of time.

Now, let us consider some of the negative implications of homophily. In many cases, groups are formed out of necessity. This necessity may be a result of employment, housing, or any of a variety of other reasons. The people in the groups may be very heterophilous with one another. In such circumstances, we should expect membership in the group to be transitory. People will prefer not to remain in the group, and if the necessity to remain is overcome, the person will leave the group. Communication within the group will be difficult, and we should not expect high productivity from groups of this type. However, if the degree of heterophily is not too great, it is still possible for effective communication to occur. To the extent that it does, increased homophily will result; and over a period of time, the group may develop a sufficient degree of homophily to operate in a highly effective manner.

If one is forming a task group, the concept of homophily should never be ignored. The best predictor of task group success is, in most cases, the homophily level of the members. This suggests, then, that the person who has the authority to select the people who will compose a task group should choose on the basis of similarity. Unfortunately, this is an over-simplification, because for the successful completion of some tasks, it is essential that high knowledge or skill levels be available to the group. Often, these levels are not available on an equal basis within a group of people. For example, in a major corporation, it may be necessary to have an expert in finance, an expert in production, an expert in management, and an expert in sales to form one major task group. Since a high level of expertise is available in perhaps only one individual, much less in several individuals, within an organization, it will be impossible to form a homophilous task group, in this instance, with any expectation of reaching an enlightened decision. The person forming the group, therefore, will have to choose between competing alternatives, neither of which is desirable.

In groups formed for social purposes, rather than task purposes, this dilemma is not present. A very substantial percentage of the groups with whom we communicate in our everyday lives have social outcomes as their main focus. Almost all of the remaining groups with whom we communicate have them as a secondary focus. In the following section, we consider some of the outcomes of social interaction.

Outcomes of Social Interaction

There are three primary desired outcomes of social interaction. They are interpersonal attraction, identification, and satisfaction. Let us consider them in turn.

Interpersonal Attraction. Interpersonal attraction is the degree to which person A likes person B, desires to associate with or spend time with person B, and enjoys being in the presence of person B. Interpersonal attraction is one of the most desired outcomes of social interaction. Not only do all of us enjoy having other people attracted to us, we also have a strong need to be attracted to others. It has been estimated that up to 90 percent of our total communication is directed toward making ourselves more attractive to another person and responding to the other person's attempts to be more attractive to us.

Interpersonal attraction passes through at least three phases (McCroskey, Larson, and Knapp, 1971). The first, or initial phase, occurs when we first meet another person. This first meeting establishes some level of interpersonal attraction between us that may be either high or low and either grow or deteriorate from that point on. The second or intermediate phase occurs after our initial contact and is heavily impacted by our communication with the other person. The third phase of interpersonal attraction exists over a long period of time and tends not to vary substantially once it has been established. Let us consider each of these phases of attraction.

1. *Initial Interpersonal Attraction.* In the initial phase of interpersonal attraction, people tend to treat other people as objects. The physical characteristics of the other person are probably the single most important element in determining the initial attraction level. Most people are initially highly attracted to beautiful or handsome specimens, and less attracted to the more common members of our species. In addition, all manner of physical properties of individuals tend to generate stereotypical attraction responses. Race, sex, height, weight, hair length and color, eye color, posture, and carriage have an impact. In short, all the object properties of people have an impact in the initial phase of interpersonal attraction. Consequently, when a group first forms, initial attraction levels are established almost immediately among members of the group. There may be some strong, positive relationships, some weak relationships, and some strong negative relationships. It should be stressed that these relationships are established prior to any extensive communication within the group. After communication has continued for a time, we pass from the initial phase of attraction into the intermediate phase.

2. *Intermediate Interpersonal Attraction.* Initial interpersonal attraction is a very transitory thing. We have all had the experience of being highly attracted to another individual, only to find out later we couldn't stand the person. Similarly, most of us have had the experience of initially disliking a person and later having him become a close friend. While initial interpersonal attraction is based primarily on the object properties of people, the intermediate phase of interpersonal attraction is based primarily upon human communication.

In order to understand how human communication in the small group has an impact upon intermediate interpersonal attraction, we need to understand the concept of "balance" in interpersonal perceptions. Heider (1946) first formulated the concept of balance; it states essentially that we are attracted to people whose orientations are similar to our own, but we are not attracted to people whose orientations

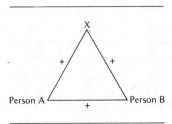

Figure 7.1. Balanced Positive Orientations toward X

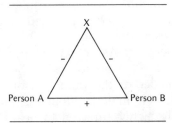

Figure 7.2. Balanced Negative Orientations toward X

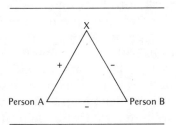

Figure 7.3. Unbalanced Orientations toward X

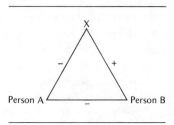

Figure 7.4. Unbalanced Orientations toward X

are unlike ours. The simple model in Figure 7.1 portrays a situation in which it is very likely that two people would be attracted to one another. In this model, person A likes X and so does person B. Since their orientations are the same toward X, it is very likely that they will develop a positive orientation toward each other. Human communication is the crucial variable here. If both person A and person B like X but do not say so, this common orientation that would form a positive bond between the two people would be unknown. If, however, person A and person B talk with one another and discover their similar orientation, the positive bond is likely to be formed.

Figure 7.2 also portrays a circumstance in which we would expect person A and person B to develop a positive bond of attraction. Both person A and person B dislike X. Even though these orientations are negative, they are shared by the two people. It is crucial to remember that attraction is based upon similarity of orientation, not whether the orientation is positive or negative.

Figures 7.3 and 7.4 portray circumstances in which we would expect person A and person B not to develop a bond of attraction. In Figure 7.3, person A likes X but person B dislikes X, and in Figure 7.4, the reverse is true.[1]

We may refer to the first two figures as "balanced," and the second two figures as "unbalanced." Interpersonal attraction is facilitated by balanced orientations and disturbed by unbalanced orientations. Human communication is the way that people discover the orientations of other people.

The impact of the desire for interpersonal attraction in small group communication can be overpowering. It is not uncommon to find a group, at least in the early part of the time they are together, spending most of it on social interaction in order to facilitate attraction among the people in the group. In some cases, of course, this is the whole purpose for the group's formation. In other cases, the group has formed to get a job done. In such circumstances, the allegedly most desired outcome is successful completion of the task. However, to the individual members of the group, the most desired outcome may very well be enhancement of interpersonal attraction.

When increasing interpersonal attraction is the most desired outcome in group communication, people tend to communicate differently from the way they might have otherwise. People may say things they do not believe in order to establish similarity of orientations and become more attractive to other members. Or, people may avoid risk-taking by not expressing a view on a question at all. They fear that if they express their opinion it will not be shared by other members of the group and thus they will be less attractive to the other members. When either of these behaviors obtain, there is sharply reduced likeli-

---

[1] It is important to note that we are not using "balance" in the same way Heider did. We claim that the last two situations in which person A and person B disagree will lead to less interpersonal attraction because their orientation toward the object is "unbalanced." This is a major modification of Heider's notion of attitudinal balance and we recognize that fact.

hood that the task goals of the group will be accomplished successfully. A task group may have to overcome the members' interpersonal attraction to one another before "real" communication can be expected. This should not be interpreted as a derogation of the value of small group communication for the purpose of enhancing interpersonal attraction. Rather, we make this point in order to stress that in some cases this goal will be antithetical to the accomplishment of the avowed purposes of the group. When an entire group adopts interpersonal attraction as the most desired outcome of their interaction, they may be destined to task mediocrity. Most of us can look around in our own environment and discover such allegedly task-oriented groups. They may be student groups that never get anything accomplished; business organizations that are very happy, but bankrupt; departmental faculties that fall ten years behind their field; or a wide variety of community-service organizations, entangled in red tape.

Intermediate interpersonal attraction, therefore, depends upon communication among people. To the extent that the communication reveals similarity in orientations, attraction will be enhanced. To the degree that the communication exposes dissimilar orientations, attraction will decline. These principles apply both to individuals and to groups, because we can develop attraction for a group in much the same way that we develop attraction for an individual.

3. *Long Term Interpersonal Attraction.* Once interpersonal attraction has passed through the intermediate phase, it has developed a considerable degree of stability. Friends tend to remain friends, and enemies tend to remain enemies. Nevertheless, attraction can vary over an extended period of time. Human communication, once again, is the primary vehicle for inducing such change; it is induced in much the same way that attraction is influenced during the intermediate phase. As the individuals or the group discover new orientations that they either do or do not share, interpersonal and group attraction levels are influenced. The reason that there is comparatively less influence on attraction during this phase lies in the "law of diminishing returns." If, during the intermediate phase of attraction, person A discovers that person B shares three orientations, and then discovers a fourth orientation on which they differ, A will be 25 percent out of balance with B. This could have a major impact on attraction level. Over a long period of time, however, person A may have discovered that he or she shares 352 orientations with person B and that they disagree on fourteen. If subsequent communication exposes a new orientation which they either share or do not share, we would expect the impact to be comparatively slight.

Since most people within any given culture have a large number of shared orientations, we should expect that there would be a fairly close correlation between the amount that two people talk with one another and the amount that they are attracted to one another. This is generally true. In fact, proximity has been found to be the best single predictor of attraction. People that work closely together or live closely together are more likely to talk to one another. The more they talk to one another, the more likely they are to expose similar orientations, and the more likely they are to be attracted to one another. While this principle holds true generally, it is not always an accurate predictor. Very often the nature of the discussion interferes. While two people may share a very large number of orientations, they may only discuss things about which they disagree, and, thus, the more they talk, the less they are attracted to one another. The principle to remember is that the degree to which we are attractive to other people is based not on how often we communicate with them, but what we say to them. Similarly, how attractive we perceive another person to be is not based on how often he talks to us, but on what he says to us. Being sensitive to the orientations of other people, verbalizing our similar orientations when they exist, and being silent about our differences in orientations will generally tend to make us more attractive to other individuals and groups.

Group Identification.   Group identification is a very important outcome of social interaction. As we indicated in the opening chapter of this book, people need to be identified with groups. This outcome is very closely associated with the outcome of interpersonal attraction; if we find that other members of a group are attracted to us, we will tend to establish a very close bond of identification with the group.

We tend to identify with groups that, through their communication with us, evidence that their orientations and ours are similar. Essentially, we discover that we are homophilous with the group and thus the group becomes an extension of ourselves, and we of it. For a group to exist over an extended period of time, such identification on the part of its members must be developed. If individuals are not identified with the group, they will seek to leave the group and ultimately cause the group's demise.

Task Satisfaction.   Although the subject of the next chapter is how groups complete decision-making tasks, task satisfaction is most closely related to the social interaction that occurs within the group. By task satisfaction, we mean the degree to which each member of the group is committed to the conclusion that the group draws. While, of course, this depends to an extent upon the kind of decision the group reaches, to an even greater extent it depends on how each group member perceives the group and the individual members of the group in relation to himself or herself. Generally, the more a person is attracted to the individuals within the group and identifies with the group, the more likely it is that the individual will be satisfied with the product of the group (Costley and Miller, 1964). When a group reaches a decision, it is often necessary for the individual members of the group to carry out the decision. Unless the individual is satisfied with the group and his or her role in it, it is most unlikely that the individual will be satisfied with the decision. Group members that are not satisfied with decisions of a group will seldom exert much effort to see those decisions through to implementation. Attraction and identification, while in some cases antithetical to reaching a good decision, are essential for the development of sufficient satisfaction to ensure implementation of the decision. The decision-making process itself is the subject of the following chapter.

SUGGESTED READINGS

Berscheid, E. and **Walster, E. H.** *Interpersonal Attraction.* Reading, Mass.: Addison-Wesley Publishing Co., Inc., 1969.

Cartwright, D. and **Zander, A.** eds. *Group Dynamics: Research and Theory.* New York: Harper & Row, Publishers, 1968.

McCroskey, J. C., Larson, C. E., and **Knapp, M. L.** *An Introduction to Interpersonal Communication.* Englewood Cliffs, New Jersey: Prentice-Hall, Inc., 1971. See Chapter III.

McGrath, J. E. and **Altman, I.** *Small Group Research: A Synthesis and Critique of the Field:* New York: Holt, Rinehart and Winston, Inc., 1966.

Rogers, E. M. and **Shoemaker, F. F.** *Communication of Innovations: A Cross-Cultural Approach.* New York: The Free Press, 1971.

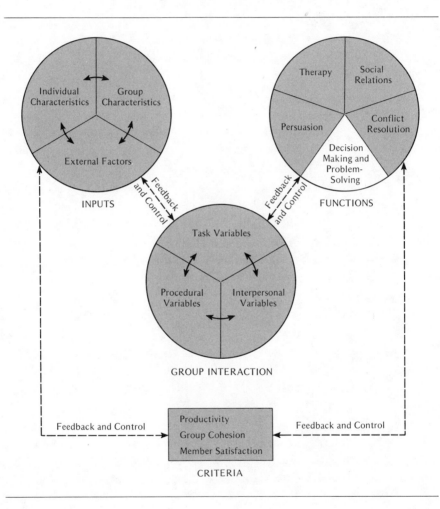

Individual Characteristics
Group Characteristics
External Factors

INPUTS

Therapy
Social Relations
Persuasion
Conflict Resolution
Decision Making and Problem-Solving

FUNCTIONS

Feedback and Control

Feedback and Control

Task Variables
Procedural Variables
Interpersonal Variables

GROUP INTERACTION

Feedback and Control

Feedback and Control

Productivity
Group Cohesion
Member Satisfaction

CRITERIA

Small Group Communication and Decision Making

MOST SMALL GROUPS, except those that are designed exclusively for social or therapeutic purposes, are confronted regularly with tasks that require the group to solve problems or make decisions. Many groups must both solve problems and make decisions. So that we may clearly distinguish between problem-solving and decision-making, let us define each of these at the outset.

Problem solving is the process in which a small group participates when it is confronted with a problem that must be overcome and when the possible alternative solutions are not known to the group in advance. Decision making is the process in which a small group engages when there is a problem that must be solved and the alternative possibilities are known to the group. The function of some groups is merely to come up with possible solutions, and the function of others is to take known alternative solutions and determine which alternative solution is preferable. And, some groups are required to engage in both problem solving and decision making.

Whenever a small group is confronted with either a problem that must be solved or a decision that must be made, the group can be referred to as "task-oriented." By this we mean that evaluation of the success of the group must be judged primarily in terms of the adequacy of the solution or decision reached by the group. Social or therapeutic goals are distinctly secondary to the task goals. This does not mean that a task-oriented group may not also achieve social or therapeutic goals. Rather, it suggests that if such goals are achieved, the achievement is comparatively unimportant in the overall evaluation of the group's success. Ideally, of course, the small group's communication should result in successful completion of the group's task *and* a group of people who are attracted to one another, identified with the group, and satisfied with the task result. Nevertheless, in any evaluation of a problem-solving group or a decision-making group, primary emphasis must be placed on successful completion of the group's task, not on the human relationships involved. This does not mean that the group should ignore interpersonal relationships while trying to find solutions or reach decisions. Rather, it means simply that interpersonal relationships cannot be allowed to dominate the interaction.

For a task-oriented group to accomplish its objectives, it is essential that the group process the available information in a rational manner and avoid, as much as possible, the strong human tendencies that tend to short-circuit our thought processes. The focus of this chapter is on appropriate thought processes that can be used in processing information to solve problems or reach decisions. Before we turn to this matter specifically, we need to consider the essential nature of human information processing so that we may understand the context in which small groups communicate about solutions and decisions.

The Nature of Human Information Processing

"Information" is a term that is familiar to almost everyone. However, to avoid confusion in the meaning that we are giving it here, we need to define it clearly. Information is knowledge about objects and events and about the relationships between objects and events.

Knowledge exists only in peoples' minds. It does not exist independently from human beings. What I "know" and what you "know" may be exactly the same, somewhat different, or even completely opposite. Therefore, in terms of small groups, information is knowledge about objects and events and about the relationships between objects and events that is held in common between members of the group. Developing a common base of knowledge within a small group requires communication. One person cannot simply transfer knowledge to another person. Rather, knowledge must be created in the other person's mind, and communication is the primary, if not the only, means for accomplishing this objective. We can say, therefore, that members of a small group have a common information base when they have a similar awareness of objects or events and hold similar beliefs about the relationships between these objects and events. Until this common information base is acquired by the members of a group, there can be no meaningful problem solving or decision making by the group.

How Information is Acquired

Information is acquired by individuals and groups in much the same way. A great deal of the information that people and groups acquire is based on their experiences in the world. We know about automobile accidents because we have seen them or even been in them. We know about the intellectual climate in our university or college because we are members of the academic community. We know something about the impact of taxes on people in our society because we must pay them.

Most people tend to put considerable faith in the information that they acquire through their own personal experiences. Unfortunately, it is impossible for any person to acquire the total amount of necessary *Empirical* information about the world in which the person exists by direct experience. Consequently, most of the information that either people or groups acquire comes through human communication. By communicating with other people, we experience vicariously what they have experienced, or what they have experienced vicariously through others. In many cases, our information that is based on vicarious experience has passed through a whole chain of communication transactions between people. The information that we have about events in history, for example, may have been passed down by various forms of communication through many generations of people. Although we must acquire much of our information vicariously through communicating with other people, we must recognize the very important difference between this type of information and that which is acquired by direct experience. Which kind is the most "valid" information is very much open to dispute. Many blacks in American society today argue that whites are simply incapable of understanding the feelings of blacks because the whites have never had the "black experience." This is a good point. Having someone tell you about being oppressed is not the same thing as experiencing oppression. On the other hand, direct experience may result in severe distortions of the experience. One will hardly ever find a marine corps recruit confronting basic training who considers it a valuable experience. However, it is certainly not uncommon to find marine corps veterans who tell us about the strong virtues of such an experience. There is considerable research, that we will not go into here, indicating that people seriously distort their perceptions of their experiences in order to meet their own psychological needs. Thus, when we acquire information from vicarious experiences of others, we should be fully aware that such information may not conform closely with reality.

Information, therefore, is acquired either through direct or vicarious experience. Both sources of information are of value, and neither is to be inherently preferred over the other.

Why Information Is Acquired. Although some information is gained simply by accident, most information is acquired because either individuals or groups seek to acquire it. Information is often consciously sought to meet specific group or individual needs. It is also sought unconsciously by individuals and groups to reinforce previous orientations. In some cases, the individual or the group may not know what is motivating their information-acquisition behavior. When information-acquisition behavior is heavily influenced by the desire to satisfy unconscious needs, the information acquired may have little relationship to external reality. Information consistent with previous orientations may be acquired, while information indicating that previous orientations are inappropriate may tend to be disregarded. Let us consider some of these barriers to information-acquisition in more detail.

Barriers to Information-Acquisition. There is an almost infinite availability of stimuli around us which can lead to information-acquisition. Consequently, it is clearly impossible for any individual or group to acquire all of the possible information concerning their world. It is essential, therefore, that individuals and groups select among the stimuli available to them. This selection process will determine which types of information the individual or the group will acquire. There are at least four natural human tendencies that often become barriers to the individual or the group who seeks to acquire all the necessary information to find good solutions or reach good decisions. Let us consider each of these in turn.

Selective Exposure. As we have noted previously, people tend to seek information that will reinforce attitudes, beliefs, or values that they already hold and behaviors in which they already engage. There is also some evidence (Mills, Aronson, and Robinson, 1959) to indicate that people either consciously or unconsciously seek to avoid exposure to information that would cast their previous orientations into doubt. Thus, in many instances, people expose themselves selectively to potential information available in their external world. This tendency has important implications for small groups that need to engage in problem solving or decision making. To begin with, if the group has been formed voluntarily, it is likely that the membership choice itself has been affected by selective exposure tendencies. People tend to join groups that they believe will reinforce them and to avoid groups that they believe will challenge their previous orientations. Thus, there tends to be, within a voluntarily formed group, an artificially high degree of homophily in orientations and associated information.

Even if the group is not severely constrained by this problem, selective exposure tendencies can affect the interaction within the group. Individual members are less likely to ask questions that would lead to information violating their previous orientations than they are to ask questions that lead to information confirming their previous orientations. In addition, group members may tend to avoid introducing information into the discussion that they think will violate other people's orientations, because they may either know or sense that to do so would reduce their interpersonal attractiveness in the minds of others.

It must be stressed that selective exposure, like the other selectivity processes to be discussed below, is a human *tendency*. While almost everybody engages in it from time to time, people also can and do overcome it. A small group concerned with problem solving or decision making must overcome this tendency or the result of their communication is likely to be less than satisfactory.

Selective Attention. While both individuals and groups may seek to avoid exposure to information that is inconsistent with their previous orientations, it is virtually certain that they will be exposed to some information of this kind. When exposure is unavoidable, there is a tendency for people in groups to pay less attention to this kind of information than they do to that which is supportive of their previous orientations. It should be stressed that this tendency is usually not a conscious one. All attention must be selective, because neither individuals nor groups can pay attention to all the stimuli in their environment at any given time. Because of this essential need for selectivity in attention, it is very easy for human needs to influence the stimuli that are selected. While four people in a group may each suggest a different solution to a problem, the ones that are in keeping with the group tradition or the past behavior of the group are likely to receive most of the attention. There is a bias in their favor. Selective attention, then, is not so much the rejection or avoidance of information inconsistent with previous orientations as it is the seeking and acceptance of information consistent with previous orientations (e.g., Gilkinson, Paulson and Sikkink, 1955).

Selective Perception. Even though individuals or groups may pay more attention to information consistent with their previous orientations than they do to information inconsistent with them, normally the latter receive at least some attention. This does not mean, however, that the individual or the group will perceive that it is inconsistent. Our prior orientations and expectations have an extremely powerful impact on our perceptions. While we may attempt to find information that "in reality" contradicts our previous orientations, we may misperceive it as supportive of information that we expected. Arnold and McCroskey (1967) did a study in which the process of selective perception was aptly demonstrated. They created three different messages on bussing to maintain racial balance in schools. The first message strongly supported bussing, the second expressed intense opposition. The third message was a combination of the first two and contained both positive and negative statements. Each of the messages was attributed to either Martin Luther King, Jr., or George Wallace. The college students were asked to record the position that they thought the message they read took on bussing school children to maintain racial balance. The students saw all three messages as supporting bussing when they were attributed to Martin Luther King, but opposing bussing when they were attributed to George C. Wallace. The students' perceptions, therefore, did not conform with the known reality of the information that had been presented to them. The perceptions did, however, conform with the students' previous orientations toward what they thought that King's and Wallace's views were on bussing. Numerous other research studies have found similar results.

In order to overcome this problem in small group communication, it is often necessary for an individual who is introducing information that is inconsistent with previous orientations to specifically stress its inconsistency. If this is not done, the research indicates a strong likelihood that the information may simply be misperceived and have little or no impact on the group.

Selective Retention. Even though information may somehow get past the barriers of selective exposure, selective attention, and selective perception, there is still no guarantee that the information will be truly acquired by an individual or a group. While it may be temporarily acknowledged, and in a sense temporarily acquired, the individual or the group may simply forget it (e.g., Levine and Murphy, 1954). People tend simply to "process out" information that is inconsistent with their previous orientations. After a period of time, they may not recall ever having been exposed to that information. In small group communication, this type of selectivity is often in evidence. While talking about the problem or the cause of the problem, the group may temporarily acquire information indicating that their previous orientations were in error. But, by the time the group gets to the point of determining solutions or making decisions, that information may have evaporated and be simply disregarded. Whenever this happens, the probability that the group will find the best solutions or make the best decisions is severely reduced.

In the previous chapter, we noted that the probability of effective communication is greatly enhanced by increased homophily among the members of the group. While this is clearly true, it is also true, unfortunately, that the greater the homophily in a problem-solving or decision-making group, the more likely it is that the group will be influenced negatively by selectivity. This is because similar people with similar orientations process information, and exclude information, in similar ways. Thus, a highly homophilous task-group constantly runs the risk of communicating well with one another, reaching a unanimous solution or decision, being highly identified with the solution or decision, and satisfied with the group's effort, but failing in the task that has been set before them—discovering a good solution or reaching the best decision.

Rational Thought Processes in Problem Solving and Decision Making

Very few people would argue with the premise that groups should try to find solutions and make decisions on the basis of reason rather than emotion. It is obvious, therefore, that a group should engage in as rational a thought process as they can while they are communicating about solutions or decisions. Unfortunately, many groups do not depend primarily upon rational means to reach their solutions or decisions, and others are not even aware of what a rational approach to problem solving or decision making would be. The purpose of this section is to describe several of the elements involved in rational problem solving and decision making.

Basic Analysis of Problems. There are three important questions that a group must confront if they are to determine rationally the best possible solutions to any given problem. If the group must also be concerned with making a final decision, there are two additional questions that they must consider. Let us consider each of these five questions.

1. *Is there a problem?* Many groups forget to ask this question and simply assume that the answer is yes. This assumption is often incorrect. But even when it is correct, merely knowing that there is a problem is not enough. The group must attempt to discover both the causes and the effects of the problem in order to know how to handle it. When a group's task involves discovering solutions, it is obvious that there is a problem to be solved. In order to be able to find an appropriate solution to a problem, the group must know the nature of the problem. Some subordinate questions that the group should ask themselves include: "What is occurring at present? What is wrong with it?

Why is it occurring? Who, if anyone, is likely to be harmed if it continues?" If these questions are approached rationally, the group should come to a good understanding of the problem and its importance. They will also be in a better position to determine whether or not any solution is needed, and if so, some of the basic elements that need to be present in the solution.

2. *Is the problem inherent?* After the group decides that there is indeed a problem, they need to consider whether or not the problem is a result of something that is an essential part of the present system, or if only a minor change might be expected to overcome the problem. For example, consider a group in a business organization that is asked to come up with a solution or solutions to a sales drop-off over the past six months. Presume that the group has decided that, indeed, sales have dropped off to such an extent that the drop places the business in danger. The important question is, of course, "Why have sales dropped? Does a whole new system of production need to be implemented? Does a whole new sales system need to be instituted?" Before such major solutions are considered, the precise cause of the problem must be explored. For example, consider a business group that actually confronted this problem. After an examination of the facts, the group found that sales had started dropping off sharply shortly after the business had changed, in order to economize, its system for handling mail. They discovered that a probable cause of the problem lay in the fact that the order department was not receiving orders until three days after they had arrived in the organization. It became clear to the group, therefore, that the problem was not an inherent one that required a major change in the organization. Rather, they simply directed a secretary from the order department to go to the mail room twice each day and sort the mail for that department and deliver it. Sales returned to their normal level within the next three months.

The point here is that a group must avoid, if we may use an old cliché," shooting flies with an elephant gun." The group must discover whether a problem is a manifestation of some inherent weakness within the current system that requires a major change or simply a minor quirk that can be easily overcome.

3. *What are the possible solutions to the problem?* After the group has determined that there is a problem of sufficient magnitude for a major change to be instituted, the group must consider alternative solutions to the problem. We emphasize solution*s*, not solution. The group that seeks only one solution will probably not find the best solution. At this point, most groups enhance their problem-solving process considerably by engaging in what is referred to as "brainstorming." We will discuss this process in the next chapter.

4. *How practical are the available solutions?* If the group is charged with decision making, they must go beyond the first three questions to

consider the possible solutions and make a decision among them. The first step in this decision-making process consists of determining whether or not proposed solutions can actually be implemented. This is a question of practicality. They must address themselves to such questions as: "Is the proposed solution legal? Can we get enough people to go along with it? What will it cost?" By carefully considering each of these questions, many allegedly possible solutions will be rejected as impractical and, thus, further consideration of them will not consume more of the group's time and effort.

5. *What are the advantages and disadvantages of the proposed solutions?* The key discussion leading to intelligent decision making revolves around this question. It is not just a question of whether or not the proposed solution will solve the problem, but rather, one that involves the total implications of any proposed solution. In the early 1960s, the leadership in Washington felt that there was a need to do something about Fidel Castro's regime in Cuba. One solution that was proposed for White House consideration consisted of sending in the marines to throw Castro out. There was little doubt in anyone's mind that this would solve the problem that the leadership felt existed. Nor was there any substantial question whether the marines could accomplish the task. The decision makers in the White House, however, rejected this solution because of a very important possible side effect, a direct nuclear confrontation between the Soviet Union and the United States. Some people argue that had the decision-making group in the White House engaged in similar rational decision-making processes concerning the Vietnamese problem, the United States would not have been engaged in a ten-year war in Indo-China. The important point to remember is that intelligent decision making depends on full exposure of all possible advantages and disadvantages associated with any proposed solution. To do less increases the probability that bad decisions will be accepted.

Recognizing and Testing Relationships Among Objects and Events

In problem-solving and decision-making it is essential that alleged knowledge concerning relationships among objects and events be tested by a group to determine whether the alleged relationships actually exist. In order to make a rational evaluation of alleged relationships, it is important that people in the small group are aware of the kinds of relationships that exist in the external world and have at their disposal appropriate tests to determine whether they exist in a given case. There are five primary types of relationships among objects and events: causation, sign, analogy, induction, and deduction. Let us consider each of these in turn.

Causal Relationships. The most frequently discussed type of re-lationship among objects and events is causal. When people reason that objects or events, or both, are causally related, it is reasoned that one thing in our environment produces another. A vitamin deficiency causes illness. Low ratings cause television programs to go off the air. Cancer and heart disease are produced by excessive smoking. Good grades are produced by intelligence and hard work. As we can see in these examples, we may reason from an alleged cause to an alleged effect, or we may reason from an alleged effect back to its alleged cause.

In the problem-solving process, it is usually considered crucial to determine the cause or causes of the effect that is recognized as a problem. It is not likely that a good solution will be discovered if the cause of the problem is diagnosed incorrectly. Consequently, it is im-portant that appropriate tests of alleged causal relationships be ap-plied. The following five tests should be considered.

1. *Are the alleged cause and the alleged effect directly related?* Shortly after World War II, two things occurred. There was extensive testing of nuclear weapons in the atmosphere, and there was unusual weather in some parts of the world. Many people argued that a causal relationship existed between these two events, saying that nuclear testing was a cause of the strange weather. However, scientists were unable to find any causal relationship between them. They simply occurred together by chance. During the same period, radiation levels were increasing in many parts of the world. Scientists were able to establish that the radiation levels were produced by atomic fallout re-sulting from nuclear tests. Eventually, this finding led to the elimination of most atmospheric tests of nuclear weapons.

In the first instance above, it was determined that there was no direct relationship between the alleged cause and the alleged effect, while in the second instance, a direct relationship was established. Had nuclear testing been discontinued because of the first relationship, the solution and decision would have been based on faulty thought process.

2. *Is the alleged cause the only or the primary cause?* It is relatively uncommon for any observed event in our world to be produced by only one cause. However, it is not at all uncommon for people to argue that X is *the* cause. A group should always seek to determine whether other causes may be present. Consider the following example. At the end of a semester before final grades have been reported, many students employ causal reasoning that fails to meet this test. They argue, "I have worked very hard this term; hard work produces good grades; therefore, I should receive an A." Hard work is certainly di-rectly related to good grades. But, it is not the only cause, and in many cases, it is not even an important cause. Native intelligence is at least

as important, and in some cases so is the bias of the instructor. A group that is trying to determine a cause of a problem must always consider the possibility of multiple causation.

3. *Is the alleged effect the only or the most important effect?* During the 1960s, and early 1970s, the United States was heavily involved in a military conflict in Indo-China. Supporters of this policy defended its continuation on the grounds that our presence there resulted (at least during that period) in the maintenance of a friendly government in South Vietnam. Few people really questioned that this causal relationship existed. However, over a period of time, decision-makers in the United States government recognized additional effects that were even more important than the maintenance of a friendly South Vietnamese government. Thousands of Americans were being killed. Hundreds of thousands were being wounded. The costs of the conflict were resulting in cutbacks in domestic programs and run-away inflation. Our image in the rest of the world was being severely damaged. Massive demonstrations were being spawned in the streets. Colleges were being closed down and students shot. Eventually, it was decided that these additional effects resulting from our Indo-China policy were of greater importance than the effect that had received primary consideration previously. Consequently, the policy was changed.

It is important to remember that just as most effects are produced by multiple causes, so are most causes producers of multiple effects. Groups involved in problem solving and decision making should always test alleged causal relationships to determine if there are additional relationships manifested by additional effects that are more important than the relationship initially established.

4. *Have other causes operated (or are they likely to operate) to prevent the cause from producing the effect under consideration?* When analyzing the problems of developing countries, it is not uncommon to hear the claim that these countries are advancing toward prosperity. This allegation is supported by the fact that the gross national production of these countries is advancing at a more rapid rate than in the United States or other developed countries. Since economic advancement of this type is normally directly related to the well-being of individual people, the causal relationship is presumably established. However, an intervening cause makes this relationship meaningless in many of these countries. That cause is population growth. Since population is increasing more rapidly than gross national production in many of these countries, the people are becoming poorer each year rather than richer.

The point to remember is that causal relationships existing under one circumstance may not exist under another. Remember the concept of multiple causation. In some cases, two causes operate in a directly opposite manner in relation to a given effect. The question then becomes, as we have indicated above, which cause is the more potent?

5. *Is the cause capable of producing the effect?* The most common error made by groups using causal reasoning is the assumption that simply because one event occurs after another event, the first event is the cause of the second. Summer follows spring, but is not caused by spring. The United States withdrew its troops from Indo-China after street demonstrations opposing the Indo-China War. These demonstrations may or may not have produced this result. Merely establishing the temporal order of two events does not establish a causal relationship. Rather, it must be established that the two events are directly related so that if one were not present, the other would not be.

Sign Relationships. Sign relationships are often confused with causal relationships, but they are essentially different. Causal relationships involve a direct tie between two events, so that the absence of one would naturally result in the absence of the other; sign relationships are merely indications that two things are related closely enough so that the presence or absence of one may be taken as an indication of the presence or absence of the other. Causal relationships may be present that underlie the observed sign relationships, but we may neither know what they are nor be able to discover them. In other instances, we may be fully aware of the causal relationships. For example, if the thermometer reads −20 degrees we may take this as a sign that the local lake is frozen. However, thermometers do not cause lakes to freeze. In this instance, we recognize that temperature conditions produce both thermometer readings and frozen lakes. If we enter a friend's home and see ashtrays placed around the living room, we may take this as a sign that our friend does not object to our smoking. This sign may or may not be reliable. One of the reasons that our friend has put the ashtrays around the room might be that he does not object to smoking and wants to make his home convenient for smokers. However, our friend may object to smoking strenuously, but prefer that smokers use ashtrays rather than his carpet!

From these examples, we may see that groups that employ sign relationships are operating from a somewhat less "pure" rational base than those using causal relationships. However, in many instances, it is necessary to operate on the basis of sign relationships. It is very important, whenever this is the case, to apply appropriate tests to alleged sign relationships. Let us consider four of these.

1. *How consistent is the sign?* Signs must be reliable and highly consistent if we are to make any important decision based on them. One sign relationship that most of us use from time to time is that cloudy conditions indicate a probability of rain. But we all know of hundreds of instances where the sky became cloudy and no rain resulted. Cloudiness is an unreliable sign. Most of us have also heard the argument

that poverty leads to juvenile delinquency. Yet, thousands of young people growing up in a poverty environment do not become delinquents, whereas thousands of delinquents come from middle- and upper-class environments. Poor solutions or bad decisions are often based on unreliable signs such as these.

2. *Are there special conditions that make the sign unreliable?* In many instances, we may be able to establish that a sign relationship is probably reliable. But certain circumstances can still invalidate the relationship. For example, an examination of history indicates that when troops mass along national borders, it is a highly reliable sign that hostility will break out between two countries, and there will be a war. Many people reasoned this way during the 1960s when Russia and China stationed thousands of troops along their shared border. No significant military conflict developed, however. The special condition of the availability of nuclear weapons, apparently, made the usually reliable sign relationship unreliable in this case. Similarly, if basketball team A has easily defeated teams B and C, who have in turn easily defeated team D, it is a generally reliable sign that team A will be able to handle team D with comparative ease. However, if the star player for team A happens to be ill, the sign relationship may be quite meaningless.

3. *Is the sign relationship reciprocal?* Sign relationships generally only move in one direction. To infer the reciprocal of the relationship is usually dangerous. For example, many people argue that poverty and poor economic conditions are the primary conditions under which Communist subversion flourishes and leads to the development of a strong Communist party. Assuming that this relationship is correct (even though it is becoming increasingly clear that it is not), to use it as a basis for concluding that foreign aid should be provided to poorer countries as a means of combatting communism is not a valid use of the sign relationship. France and Italy have experienced strong growth in their domestic Communist parties, but few people would say that they are in the throes of poverty. Similarly, even though it may be safe to reason that since the thermometer reads −20 degrees, the local lake is probably frozen, it is not reasonable to argue the reverse—the local lake is frozen, therefore, the thermometer probably reads −20 degrees. The thermometer may read −30 or even +40 degrees. The relationship that is reliable in one direction is quite meaningless in reverse.

4. *Are there other signs leading to the same conclusions?* The main weakness in the use of sign reasoning on the part of groups lies in the fact that conclusions often are based on single signs. There may be many other sign relationships present, some of which point in the opposite direction. These must be taken into account. For example, a declining stock market is certainly a sign of economic difficulty, but a rising gross national product, increasing personal income, and a re-

duction in inflation are all signs of a healthy economy. To reach a solution of economic problems or make a decision about the state of the economy on the indications of the stock market, therefore, would probably be unwise.

Analogical Relationships. When groups use analogy as a pattern of thought, they reason that if two or more things are alike in one or more respects, they are also apt to be alike in other respects. For example, we are using analogy if we reason that since economic conditions today are similar to those in 1932, and the voters elected a new President in 1932, the voters are likely to elect a new President this year as well. In essence, analogy is simply an extended use of sign relationship. The reasoning pattern works thus: since it can be demonstrated that a sign relationship exists in one case it is likely to exist also in a second case. Consider the following tests for analogies.

1. *Are there significant similarities between the things under comparison?* The crucial element in an analogical relationship is the essential similarity of things under comparison. At least one significant point of similarity is essential before an analogy can be drawn. But, beyond this, for an analogy to be strong, there should be many additional similarities as well. In general, the more similarities the better.

2. *Are the points of similarity important to the comparison?* It does not necessarily follow that just because two things have something in common the similarity is important to the issue under discussion. For example, England and the United States have many similar characteristics. They have a similar economic system, are primarily inhabited by English-speaking people, and maintain strong military forces. But, if we use these similarities to conclude that socialized medicine would be as successful in the United States as it has been in England, we may be drawing an invalid analogy. The important similarities needed for drawing a conclusion about a medical system are related to the country's health needs, medical facilities, and social system. Unless significant similarities can be established on these levels, the analogy between the two countries could very easily lead to a false conclusion.

3. *If there are points of difference between the things that are being compared, are the differences important?* In many cases, analogies compare two objects or events that are very similar on many important levels, but the analogy can be invalidated by a single point of difference. Several years ago candidates for mayor in Honolulu were confronted by a major issue—whether new schools should be built as single-story buildings or as multiple-story buildings. One candidate drew an extended analogy based on numerous studies conducted in mainland cities indicating that in every case single-story construction was less expensive than multiple-story. The case appeared to be overpowering. However, the opposing candidate demonstrated the in-

validity of the analogy by showing a single point of difference between Honolulu and mainland cities. It was the difference in the cost of acquiring land. Since land costs in Hawaii varied from 300 to 1000 percent higher than in the mainland cities that were being compared, it was clear that multiple-story construction was, in this instance, less expensive. Groups that are basing their conclusions on analogical relationships, therefore, must be careful to explore all points of similarity and difference among things under comparison before drawing final conclusions.

Inductive Relationships. Inductive relationships are normally referred to as generalizations, and generalizations are based on examples. It is reasoned that what is true of representative examples from a group will be generally true of the group. For example, if a representative group of cities that have strong gun laws have less crime than other cities, it may be generalized that strong gun laws are a deterrent to crime. The only way that we can be absolutely certain that a generalization is valid is to examine all possible examples. Since this is almost never possible, and since problem-solvers and decision-makers must inevitably use inductive relationships in reaching conclusions, it is vital that appropriate tests be applied to generalizations. Consider the following tests.

1. *Are the examples relevant to the generalization?* The first and simplest test of a generalization is to determine whether the examples upon which it is based are even related to it. Several years ago it was argued that military aid was an effective means of preventing Communist groups from overthrowing friendly governments. Examples were provided where military aid was given to countries and there were no successful rebellions. Further examination, however, indicated that the amount of aid provided in the countries used as examples never exceeded 5 percent of the countries' military budget. It became obvious, therefore, that the examples did not support the generalization.

2. *Are there enough examples?* A single example is seldom sufficient to provide an adequate basis for a valid generalization. The discovery of one example of waste in a program does not justify the generalization that it is a wasteful program. If a generalization is valid, there should be an extensive supply of examples illustrating its validity. If there are not, there is a strong possibility that it is false.

3. *Are the examples typical?* In some cases, a fairly sizeable number of examples can be collected that lead to a generalization, but the generalization is still not valid if the examples are not representative of the total situation. For example, for many years it was taken almost on faith that the use of marijuana led to the use of hard drugs such as heroin. Supporters of this generalization had little difficulty finding a

sizeable number of examples of people who started out using marijuana and eventually moved on to harder drugs. Over a period of time, however, this generalization came under question and was finally rejected as invalid. It was found that only a small minority of people who used marijuana moved on to harder drugs. The supporters of the generalization had drawn all of their examples from this small minority, while the large majority of the examples pointed to the invalidity of the generalization.

4. *Can negative examples be explained?* It is comparatively rare for every possible example to point to the same generalization. In most cases, there are at least some examples that point in the opposite direction. Before we can draw a valid generalization, therefore, we must be able to account for the existence of these negative examples. The existence of any sizeable number of inexplicable negative examples is a clear indication that a generalization should not be accepted.

Deductive Relationships. Deduction is based on a generalization about a class of objects or events, and deductive relationships depend upon classification. This classification is applied to a specific instance, and a conclusion is drawn concerning it. For example, if we start with the generalization that most Republicans are supporters of civil rights legislation, we may then reason that since Mr. Williams is a Republican, he is probably in favor of civil rights legislation. To be completely valid, the generalization that serves as a starting point must be exclusive and all encompassing. The example we have just used would not be sufficient, since we know that some Republicans do not support civil rights. Unfortunately, groups that are engaged in problem solving or decision making seldom have perfect generalizations from which to operate. Rather, the starting points in deductions in small group communication are normally "probabilistic" generalizations, such as our Republican example above. Consequently, any conclusions drawn through deduction will also be "probabilistic." It is essential, therefore, to test these deductions to determine how likely the conclusions are to be correct. Three tests should be applied.

1. *Is the group identified in the generalization homogeneous?* Any generalization that is used as a starting point identifies some class or group, such as "Republicans" in our example above. The first test, therefore, is to determine whether the class or group actually exists. For example, if it were found that the class "Republicans" included people that were so diverse that any two given members of the class could have little or nothing in common, any conclusion that was drawn would have a low probability of validity.

2. *Does the group or class profess the characteristic attributed to it in the generalization?* Since deduction begins with a prior generaliza-

tion, the generalization itself must be tested. The tests for generalization discussed above should be applied.

3. *Does the individual instance under discussion belong to the class described in the generalization?* It is vital that the specific case that is discussed be established as a member of the group or class described by the generalization. For example, if Mr. Williams in our example above were found to be a Democrat, any conclusion we might draw from the generalization concerning Republicans would have no validity.

Recognizing and Testing Evidence

The recognition and testing of relationships among objects and events depends on more than the reasoning processes involved. It is also necessary that the group concerned with problem solving or decision making recognize and evaluate evidence that allegedly supports relationships. There are essentially four kinds of evidence that may come under consideration: tangible objects, opinions, factual examples, and statistics.

Tangible Objects. Tangible objects are physical evidence. Things such as photographs, a piece of equipment, and written records may serve as this type of evidence. It is probably the best evidence when it is available, but small groups involved in problem solving and decision making will seldom have any significant number of tangible objects available as evidence.

Opinions. Opinions expressed by members of the small group are not generally regarded as evidence. Unless one of the group members is an expert on the subject that is being discussed, most opinion evidence must be drawn from people outside the problem-solving or decision-making group. Normally, groups must depend, to some extent, on the opinions of outside experts in their deliberation.

Factual Examples. Factual examples normally serve as the core of evidence available to a small group. These examples serve as the basis for almost all of the relationships we have discussed in the previous section.

Statistics. Statistics are merely a quantification of factual examples. Figures concerning production, population growth, tax rates, and so forth represent a collection of a large number of factual examples that have been reduced to numbers so they can be more easily managed. Statistics often form a very important portion of the evidence available to a group.

One of the major parts of any problem-solving or decision-making discussion is the evaluation of available evidence. The following tests should be considered in the process.

1. *Is the source of evidence competent?* Evidence, other than tangible objects, always comes from someone. The most important test of evidence, therefore, is the source of the evidence. Is the individual or the group responsible for the evidence competent? Is the source an expert in the subject matter of the evidence? If not, the source may be reporting inaccurately. It is important that we avoid confusing status with competence. A United States senator is a high-status person, but on a given question, the senator may have little or no competence.

2. *Is the source trustworthy?* Just because a source of evidence is competent, it does not follow that all evidence the source provides is valid. The term "credibility gap" has become common in our society. Very often, people are in a position to report evidence accurately, but because of their own motivations may choose not to do so. The group should always consider the motivations of the person providing evidence to see if they might have an influence on what is reported.

3. *Is the evidence consistent with other evidence?* A group should seldom make a decision based on a single piece of evidence. If a conclusion is correct, there is probably a wide variety of evidence available to support it. This evidence should be sought. If new evidence is discovered that is inconsistent with previous evidence, it is a clear indication that any tentative conclusion is in need of revision.

4. *Is the evidence relevant to the point at issue?* A group has to take care that they are not overwhelmed with a mass of evidence. Sometimes a group member will provide a large amount of evidence in support of a conclusion that he or she wishes to draw. The group must take care not to be overly impressed with quantity as opposed to quality. A large amount of evidence supporting a given conclusion is certainly justification for accepting the conclusion. But the key variable in this statement is not "a large amount of evidence." It is, rather, "supporting the conclusion."

Barriers to Rational Problem Solving and Decision Making

Generally groups discover better solutions and reach better decisions than individuals do. When a group communicates about a problem or about possible decisions, the likelihood is increased that some member of the group will be able to spot a false relationship or poor evidence that an individual might overlook. Nevertheless, problem-solving and decision-making groups must be on guard constantly against fallacious reasoning that can creep into the discussion and reduce or destroy what could otherwise be a successful product of the group. In this section we will discuss some of the most common errors in rational thought that are made by both individuals and groups. It is not possible in the space available to go over all of the possible fallacies that confront small group thought processes. The reader is encouraged to go beyond our discussion here and read W. Ward Fearnside and William B. Holther's excellent book, *Fallacy—The Counterfeit of Argument* (Prentice-Hall, 1959).

Faulty Generalization. One of the most common fallacies that affects the reasoning of groups is the faulty generalization. We have previously considered several tests of generalizations, but two important points are worth repeating here. The first type of faulty generalization is the hasty generalization, based on too few examples, particularly when only one example is cited. The second is the unrepresentative generalization. This type of generalization occurs when the examples drawn upon are not representative of the class to which the generalization is applied. An example of this would be to poll people concerning their preferences for a political candidate, but to poll only those that are discovered in a supermarket. If the generalization is drawn that so and so is likely to be elected, the generalization would ignore the fact that a significant portion of the population who are likely to vote are not likely to be in a supermarket.

Faulty Causation. Conclusions that are drawn on faulty causal premises are generally the result of confusion with sign relationships. Consider the following example. A young boy becomes ill in the early evening after dinner. The mother or father concludes, "It must have been something that he ate." While it may, indeed, have been something the young boy ate, it is not much more likely to be the cause than anything else. Illness after dinner is a fairly reliable sign that something eaten has disagreed with the individual, but it is insufficient to establish a causal relationship. Symptoms of illnesses of any kind can occur at any hour of the day, and are just as likely to occur in the early evening as at any other time. Thus, while the causal relationship attributed by the mother or father may be correct, it is just as likely that it is fallacious.

Post Hoc Reasoning. Post hoc reasoning is also faulty causal reasoning, but of a particular type. *Post hoc* reasoning draws conclusions on the basis of temporal order alone. Most superstitions are based on this type of reasoning. Walking under a ladder does not cause someone to have bad luck, but for many people, if they have bad luck after walking under a ladder, they attribute it to this cause. If such reasoning were valid, astrology would be a science instead of a superstition, because configurations of stars and planets are certainly antecedent to every event in the world. Unfortunately, this reasoning is not valid. Establishing the temporal order that one thing occurred before another can only establish the possibility that the first thing caused the other, it cannot establish that a causal relationship actually exists.

Emotional Language. Language colors our thoughts, and in many cases, determines how we think. The use of highly emotional language in small group communication is very likely to interfere with the rational deliberation of the group. It is one thing to say that a news release from the White House is "incorrect." It is quite another to say that the news release is a "lie." Correctness or incorrectness can be established with objective evidence. But, if a person makes an incorrect statement, it does not mean he is lying. Lying infers conscious misstatement, something that is usually difficult, even impossible, to establish. The use of words such as "lying" introduces connotations into a discussion that usually cannot be verified. If the group does not recognize and reject such connotations, their thought processes are likely to be faulty and lead to bad conclusions.

Appeal to Authority. Appeal to authority is sometimes referred to as the "ipse dixit fallacy." It's the use of someone's opinion as fact, without establishing that the person is competent to render a valid opinion. Webster's dictionary says that a "cat" is a member of the feline species, therefore, that is what "cat means." Each of us can probably list at least a dozen other meanings for this common word. Whenever a source's opinion is used in a discussion, even a source like Webster, the tests for evidence discussed previously should be applied.

Damning the Origin. This fallacy is almost the exact reverse of the previous one. This is the rejection of a piece of evidence simply because of the source of the evidence. John Brown is a notorious rogue. Since he says that it will rain tomorrow, we conclude that it probably will not. Whenever possible, a group should carefully analyze evidence independently of its source. This is not to say that the source is irrelevant, but rather to indicate that even a bad source can often provide valid evidence.

Appeal to Tradition. "We've always done it this way before, so we should do it this way again." This is probably the most common fallacy that intrudes on rational problem solving and decision making in ongoing groups. Simply because something has been done a certain way in the past, it does not follow that it is either a satisfactory or desirable way of doing it in the future. Any solution should be tested for its advantages and disadvantages. It is neither an advantage nor a disadvantage in itself for something to have been done previously.

The Band Wagon. "Fifty million Frenchmen can't be wrong." "But mother, all the girls are wearing their skirts shorter now!" Simply because a large number of people hold an opinion, it does not follow that the opinion is valid. We should always remember that a large number of Germans thought it was a good idea to exterminate Jews in the 1940's. A few hundred years previous to that, the majority was fully in agreement that a troublemaker named Jesus should be eliminated. Majority opinion, therefore, should not be taken as an argument for or against a solution or decision. The decision should be evaluated on its own merits.

Ad Populum Reasoning. *Ad populum* is an appeal to the under-dog or the common people. Many political candidates use this type of reasoning to explain why they should be elected. They have lived all their lives in this state or district while their opponent is a "carpet-bagger." "Middle America knows that I am right, even if the Eastern establishment press doesn't." Neither of these examples of "reasoning" have any validity. They simply appeal to prejudice and have no place in rational problem solving or decision making.

The Call for Perfection. One of the biggest barriers to intelligent problem solving and decision making is the irrational call for perfection. Very few solutions or decisions will have entirely positive results and no negative ones. Similarly, it is often possible to overcome part of a problem but not the whole problem. "You can't legislate racial equality." This line of reasoning was used by many people in the United States during the 1950s and 1960s as an excuse for opposing laws designed to overcome racial discrimination. It was an irrational attack on a solution that was never intended to completely overcome the problem, but only to make a significant inroad. To reject solutions only because they are not perfect will often cause a group to fail to accept any solution at all, when they could adopt one that would go a long way toward overcoming a problem.

It must be stressed that the fallacies discussed above are only a few of the most common that confront problem-solving or decision-making groups. If people are aware of them, however, and work to avoid them, a significant improvement in the thought processes of the group should be expected. Another significant aid to rational thought in small group communication is structuring the communication itself in an organized way. Some of the ways of structuring problem-solving and decision-making groups in order to facilitate rational thought are considered in the following chapter.

SUGGESTED READINGS

Barker, L. L. and **Kibler, R. J.** *Speech Communication Behavior—Perspectives and Principles.* Englewood Cliffs, New Jersey: Prentice-Hall, 1971. See Chapter IV.

Fearnside, W. W. and **Holther, W. B.** *Fallacy—The Counterfeit of Argument.* Englewood Cliffs, New Jersey: Prentice-Hall, Inc., 1959.

Michalos, A. C. *Improving Your Reasoning.* Englewood Cliffs, New Jersey: Prentice-Hall, Inc., 1970.

Phillips, G. M. *Communication and the Small Group.* 2d ed. Indianapolis: The Bobbs-Merrill Co., Inc., 1973. See Chapter IV.

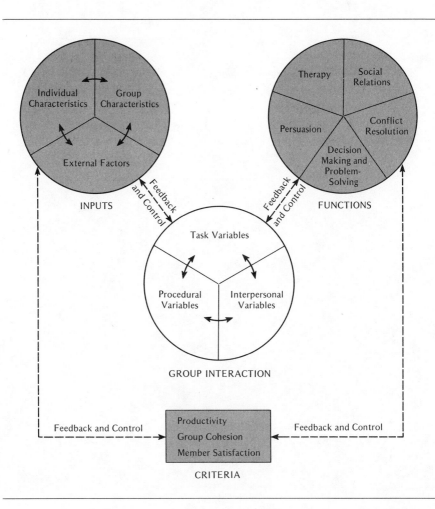

INPUTS

Individual Characteristics

Group Characteristics

External Factors

Feedback and Control

Therapy

Social Relations

Persuasion

Conflict Resolution

Decision Making and Problem-Solving

FUNCTIONS

Feedback and Control

Task Variables

Procedural Variables

Interpersonal Variables

GROUP INTERACTION

Feedback and Control

Productivity

Group Cohesion

Member Satisfaction

CRITERIA

Feedback and Control

Organizing
Small Group
Communication

S OME GROUPS are highly organized and structured, others have
much less organization, and some are almost chaotic. For many
groups, there is little or no need for organization of their communication. For example, a social group does not need to structure its communication. In fact, if structure were imposed on such a group, it
might actually get in the way of accomplishing its objectives. Task
groups, however, have a very great need for organization and structure
if they are to accomplish their objectives.

Research concerned with task groups has consistently indicated the
desirability of organization and structure. Organized groups tend to
discover more possible solutions, to reach better decisions, and to be
more satisfied generally with the decisions they reach. The organization and structure of small group communication may cause the group
to take longer to accomplish their tasks. However, this is the only
negative element and is usually not too important. One might ask, "Do
you want it fast, or do you want it good?" A poorly structured group

may reach a quick decision, but it is very unlikely that it will be a quality decision.

A wide variety of patterns have been observed in effective groups. It seems clear that there is no one pattern that is inherently superior to all the others. However, as we have indicated, *some* pattern is better than *no* pattern. In this chapter, we will describe some patterns that have been found to be particularly useful.

A Structure for Problem-Solving Tasks

Almost four decades ago, John Dewey published a book entitled *How We Think* in which he described a basic thought process that he believed was most commonly used by individuals when they were confronted with problem-solving tasks. Dewey's description has led to an organizational pattern that is recommended by many writers concerned with small group communication. This pattern has three essential steps: identification of the problem, analysis of the problem, and determination of possible solutions.

Problem Identification. The first step in problem solving is identification of the problem. The group must determine the essential nature of the problem itself. Is it a new problem? Is it a problem that is severe? Have attempts been made previously to solve the problem? What is likely to happen if nothing is done? Answering these questions permits the group to determine whether they are concerned with something vital or something more trivial.

Let us consider three groups that discussed the topic of "student participation in university governance" to see the different conclusions that groups can draw concerning the same problem. We will not attempt to evaluate or compare the groups' conclusions, but you may find it interesting to do so. Group A was composed of five university students, Group B was composed of five university faculty members from different departments, and Group C included two students, two faculty members, and one administrator, the vice-president of the university.

Group A: The basic problem is the students' lack of opportunity to influence their own environment. This has been a recent development that has occurred since the enrollment in the university has grown to its current large size. It is a very severe problem in that many students are alienated from the university. There have been no attempts to solve the problem; the administration has ignored all student requests. If the problem is not overcome, more students will become alienated, and our present poor-quality educational program will continue to exist.

Group B: The basic problem is student demands for control of the university. This is not a new problem, it has occurred throughout the history of the university from time to time. The problem is not severe because only a few students really care. There has been an attempt to solve it by putting some students on university committees. If nothing further is done, students will continue to complain for awhile and then forget the issue.

Group C: The basic problem is a lack of understanding and cooperation among students, faculty members, and the administration. It is a relatively new problem; when the university was smaller, there was a lot more interaction, understanding, and cooperation among the elements in the university. It is a very severe problem. There has been an attempt to solve it by instituting university committees composed of faculty members, administrators, and some students. If the problem is not solved, it is likely that the groups will become more alienated from one another and the possible benefits of cooperation among the groups will be lost.

Problem Analysis. After the problem has been defined, the group must seek to develop a thorough understanding of the problem. How long has the problem existed? Who or what is affected by the problem? Is it becoming more or less severe? What are the causes? What are people's attitudes towards it? Essentially, the problem-solving group has to confront the traditional journalist's questions: Who? What? When? Why? How? Where?

As we noted in the previous section, three different groups who are discussing the same question can identify an existing problem in very different ways. They can also develop very different analyses of the problem. Consider the conclusions arrived at by our groups.

Group A: This problem has existed ever since the enrollment underwent rapid growth in the 1960s. The people affected by the problem are the students, and the problem is getting more severe all the time. It has been caused by the faculty's and administration's lack of concern for the needs of students, who are very upset and concerned about the quality of the education they are receiving. They believe that they have more insight into what they need to learn than the administrators who are not even familiar with them.

Group B: The problem began about six months ago when a group of students who were dissatisfied with the military policy of the federal government began demonstrating on campus. This group sought to blame the University as a contributor to the nation's problems and started demanding change. Not very many people are affected by the problem at present, though some classes have been disrupted by demonstrators. The problem is becoming less severe since the government has withdrawn troops from Indo-China. The attitude of most students is apathy and most faculty members are completely unconcerned.

Group C: The problem has existed to some extent for almost ten years. As the university has grown, the various groups in the university have become more distant from one another and have had decreasing opportunities to interact. The primary cause of the problem is the size of the university enrollment. Most of the people in the university are aware of the problem and feel that something should be done to overcome it.

Research suggests that the group should not move on to consider any possible solution until the problem has been thoroughly analyzed. Otherwise, while talking about possible solutions, the group will discover elements of the problem that they do not understand and will have to return to the problem-analysis phase. This will lead to disorganization within the group and may interfere with rational thought processes.

Discovery of Possible Solutions. The final phase of the problem-solving process is the generation of possible solutions. Deciding which solution is the best of the possible ones is not part of this process, but belongs rather in the decision-making process. The group that handles this discovery phase effectively exhausts all possibilities of solutions. They leave no stone unturned.

Since our three groups have identified and analyzed the problem differently, it should come as no surprise that they will come up with different alternative solutions. Let us consider the results of their efforts.

Group A: Possible solutions:
1. Reorganize the university's senate so that it is composed of 50 percent students and 50 percent faculty.
2. Appoint four students and two faculty members to the nine-member board of regents.
3. Reduce the enrollment of the university to correspond with the level in 1957.
4. Fire the dean of students.
5. Fire the president.
6. Establish a curriculum committee for the university that includes a majority of students.
7. Abolish all regulations imposed on students except those directly related to academic matters.
8. Abolish required courses.

Group B: Possible solutions:
1. The administration should maintain a low profile until the demonstrations and complaints have run their course.

Group C: Possible solutions:
1. Form a university senate composed of all the various groups in

the university, including students, faculty, administrators, and civil service employees.

2. Establish committees in the university that include elected faculty and student members.

3. Appoint a committee to investigate the possibility of limiting future enrollments.

4. Establish departmental curriculum committees at every level composed of both elected students and faculty members.

5. Elect students to serve as assistants to all administrators in the university.

The problem-solving process, therefore, should pass through three relatively discrete phases. First, the group must clearly identify the problem with which it is concerned. Then, the group must be certain that it develops a thorough understanding of the nature of the problem, its causes and effects. And, finally, the group must attempt to determine all the possible solutions that could be employed to solve the problem. If this simple process is followed, the probability of effective problem solving is greatly enhanced. We will take a closer look later at the behaviors of our three groups.

A Special Problem in Problem Solving

Very often a task group develops a highly critical orientation during the problem analysis phase of their discussion. This is highly desirable, but it can lead to problems when the group is trying to generate possible solutions. This is not a time when critical evaluation is either needed or particularly valuable. A technique sometimes referred to as "brainstorming" has been found to be effective for many groups.

Brainstorming has two essential elements. First, all critical evaluation is temporarily suspended. Second, all discussion, except for clarification, is suspended. When a group is brainstorming for possible solutions, one member of the group is designated to keep a record of all the possible solutions suggested. Each group member verbalizes any possible solution that comes to mind, no matter how "off the wall" it may be. Brainstorming has been found to be a very effective method of generating possible solutions. Not only are more solutions proposed, but also more good solutions.

Another technique is also used in conjunction with brainstorming by some groups that have a very sizable membership. Since it is difficult for groups of more than five or six people to engage in brainstorming, larger groups sometimes find it effective to break themselves down into smaller groups, sometimes called "buzz groups." These smaller groups engage in brainstorming independently from one another and then come back into the larger group to compose one integrated list of possible solutions.

While brainstorming and buzz groups are particularly effective for the generation of possible solutions, they can also be employed effectively, at times, during the problem analysis stage in order to discover possible causes or effects of a problem.

Structuring the Decision-Making Process

As we have indicated previously, decision making must follow problem solving. A group may begin their interaction at the decision-making level if they, someone else, or some other group have already gone through the problem-solving process and have generated alternative solutions. In other circumstances, a group may move from the problem-solving process to the decision-making process during the same period of interaction. It is very important, however, to keep these two processes separate. If they are not carefully separated, the group is very likely to fall into disarray and unproductive communication.

Figure 9.1 presents a model of the decision-making process. Many other similar models have been suggested, and this model should not be considered the only procedure that a group can follow to reach effective decisions. However, this model is probably as good as any. Let us consider each of the steps in the model.

Recognition of Alternative Decisions. The first step in the decision-making process requires the group to be fully aware of all alternative decisions available. If it is not, the problem-solving process has been either inadequate or incomplete, and the group should return to it.

In the case of our three groups who were concerned with student participation in university governance, all three should return to the problem-solving phase. A comparison of the three individual lists of proposed solutions indicates that each of the groups failed to consider some alternatives generated by the other groups. If, however, the groups had been more diligent in their generation of possible solutions, they could now move on to the next step in the decision-making process.

Determination of Criteria for Acceptable Decisions. Once all the alternative decisions available are recognized, the group needs to establish criteria for evaluating them. Evaluation should never begin prior to the establishment of criteria. Otherwise, the group is very likely to be inconsistent in the criteria applied to different alternative decisions. The specific criteria that should be set depend on the topic of the discussion. Things such as cost, impact on the organization, and so forth provide the basis for appropriate criteria.

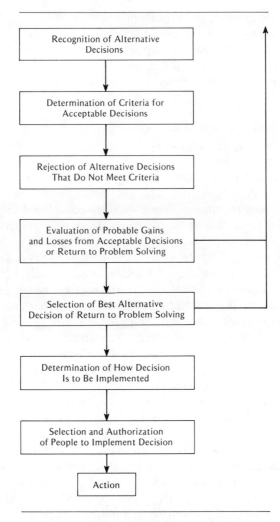

Figure 9.1. A Model of the Decision-Making Process

Let us see what kind of criteria our three university governance groups came up with.

Group A: Criteria for an acceptable solution:
1. Students must be able to veto irresponsible decisions of faculty or administrative committees.
2. Students must be able to determine their own curriculum.
3. No student should be required to take any particular course.
Group B: Criteria for an acceptable solution:
None.
Group C: Criteria for an acceptable solution:

1. It must provide an opportunity for the various groups within the university to interact with one another.
2. It must permit each group within the university to participate in all decisions that affect the group.
3. All people representing a group must be elected by the group involved.

Rejection of Alternative Decisions That Do Not Meet Criteria. The next step in the decision-making process is to evaluate the alternative decisions in terms of the criteria that have been established. During this decision-making phase, inappropriate, ineffective, and irrelevant decisions will be rejected. If the group finds that there are no alternatives remaining after they have completed this process, they must return to problem-solving to generate new alternatives.

Evaluation of Acceptable Alternative Decisions. During this phase of decision-making, the group should analyze intensively the probable impact of the alternative decisions. The group should consider all probable gains and all probable losses that could accrue from each alternative decision. This phase of decision-making is very similar to the problem analysis phase of the problem-solving process, since each alternative decision is examined not only in terms of whether or not it will solve the problem but also in terms of whether or not it might create new problems.

Let us again consider our university governance groups. Only two are still functioning, Group B has already decided on its course of action.

Group A: The evaluation of alternatives. The first proposed solution was evaluated as a desirable alternative since it met the established criteria. It would provide student control over their environment. The second alternative was rejected because it did not meet the criteria on control. Students would still be in a minority. The third alternative was rejected because such a severe reduction in enrollment would adversely affect many current students. Alternatives four and five were rejected because they did not provide any assurance of overcoming the problem. The people appointed to replace the dean and the president might be worse than the present holders of the positions. Alternatives six, seven, and eight were all considered desirable, even though it was recognized that alternative seven did not meet the criteria for a solution to the problem.

Group C: The first and second alternatives were determined to be desirable since they met all the criteria established for an acceptable solution. The third alternative was rejected because it could have no immediate impact on the problem. The fourth alternative was considered desirable since it met all the criteria for a solution. The fifth alternative was rejected because it was decided that one student would not have the time to devote to such a task.

Selection of the Best Alternative Decision. After each of the alternative decisions has been carefully analyzed on the basis of probable gains and losses, the various alternatives must be compared in terms of their gains and losses. The group then must reach a decision on the basis of which alternative decision will provide the greatest gain with the minimum loss compared to other alternative decisions. If, among all the available alternatives, no alternative provides a probability of greater gain than loss, all alternative decisions should be rejected and the group should return to problem-solving.

Let us look again at our three groups, since each has now reached a decision.

Group A: It was decided that the university should reorganize the university senate so that it would be composed of 50 percent students and 50 percent faculty. This was believed to be the best decision because it would permit implementation of all the other solutions as well.

Group B: It was decided that the administration should maintain a low profile until the demonstrations and complaints had run their course. This decision was reached because it was felt that the problem was a minor one that would go away of its own accord if left alone.

Group C: It was decided to combine three alternative solutions into one. Thus, the group concluded that a representatively elected university senate including students, faculty, administrators, and civil service employees should be established. It was further decided that the senate should form committees concerned with all important university matters that would include both faculty and student members, and that the University Senate should direct each department to form curriculum committees composed of elected students and faculty members.

Determining Means of Implementation. Presuming that the group has been able to decide on an alternative that will probably provide more gains than losses and is superior to any other alternative, the group must now determine how this decision will be carried out. The concern here is not whether or not the decision that has already been determined is good or bad; it is how the group is to get the job done. During this phase of the group's communication, the group may be concerned with such matters as what committees are needed, whether or not new employees are needed, whether or not the group can divide the work up among themselves, and so forth.

Let us see how our three groups decided to implement their decisions.

Group A: It was decided that there was no way for the group to implement the decision they had reached since they had no power. Consequently, two members of the group indicated that they intended to organize a rally of students to demonstrate against the administration of the university.

Group B: It was decided that a letter to the university president should be drafted with the committee's recommendation and delivered to him.

Group C: It was decided that only the president of the university could actually begin implementation of the decision reached by the group. Consequently, the group decided that it was imperative that they schedule a meeting with the president as soon as possible.

Selection and Authorization of People to Implement Decision. The final step in the decision-making process is the selection and authorization of the people who will carry out the decision. At this point, the only concern that remains for the group is final implementation of the decision.

Group A did not have to concern itself with this step in the decision-making process, since its discussion was terminated a step previously. Group B appointed one of the members to write and deliver the letter to the president. Group C delegated the administrative member of the group to attempt to schedule a meeting with the president.

Action. The final outcome of the decision-making process is action; people designated by the group carry out the decision reached by the group. Of our three groups, which one(s), if any, do you think resulted in action?

We have intentionally used as our example three groups with different types of members who have different orientations, and who make some different errors in the problem-solving and decision-making processes. Many of these errors have little to do directly with the organizational pattern that was employed. However, the causes of these problems have been discussed extensively in the previous chapters in this book. Before going on to the next chapter, it would be useful for you to examine carefully the products of these three discussion groups in relation to what you have learned throughout the preceding eight chapters. By diagnosing the problems of these groups, you may be able to avoid the same problems in groups of which you are a member.

Structuring Continuing Group Interaction

The material that we have discussed above concerning problem-solving processes can be applied to a group meeting only a single time or to groups that meet over a period of days or even years. However, groups that have extremely complex tasks requiring long periods of interaction, over weeks or months, present a special problem. In many cases, the overall task must be broken down into smaller parts in order to be manageable. In some cases, all of these smaller parts must be confronted by the same small group. When this happens, the group must take care not to confront too many of these subproblems during the same interaction. A better structural pattern would be to consider various subproblems during different interactions.

It is also common in a large organization to form a sizable number of small groups that are each concerned with subparts of an overall task. These groups must be carefully coordinated or their efforts may simply end in confusion rather than intelligent decisions. As in the case of the individual group confronting a task, a collection of groups must have structure if good decisions are to be reached. Most of the principles that are outlined in this book are relevant to the communication problems of large organizations, but specific consideration of these problems is beyond the range of our consideration.

For any task group to adhere to any organizational pattern, it is essential that the group have good leadership. When effective leadership is present, the group will not be diverted from its organizational structure. The characteristics of leadership are the focus of the following chapter.

SUGGESTED READINGS

Brilhart, J. K. *Effective Group Discussion.* Dubuque, Iowa: William C. Brown Company, Publishers, 1967. See Chapter III.

Dewey, J. *How We Think.* Lexington, Mass.: D. C. Heath and Company, 1933.

Heimstra, N. W. and Ellingstad, U. S. *Human Behavior—A Systems Approach.* Belmont, California: Brooks/Cole Publishing Company, 1972. See Chapter VIII.

Zelko, H. P. *The Business Conference: Leadership and Participation.* New York: McGraw-Hill Book & Education Services Group, 1969. See Chapter VIII.

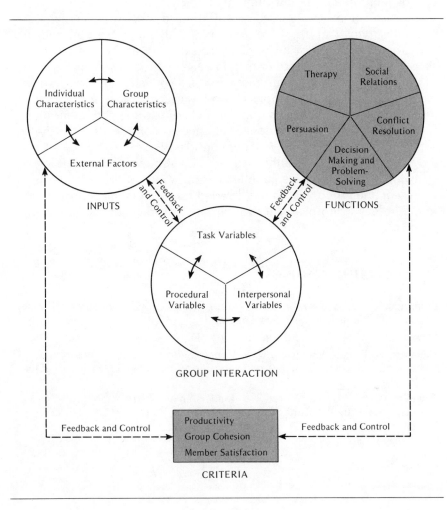

Leadership in the
Small Group

FROM ANTIQUITY to the present, much of the discourse of influential thinkers has been concerned with the power of some individuals over others. The recorded histories of civilizations, religions, and of entire eras often reflect little more than biographies of their "leaders." In this century, leadership has been the concern of scholars in a variety of disciplines such as psychology, sociology, management, and communication to name but a few. Understanding what leaders do, what functions they serve, and specifying how leaders best function in a small group is analogous in difficulty to nailing jello to a wall. However, that is our purpose in this chapter and one we consider extremely worthwhile, for leadership plays an important role in all functions of small group communication that we have previously discussed.

We begin this task by looking at some of the ways leaders and leadership have been defined. Each of these definitions is described and critiqued in terms of its usefulness in understanding group communication.

The Leadership-Trait Approach. One of the earliest approaches to leadership can be called the "great person theory," an attempt to discover specific traits or characteristics that are inherent in leaders. This approach has taken writers on a journey from physical characteristics to intelligence to personality syndromes to abstract descriptions of leaders.

Gowin (1915) in the early part of this century found that insurance salesmen were taller than policy holders, bishops taller than clergy, university presidents taller than college presidents, and salesmanagers taller than salesmen. In fact, recruiters for modern organizations must still believe that height is a predictor of success, since an analysis of starting salaries for college graduates in recent years indicates that males over six feet start with a significantly higher salary than those "unfortunate" enough to be shorter. We find it difficult to quarrel with this given that the two male authors of this text are six feet two and the female is five, nine. Obviously, something is operating here. Many studies show that leaders are generally bigger (taller and heavier) than followers. Other studies have found that leaders are better looking and have a higher level of energy, of one sort or another.

Numerous people have demonstrated that leaders have more general intelligence than nonleaders (Mann, 1959; Gibb, 1947). However, this does not hold in all small group situations. It is not surprising that in positions where mental skill is important, intelligent people assume leadership positions, but in other groups requiring little communication, routine tasks, or both, intelligence is less valued. Another factor, homophily, which we have already discussed, may alter these conclusions. Great differences between the intelligence of one group member and the others work against both obtaining and holding a leadership position. This could happen because the highly intelligent leader has different goals and purposes than the group members or because he bypasses them as a result of communication on different conceptual or language levels. Certainly the results of a number of political elections would confirm this speculation. Gibbs offers a provocative, albeit disturbing, comment about this: "The evidence suggests that every increment of intelligence means wiser government, but that the crowd prefers to be ill-governed by people it can understand" (Gibb 1969, p. 218).

Several personality syndromes have been found that are associated with leaders. They have been shown as more *self-confident* than nonleaders (Drake, 1944; Gibb, 1947), less *anxious,* and more *deliberate in their will control* (Cattell and Spice, 1954). Moreover, they seem to have a great need for *dominance* and are motivated by desires for power, prestige, and status. Taken as a whole, these personality syndromes suggest that leaders obtain their position because of a need for power and a confidence in their abilities to obtain and hold their dominance.

While many group discussion texts have popularized the notion that extroverts are more commonly leaders than introverts are, research does not clearly support this contention. In fact, our findings indicate that too much extroversion lowers credibility (Heston, 1973), and we expect that it might reduce leadership effectiveness if it goes beyond a point acceptable to the majority of group members.

Some people have suggested traits describing leaders that are much more nebulous than physical properties, scores on IQ tests, or measures on personality tests. An early writer Galton (1941) suggested that a leader had certain qualities of eminence such as "knowledge, cleverness, force, tact, loyalty, initiative, and courage." Bogardus (1950) cites five universal leadership factors: "imagination, foresight, flexibility, versatility, and inhibition." Others use ambiguous terms such as "persuasiveness, intuition, and initiative." These labels provide little help to the person who wishes to have a better understanding of leadership behavior. We are at a loss how to instruct a person to develop any of the attributes. We can neither describe the behaviors that lead to "persuasiveness" or "intuition" nor can we prescribe how a person develops such attributes. Therefore, we think that much of this work is of little value to the fledgling group member.

We do not deny that some of these traits influence the choice of a leader and what he does; there is considerable evidence to suggest that leadership is more than just the function of a given situation. Individual differences clearly affect group situations and the perceptions of others. However, the trait approach to leadership is no longer a popular avenue for scholars attempting to explain leadership. Other approaches seem to have more utility and recognize that many situational variables influence the group.

Leadership Style. Another related attempt to delineate leadership characteristics is similar to the trait approach but differs in some ways. This approach, instead of seeking inherent characteristics in the leader, centers on the behavior of the person in a leadership position. It does not matter if the leader is really aggressive or dominant; his style of leadership is aggressive if he behaves aggressively with the other group members. This approach has yielded labels not unlike those in the trait approach. A leader is said to have a facilitating style, aggressive style, or authoritarian style. And this approach faces the same problems encountered in the trait approach. First, the terms describing style are so ambiguous that they are unusable in helping one learn about leadership. Second, there does not seem to be a universal leadership style that is effective in all social and cultural situations. The aggressive, ambitious Manus tribal leader in Oceania would probably have been loudly rejected by plains Indians who valued group welfare and conformity to group wishes. Similarly, a businessman with what would be called a certain style of leadership in a business organization would not necessarily fit into a college or university position. There is no clear understanding of leadership style as it is or as it should be across all situations.

Task Approach.   The task approach to defining leadership states that the task faced by the group is the primary determinant of the leadership and group behavior that is likely to occur (Heise and Miller, 1951). The central notion of this approach is that groups working at different tasks require different kinds of leadership. Although there is no doubt that the leader of a therapy group must behave differently from the leader of a more task-oriented decision-making group, there are probably many similarities in required behavior.

We will resist the urge to list the kinds of behaviors that a leader should perform in differing task situations. Obviously, people must adjust to the task the group is working on, that much we know. However, there is a great deal of evidence to suggest that a strict task-orientation can cause severe problems both in a small group and in a large organization. A great deal of what we hear about the dehumanized working climate is probably the result of leaders who are task-oriented at the expense of the people in their work groups. Frequently this is resolved by having a *task leader*, often appointed to the position by someone with authority, who provides behavior that is designed to produce a product or make a decision. In addition, another person becomes the *socioemotional* leader of the group. This person can reinforce or reward people on a personal level, take care of the emotional well-being of the group, and behave in ways designed to reduce tension and provide orientation for the group. Actually, the informal socioemotional leader can become more powerful than the task leader and exert control over the group in all areas. A strong socioemotional leader can rely on the loyalty of group members to produce a slowdown or block a decision. The wise leader will recognize that there are many things required of him·and attention to the task alone may cause him problems.

A Behavioral Definition.   Perhaps a more useful way to define leadership is to explain the behaviors that go on in a group. In another chapter we have talked about the behaviors required for effective participation; they apply to the leader as well as the nonleader. However, there are some behaviors that a leader can exhibit that might be worth considering. Most of these behaviors have been shown to be important in a variety of settings such as industrial work groups, decision-making groups, and social groups. Hemphill (1950), Halpin and Winer (1952), and others have discussed leadership. The following list represents some of their findings and represents our thinking about the best way to categorize leadership functions.

1. *Initiation:* The leader should and does originate and facilitate new ideas and practices. It is also his duty to resist new ideas when he feels that they are inappropriate.
2. *Membership Function:* Part of the behaviors of a leader are aimed at making sure that he is also a member of the group. This is done by mixing with the group, stressing informal interaction, and taking care of socioemotional needs.
3. *Representation Function:* Often a leader has to defend group members from external threats or act as their spokesman to outside groups.
4. *Organization Function:* A leader is often asked to structure his own work and that of others. He can be responsible for some things we have discussed earlier, like agenda setting.
5. *Integration Function:* This function requires conflict resolution or management and is concerned with creating an atmosphere conducive to individual happiness.
6. *Internal Information Management:* The leader must, at times, facilitate information exchange among the group members and seek feedback on how well the group is doing. And he must often inhibit the free flow of information to protect specific individuals. You will recall in the chapter on therapy, we suggested that one leadership function in laboratory groups is ensuring that people are not personally harmed by information from other people. When information is not needed by all members, the leader functions to ensure that those who need to know are informed.
7. *Gatekeeping Function:* When a group has to deal with other groups or organizational units, the leader functions as a filter and manager of information *entering* and *leaving* the group. This is a somewhat different function from monitoring the internal communication. If too much information is present, conflict can result as we have already said; this filtering process can reduce that possibility. Sometimes a group wants to say things that they do not wish other people to hear. Gripe sessions often provide cathartic benefits to group members, and the leader reports to others while protecting member anonymity. These two information control functions are of increasing importance in contemporary society. In fact, one principal activity of a decision maker in organizations is controlling the flow of information. We are sure that the discerning reader is already aware that this function is one that can be a positive aspect of group life or a source of problems.

8. *Reward Function:* The leader performs evaluative functions and expresses approval or disapproval of group members. This can be done by material rewards such as pay increases or by conferring status, praise, or recognition. Many group members are extremely sensitive to the leader's reward power and much of their behavior, verbal and nonverbal communication, and work output is designed to bring them rewards from the leader.

9. *Production Function:* When the leader is responsible for getting a task accomplished, much of his communication behavior is designed to elicit more effort and achievement. Of course, all the other functions we have discussed can lead to more production, although there is no necesssary causal link. Happy workers are *not necessarily* more productive; so a task orientation is necessary to some degree in task groups.

Throughout this discussion, we have attempted to express the idea that effective participation by leaders and nonleaders is very similar. We urge our readers whether they are leaders or members of a small group to consider carefully our suggestions in the next chapter.

COMMUNICATION AND POWER: DEFINING CHARACTERISTICS OF LEADERSHIP

Perhaps a more useful approach to leadership would be to analyze it from a power point of view (Collins and Guetzkow, 1964). Although specific traits and leadership styles may be important, it is our belief that much can be gained by looking at leadership as power that one member has over another. According to this view, leadership is a residual effect: everyone has the potential to be a leader, but through the group's interaction, a power hierarchy, with a leader at the top, is established. Within this framework, we are able to specify certain communication behaviors that allow a person to establish and maintain his power over others. However, this section is primarily concerned with a detailed look at communication as an input to gain power and as an output once a leadership position has been established.

Before looking at the specific communication behaviors demonstrated by the aspiring leader, we would remind the reader of the discussion of power relationships in Chapter 3, where we were concerned with their effects on persuasion. In that chapter, we indicated two sources of power: external and internal. Leaders who have attained power externally by being designated to their positions will engage in some different communication behaviors from those who emerge (i.e., garner internal power) as leaders. We will begin by looking at leader communication behaviors in general and move on to the appointed-emergent leadership distinctions later.

The potential leader may be first identified in the early stages of a group by his *campaigning behavior.* He tends to communicate primarily with low-status members to establish his power base. His interactions at this point may function in rewarding, recognizing, and reinforcing low-status members, to establish his similarity and credibility, and to build interpersonal attraction, all of which strengthen his power. Once he has sufficiently established his power, he will shift to interacting primarily with high status members. Moreover, he seeks feedback from high rather than low-status members, which can encourage the formation of cliques. This behavior, however, serves a positive function since it clarifies the status hierarchy, thus reducing ambiguity and its consequent frustration.

The leader's communication patterns also serve to create the group's personality and to generate group norms, both of which contribute to the uniqueness of the group. Through his language, interaction patterns, and use of rewards and punishments he will strongly influence the group's identity and habits.

While the leader is instrumental in establishing group norms, he will be allowed to deviate more often. This is called *idiosyncratic credit.* It works rather like a bank account: the more power or conformity to norms, or both, that you demonstrate, the more credit you build up toward deviations. Because the leader has the power and tends to set the standards, he has more freedom to deviate from them. Thus the leader, at times, may express more extreme positions than other group members. When he deviates, more communication will be directed toward him (Collins and Geutzkow, 1964). By contrast, low power or unaccepted members who deviate may find more communication directed toward themselves initially, but over the long run, they will receive *less* communication, eventually becoming isolated.

As for the general frequency and content of a leader's communication, he initiates and receives more communication, makes more interpretations, provides more information for carrying out activities, proposes more solutions and courses of action, participates more actively in diagnosing problems and exerts more influence (Carter, Haythorn, Shirver and Lanzetta, 1950). The nature of the task also affects the leader's communication patterns. On reasoning tasks, leaders frequently ask for information or facts; on discussion tasks, they ask for opinions, give general information, and express agreement or approval; on mechanical tasks, they indicate a desire to get things done.

Differences exist among leaders depending on whether they are appointed or emergent (Carter, Haythorn, Shirver, and Lanzetta, 1950). Appointed leaders tend to adopt the role of coordinator, although they demonstrate strong attempts to lead. Emergent leaders, on the other hand, are more aggressive, energetic, authoritarian, forceful and dominating. Emergent leaders are more likely than appointed leaders to advocate their own ideas.

A leader may be differentiated from nonleaders on the basis of traits and skills. Moreover, orientations toward freedom and control may influence communication and group behavior. However, we believe that what separates leaders from nonleaders is their communication behavior. The last section has described some general communication behaviors engaged in by leaders of different sorts. We urge you to observe groups that you participate in to test the validity of our descriptions, recognizing, of course, that differing orientations and contexts cause some differences in communication behavior. The next step is to determine more carefully which combinations of traits, orientations, and communication behaviors result in the best group outcomes for each of us. The next sections look at the effects on groups of differing orientations and communication behaviors of those in leadership positions.

DIFFERENT LEADERSHIP ORIENTATIONS

No chapter on leadership would be complete without a discussion of the concepts of *freedom* and *control*. All the functions we just finished discussing can be fulfilled either by an autocrat who wishes complete control or by a democrat who wants freedom and participative decision-making. We will discuss five different orientations toward leadership including the behavior of the leader and its effects on such matters as communication, production, and morale. The five leadership orientations are labelled *bureaucrat, autocrat, diplomat, democrat,* and *laissez-faire.* Although other writers such as Gibb (1969), Haiman (1950), and Shaw (1964) have discussed leadership orientations, the following classification is our analysis of the work of several authors who have influenced us.

The Bureaucratic Leader. This type of leader has a frame of reference toward the group that is best characterized by the word "they." His orientation is impersonal and his orientation is rule-centered. If the group behaves according to preestablished rules, the leader is satisfied. The motivation that induces a bureaucrat to accept a position of leadership is personal security. For example, the bureaucratic leader often takes a promotion for increased job security rather than power. His main objective is to develop the group as a system governed by formal rules; this constitutes his base of authority.

His communication with other group members is infrequent and impersonal. The demands made on the members are ones of loyalty to a larger system (the overall bureaucracy), and avoidance of communication is typical. Identification with group members and their problems is minimal and his relationship with them is official, as opposed to personal.

The group members tend to be apathetic and turn to operating with minimal effort to achieve task results. Any of us who have had to deal with large bureaucracies are aware of the problems that this leadership orientation produces.

The Autocratic Leader has a self-centered "I" approach to group communication. His reasons for becoming a leader are based on the need for power and prestige. All determination of policy is done characteristically by the leader. Control of information both within and outside the group is a high priority function of this type of leader. Rules are followed and relied on when they serve the interests of the autocrat; therefore future behaviors are uncertain to a large degree. Obedience of the nonleaders is demanded by the autocrat and controls and sanctions are frequently used to ensure compliance with the leader's wishes.

His communication with nonleaders is often filled with detailed "personal" praise or criticism, or both, of each member. Members receive one-way communication and feedback is usually neither desired nor expected. Authority of the leader's position is communicated and compliance demanded. People must be continually watched to ensure that tasks are completed. Negative attitudes and antagonism are likely outputs.

The Diplomatic Leader is a manipulator and can be characterized as the Machiavellian we discussed earlier. He seeks the position of leadership for personal gain and recognition. He seeks to use a variety of tactics to manipulate the nonleaders to his desired ends. Often there is an illusion of participation or democracy. Many times this type of leader enters a group discussion with a "hidden agenda." For example, he knows exactly the decision he wants the group to make but is willing to allow discussion so that members will believe that they have made the decision. He engages in superficial two-way communication and attempts to make the group feel that he is seeking feedback. He can be democratic or autocratic depending on his evaluation of the best way to manipulate the situation. This style can lead to competition because the leader often pits one member against another. When the leader's true philosophy is exposed, antagonism is the likely result.

The Democratic Leader has the "we" orientation and works hard to maintain the membership function. He believes that development of the group can lead to better decisions and more productivity.

He accepts a leadership position because of his desire to serve the group. He tries to identify with the group and encourages peers to exercise discipline and social sanctions. His contact with members is frequent and he sincerely wants corrective feedback. The following is a good summary of the democratic philosophy:

> The democratic leader seeks to evoke maximum involvement and the participation of every member in the group activities and in the determination of objectives. He seeks to spread responsibility rather than to concentrate it. He seeks to encourage and reinforce interpersonal contacts and relations throughout the group structure so as to strengthen it. He seeks to reduce intragroup tension and conflict. He seeks to avoid hierarchical group structure in which special privilege and status differentials predominate (Krech, Crutchfield, and Ballachey, 1962, p. 435.)

This kind of leader is objective or "fact-minded" in his praise and criticism. He tries to be a regular member without doing an unfair share of the work. Haiman gives several reasons for claiming that this style of leadership is superior; it encourages more member participation, and people understand best things that they have actually experienced and are influenced most by processes in which they have participated. Therefore, change is more enduring and the controls that ensure continued behaviors minimized.

Laissez-Faire Orientations. This leadership orientation is close to a nonleader style. There is complete freedom for group *or* individual decision with a minimum of leader participation. The leader supplies information, material, or advice *when asked* but rarely takes part in discussions or communication of any kind. The members make all decisions and the previously discussed leadership functions are handled by members if they are attended to at all.

THE EFFECTS OF DIFFERING ORIENTATIONS

Perhaps a summary of research findings would help illuminate the expected effects of these orientations. These findings are somewhat tentative but can serve as guidelines for choices of leadership orientation (White and Lippit, 1968):

1. Laissez-Faire is not the same as democracy. It is characterized by less work and lower quality work. People often feel that the group lacks purpose and withdraw from further participation.
2. Democracy can be efficient but the amount of work done in autocracy tends to be greater. Work motivation is stronger and does not require the presence of the leader. Originality and creativity are more frequent in democracy.

3. Autocracy can create discontent that does not appear on the surface. More discontent is expressed toward the leader although members continue to be submissive to his authority. Conversations are less varied and boredom and/or frustration causes turn-over, absenteeism, and other dysfunctional behaviors. Communication is directed to the immediate solution of problems.
4. There is more group-mindedness and friendliness in groups with democratic leaders. The pronoun "I" is less frequently used and mutual praise among group members is more frequent. Cohesiveness and morale are higher. There is less disruption of group activities when the leader is absent.

Fiedler (1965) has tried to take the research and make statements about the situations in which different leadership orientations are most effective.

When Effective	
Authoritarian	*Democratic*

When leader has power *and* good relations with members *and* a clearly structured task.
 	
or
 	
When leader lacks power *and* does not enjoy the confidence of the members *and* the group task is ambiguous.
	The moderately favorable situation where
	    the group faces an
	    unstructured task
	
	or
	
	where leader-member relations are tenuous

This model obviously needs explanation. The most favorable situation exists if an authoritarian can structure the task, have the power to implement the plan, and enjoy the continued personal liking of the group; if these conditions are present the group will be highly productive. Also, under the most unfavorable conditions, the authoritarian style may be most effective in controlling conflict and getting a task done. Democracy might, in this case, lead to endless discussion and interpersonal difficulties. The democratic style and its benefits have been discussed in detail. One of the problems with the Fiedler model lies in the fact that it is difficult for an authoritarian, given his desire for control, to maintain good interpersonal relationships. Therefore, the favorable case might be too ideal and unattainable in most groups; this would suggest that democratic leadership is applicable in more situations than Fiedler claims.

We want to end this section with a word of caution. Probably no leader is a pure autocrat, democrat, diplomat, or bureaucrat. All leaders behave in ways that fit in each of our classifications so we can only talk about general tendencies or most frequent behaviors. All orientations have obvious strengths *and* weaknesses. The autocrat can alienate people, while the democrat can delay decisions and keep people engaged in endless discussions and meetings. Situational variables help dictate the orientations that a leader will take. When quick decisions are mandatory, democracy can be unworkable; other situations require replacement of a leader that is too autocratic. The leader must properly diagnose the situation so that the appropriate balance between freedom and control can be achieved. Therefore we urge caution and analysis *prior* to adopting a given orientation.

SUGGESTED READINGS

Bass, B. M. *Leadership, Psychology, and Organizational Behavior.* New York: Harper & Row, Publishers, 1960.

Fiedler, F. E. "The Contingency Model: A Theory of Leadership Effectiveness," in *Advances in Experimental Social Psychology, I,* edited by L. Berkowitz. New York: Holt, Rinehart and Winston, Inc., 1965: 538–551.

Gibb, J. R. "Leadership" in *Handbook of Social Psychology,* Vol. IV, edited by G. Lindzey and E. Aronson. Reading, Mass.: Addison-Wesley Publishing Co., Inc., 1969: 205–282.

Petrullo, L. and **Bass, B. M.** eds. *Leadership and Interpersonal Behavior,* New York: Holt, Rinehart and Winston, Inc., 1961.

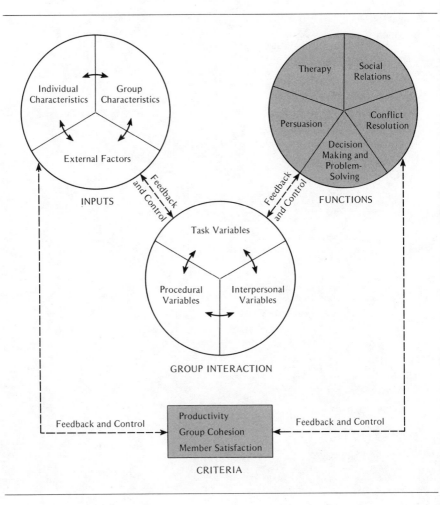

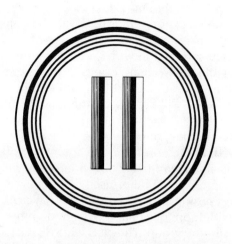

Effective Participation in Small Group Communication

HOW OFTEN have you found yourself in a conversation like the following?

"How did the meeting go today?"

"Same as usual. John and Jim began arguing immediately and made accusations throughout the discussion. No one had prepared anything before the meeting. Al kept trying to take over, Pete continually interrupted with questions or wisecracks, and the girls refused to participate because they said no one listened to them anyway."

"What did the group decide?"

"That we shouldn't have met."

The usefulness or uselessness of group discussion is dependent on effective participation by its members. When problems occur such as those hinted at in the example above, the utility of groups is largely negated. Throughout the preceding chapters, numerous explicit and implicit recommendations have been made on ways of overcoming similar problems. They have laid the groundwork for this chapter, which is designed to distill the previous conclusions into some specific recommendations for making group participation as effective as possible.

Before examining how the individual can improve his communication in a group, one major prerequisite should be considered—the relationship of effort to reward. The willingness of group members to participate and their satisfaction with group outcomes is partly dependent on this variable. Individuals bring to the group their personal anticipations of the amount of effort they will expend compared to the amount of reward they will receive. If the amount of effort required becomes disproportionate to the amount of reward received, willingness to be involved in the group decreases. The person who reluctantly volunteers for a committee on the expectation of working four hours, then finds himself involved in a twelve-hour task with no increase in personal benefit is unlikely to be pleased by the development. The student working on a group project who could have produced a higher quality product with more personal recognition on his own will be less willing to work with the group. The club whose social activities require more effort in planning than the amount of enjoyment they bring will not long remain a viable social organization. Or the party to a negotiation who can only lose by compromising will be unwilling to participate in discussions of the problem. All these examples show how important it is that the amount of effort required by a group balance favorably with the reward received by each member. This is a group responsibility; an individual cannot, himself, change the effort/reward ratio. The group must, therefore, select its responsibilities and design its activities so that the members are collectively and individually satisfied with the relationship. Under circumstances in which it is impossible to balance favorably effort and reward, the reasonable alternative is to use something other than a group approach.

With this overall prerequisite in mind, we can begin considering what the individual should do to improve his communication in a group. The recommendations can be viewed from the functional approach first introduced in the opening chapter of this text. Using this format, we look first at the inputs the good participant brings to the group, the communication functions he performs during interaction, so that the group can achieve its functions, and how he responds to the group's outcomes. We realize that breaking up small group communication into three separate parts is an artificial distinction. Small groups are a process and all these parts interact with and affect each other. Obviously, the people variables affect both communication and outcomes; likewise, the group's communication can affect people. However, by making this separation of components, albeit artificial, we can systematically examine the situation in order to make suggestions for effective participation.

INPUTS

The inputs we are concerned with here are the qualities that a person should bring to a group discussion if he is to be an effective participant. There are many individual inputs in a group over which a person has no control, such as his age, sex, and personality. We will confine our recommendations to inputs that the individual can control.

Orientations

Of primary importance are a person's general orientations toward group processes and group members. These attitudes that a person has upon entering will determine a group's effectiveness. We feel there are eight orientations that, if adopted by members of a group, will facilitate a productive, satisfying outcome.

1. *Responsibility.* Participants in a group must accept responsibility for seeing that the group's activities run smoothly. This means that each person shares in the planning and conduct of the group and makes an effort to resolve problems. Essentially, this orientation means that each member takes on leadership responsibilities even though he is not the leader. Rather than passively waiting for someone else to do what has to be done, he actively seeks and accepts responsibilities. In an effective group, there are no absolute followers, only different levels and kinds of leadership. The notion of active participation itself assumes responsible involvement of all members. The orientation of responsibility negates the philosophy of "letting George do it."

2. *Commitment.* Going hand-in-hand with responsibility is the orientation of commitment. The good group member is willing to commit himself to the group process and product, whatever the outcome (assuming it doesn't violate his personal ethics). He is willing to devote time and energy to the group's activities. He gives as well as takes. This is basically a question of loyalty. Prior to any particular group meeting, each member should determine for himself if he is really committed to the group's membership and activities. The individual who has no initial commitment to a group, whose entering attitude is one of "wait and see," is not likely to be an asset. In times of stress, he is more likely to "abandon ship" than to address the problems seriously. If a person voluntarily chooses to be a member of a group, he has an obligation to maintain a commitment to it in return for the benefits he gains by membership.

3. *Open-Mindedness.* The orientation of open-mindedness is willingness to listen to other points of view. The effective group participant comes to a group meeting with an open mind and is willing to consider a broad range of ideas and suggestions from others. He takes a

provisional attitude about his own positions. An important element of open-mindedness is the absence of a hidden agenda. A hidden agenda, as we explained in Chapter 10, is a secretly held preference that governs an individual's behavior. The person with a hidden agenda tries to manipulate the group to take the direction he wants, without appearing to do so. He has already made a private decision about the outcome he desires, which means that he is not approaching the group with an open mind. The real detriment of the hidden agenda is that it usually evolves from ulterior motives that are never exposed to the group. Otherwise, the person would openly present his preference and his rationale for group evaluation. The hidden agenda may produce decisions that have an unsound basis if the person is successful in manipulating the group. This orientation may bring personal satisfaction but it is not the mark of a good group member.

4. *Flexibility.* Related to open-mindedness is flexibility. The member who enters a group with this orientation has decided in advance that he will be open to change. He has chosen to avoid taking rigid stands on issues. Similarly, if the group finds his behaviors unacceptable, he is willing to improve them. For instance, if he is criticized for monopolizing the group's communication, he does not rigidly defend his right to talk as much as he wants. The flexible member tries to adapt to the best interests of the group.

5. *Objectivity.* Also related to open-mindedness is objectivity. The objectively oriented group member expects to make unbiased, impartial judgments. This does not mean that he completely suppresses his subjective, emotional reactions. He tries, rather, to balance them with objective observations. He doesn't get carried away with irrelevant emotional considerations. He attempts to make rational, reasonable decisions. This requires maintaining a "proper perspective," that is, neither becoming too embroiled in problems to maintain objectivity nor remaining too distant and uninvolved to be fully aware of their nature. Objectivity is part of our image of the ideal, rational man. As happens with any ideal, we often fall short of this goal. One way we can try to improve our objectivity is by listening to understand rather than listening to argue. Our biases frequently cause us to listen to others' views so that we can refute them, rather than listening to really understand what is being said. If we listen attentively and objectively to another's arguments, rather than trying to build a case against them, we will make more progress in group discussions.

6. *Cooperation.* The relative merits of cooperation and competition have been discussed in an earlier chapter. While competition brings personal satisfaction at times, a group is usually more successful if its members choose to cooperate. Cooperation dictates that each member decide that any personal gains from competition should be subordinated to the group's best interest. Of course, there are times that

an individual's personal convictions may require that he refuse to co-operate with the group, and competition may be healthy in special circumstances. This does not deny the basic premise that cooperation generally produces better group outcomes, more cohesion, and greater member satisfaction.

7. *Acceptance.* The orientation of acceptance is a general willingness to accept others for what they are and to support rather than criticize. A group that adopts an accepting orientation has a more relaxed atmosphere, greater participation (especially by hesitant members), and greater member satisfaction. If a group develops a critical nonaccepting atmosphere, defensive communication and conflict result. Each member has a responsibility to engage personally in supportive communication.

8. *Equality.* The final orientation, equality, rejects notions of superiority. The participant with the orientation of equality feels that a group will be more successful if he responds to others as equals, rather than establishing his superiority over them. The group that adopts this perspective deemphasizes status differentials. People in positions of strong power and status avoid attitudes of superiority in their communication. This kind of communication pattern should not be confused with eliminating power and status differentials. The existence of a status hierarchy does not preclude communicating with others on an equal basis. Unfortunately, our personal needs for achievement and recognition cause us to seek ways of demonstrating our superiority. These motivations need to be overcome if group communication is to succeed.

These eight orientations should be goals for each group member to achieve. If individuals bring these orientations to a group, the chances for satisfying, productive communication will be heightened.

Criteria for Satisfaction

A second major input of the good group participant is predetermination of his criteria for satisfaction. Often we enter a group without really knowing what we expect. This uncertainty can lead to disappointment in the group's outcomes, because we develop postexpectations that are greater than what could have been realistically achieved. It seems, therefore, good sense for a person to make some decisions, prior to a group experience, about what he expects to get out of it. After realistically assessing the nature of the group, he should determine how much effort he is willing to expend in exchange for an appropriate reward. He should decide on the standards or criteria that will have to be met to receive satisfaction. By predetermining realistic criteria, each member has something with which to measure group output. Advance personal decision making of this nature should reduce unrealistic expectations and disappointments later.

Attitudes and Ethics

Besides clarifying his expectations, each member should enter a group with a clear understanding of his own opinions and values. He should devote some time to analyzing his own attitudes and the ethical standards that he wants to maintain. Careful deliberation of one's position prior to a group experience can prevent inconsistency or embarrassment later. We wonder if the injurious actions of mobs are not partially due to the failure of the participants to know their own thoughts in advance or to decide on the behaviors they condone. People who take the time to analyze their own values and beliefs may protect themselves from "the morning after" regrets.

Information

A final input that a good participant should have in task-oriented groups is adequate information. You can't fill a cask from several empty vessels. Neither can you produce decisions without adequate knowledge. The effective participant seeks to acquaint himself with a broad range of opinions and evidence. Moreover, he organizes and synthesizes this material prior to a group meeting so that he can effectively present it to a group. Often the group divides its labor so that each person is responsible for acquiring information on a specific topic. This should not prevent the conscientious participant from gathering as much information as he can in advance to give him general knowledge on the issue. We cannot overemphasize how essential it is to have adequate information for the group process to work. A key measure of a participant's effectiveness is how well-informed and prepared he is.

INTERACTION

All the inputs discussed above also imply effective behaviors during the interaction process. A person's orientations are evidenced by his actual communication during the group's interaction. Likewise, his expectations, attitudes, ethics, and knowledge influence his behavior. Over and above these considerations there are several others that should be recommended for effective behavior during group interaction. These involve communication roles, language, communication networks, and feedback.

Within a group, there are several roles or functions that need to be fulfilled if the group is to complete its task and maintain its cohesiveness. These are classified as task and maintenance roles. A third category are dysfunctional, self-centered roles that need to be avoided.

These three categories include the range of constructive and destructive functions that group members may perform (Benne and Sheats, 1948). We will discuss each of these individually.

Group Task Roles

These roles involve the communication functions necessary for a group to accomplish its task, whether it is decision making, problem solving, education and information exchange, or conflict resolution. Not all, but most, roles are required in each situation. No roles should be played by a single individual; each person should perform multiple functions. The good participant will fulfill most, if not all, of these roles.

1. *Initiator*—proposes new ideas, procedures, goals, and solutions. He gets the group started. Since getting started on any task is usually difficult, his is an important role. New ideas and perspectives are also essential to the continued life of a group.

2. *Information giver*—supplies evidence, opinions and relates personal experiences relevant to the task. We have discussed earlier the necessity of an abundance of information. In addition to quantity, quality information is needed. The quality of a decision or solution can be no better than the information that produced it. No information may be better than erroneous or biased information.

3. *Information seeker*—asks for information from other members and seeks clarification when necessary. This role is equally as important as giving information; if we fail to ask others for their information, relevant evidence may be overlooked.

4. *Opinion giver*—states his own beliefs, attitudes and judgments. Usually, there are a few people in a group who are more than willing to present their opinions. The concern is that everyone, including the introverts and communication apprehensives, give their views. Group effort has an advantage over individual efforts; it produces both a wider range of ideas and more creative contributions. This principle presupposes that all members participate. The ineffective participant withholds his opinions out of fear of criticism; the effective member expresses them.

5. *Opinion seeker*—solicits the opinions and feelings of others and asks for clarification of positions. Too often, we are so concerned with presenting our own views that we neglect to ask the opinions of others. The effective participant actively seeks others' attitudes and convictions, especially those of members who are hesitant to speak. Questioning for both opinions and information can play a vital role in group communication. It should not be overlooked as an effective discussion technique.

6. *Elaborator*—clarifies and expands the ideas of others through ex-

amples, illustrations and explanations. As long as his elaborations are relevant to the task, this role is valuable. It is especially useful with others who are unable to express their own ideas adequately.

7. *Integrator*—clarifies the relationship between various facts, opinions, and suggestions and integrates the ideas or activities of other members. The integrator ties together elements that might otherwise seem unrelated and disjointed. This linking function makes contributions as useful as possible by incorporating ideas that might otherwise be disregarded.

8. *Orienter*—keeps the group directed toward its goal, summarizes what has taken place and clarifies the purposes or positions of the group. Essentially, he insures that the group has a direction and that it heads in the "right" direction. Without orientation, a group may easily "get off the track" onto trivial or irrelevant issues. This role is necessary to define or clarify continually the group's intermediate and ultimate goals so that the group's activities can be checked, at any given time, for consistency with the desired outcomes.

9. *Energizer*—stimulates the group to be energetic and active. By this person's communication and example, he motivates the group to reach a decision or to be more involved. The energizer's drive contributes to greater group efficiency and productivity.

Group Maintenance Roles

These roles build and maintain the group's interpersonal relationships. They determine the socioemotional atmosphere of the group. If these roles are not performed, conflict may arise and group cohesiveness is reduced; if they are performed, the group interacts more smoothly, with greater satisfaction as an outcome.

1. *Encourager*—praises and agrees with others, providing a warm, supportive interpersonal climate. The accepting orientation, discussed as an input, is evidenced by how well a person shows encouragement and support for others. This function is valuable in producing solidarity in the face of conflict.

2. *Harmonizer*—attempts to mediate differences, introduce compromises, and reconcile differences. The harmonizer's conciliatory communication is directed toward reducing conflict and encouraging a pleasant socioemotional atmosphere.

3. *Tension reliever*—introduces a relaxed atmosphere by reducing formality and interjecting humor. This role, like the harmonizer, must be filled when conflict arises. This is not an easy assignment; when tension increases, people become less flexible and more emotionally involved. The effective participant attempts to suppress his own emotional reactions while trying to deemphasize the conflict for others. If

he is good at telling jokes or making others see the humor of a situation, his intercession may go a long way in relieving tension.

4. *Gatekeeper*—controls the channels of communication, providing proper balance in the amount of participation of each member. The gatekeeper encourages those to talk who might otherwise not speak, while cutting off those who tend to monopolize the discussion. In conflict situations, he attempts to reduce the amount of communication by highly dissident or argumentative members, while increasing participation by more moderate, conciliatory members. However, if the situation warrants a confrontation, the gatekeeper opens up channels to the opponents so that the catharsis can take place. His overall purpose is the satisfactory continuation of the group. By his attention (or lack of it), by his body orientation and eye contact, and by the members he addresses, he can control the flow of communication.

5. *Follower*—acquiesces to the wishes of others. Although we do not generally recommend the follower role, in circumstances where the group's cohesion is disintegrating, this role is constructive in furthering maintenance of the group, because it does not contribute to conflict. It serves, rather, as a neutralizing element. The good participant may be advised, therefore, to adopt this role under stress situations, as long as he is following a leader who is trying to resolve conflict. If he is following one of the disruptive members, this role becomes a destructive one.

Dysfunctional Roles

We have recommended that the effective participant function in as many of the task and maintenance roles as possible. The roles that are about to be discussed are ones that the good participant should avoid. They are self-centered roles played by a person who is more concerned about personal needs than the group's interest. These roles reduce group productivity, cohesion, and satisfaction.

1. *Blocker*—constantly objects to others' ideas and suggestions and insists that nothing will work. He is totally negative. As the name implies, the blocker prevents progress. He may belabor points that the group has finished discussing or repeatedly oppose recommendations. The blocker is always complaining, always dissatisfied. He is the type you forget to inform about meetings or plan them during times when he is busy.

2. *Aggressor*—insults and criticizes others, shows jealousy and ill will. Like the blocker, the aggressor is discontented and disapproving. His malevolence is evidenced by jokes at others' expense and efforts to deflate others, whom he distrusts and dislikes. He may have alienated or anxious personality traits.

3. *Anecdoter*—tells irrelevant stories and personal experiences. He is a little like the elaborator, only he gets carried away with irrelevant anecdotes. He is motivated by a need for attention (as are the others who take disruptive roles). While the stories and jokes may be entertaining, they retard group progress.

4. *Recognition seeker*—interjects comments that call attention to his achievements and successes. He boasts while trying to appear not to do so. For example, the recognition seeker might say, "When I won the state swimming meet, I noticed that that problem was occurring . . ." He needs the sympathy and recognition of others.

5. *Dominator*—tries to monopolize group interaction. He wants to lead the group and will use whatever tactics he feels necessary, such as flattering, interrupting, and demanding to get his own way. He has the "spoiled brat" syndrome: he is not happy until he is running things his way.

6. *Confessor*—uses the group to listen to his personal problems. The confessor seems compelled to reveal his shortcomings, fears, and needs to the group. He involves the group in his problems, using it for catharsis. Unless the group is intended to be therapeutic, this role is disruptive, sidetracking the group from its goals.

7. *Special-interest pleader*—represents the interests of a different group. He pleads for favors or attention for the group whose interest he represents. The special-interest pleader's loyalties lie outside the group.

8. *Playboy*—distracts the group with antics, jokes, and comments. He is uninvolved with the group's purpose, preferring to entertain himself and the other members through his horseplay or sarcasm. The label "playboy" does not derive from his flirtatious behavior, although this may be part of it, but for his affinity for "play" rather than "work." Nor should the label imply that only males are guilty of this behavior; females can be playboys just as easily.

Each of us may recognize within ourselves some tendencies toward these dysfunctional behaviors. If we are to be effective participants, we must consciously control these inclinations, while striving to perform the more constructive task and maintenance roles.

Language

A second deciding factor in effective participation is a person's sensitivity to his own use of language and the language of others. An entire field, called general semantics, has evolved around the study of the effects of language on our daily living (cf. Johnson, 1946, and Korzybski, 1941). It seems especially appropriate to include some mention of general semantics at this point since unawareness of the influence of language can unalterably muddle a group. While it is beyond the scope of this chapter to explore the topic in depth, we have selected a few language problems for consideration because we feel that groups are particularly susceptible to them. Problems that are simple to begin with may be quickly escalated in a group because of the number of people involved.

Judgments based on inferences rather than facts. By now you have probably had at least one English class that warned you about the dangers of using inferences. It is also likely that it had little impact on you. It is probably naive of us, therefore, to try to make the problem meaningful; nevertheless, we will try.

Inferences are statements that can be made at anytime without direct observation or that go beyond what is actually observed. Inferences act as complete statements about reality. Facts, on the other hand, are bound by actual observation and the specific time the observation is made. They are, by their nature, incomplete statements of reality because nothing can be observed in its entirety. Observations are limited by the gross abilities of the human eye. The statement, "Carol has blond hair" is a fact (if observed); the statement "Carol bleached her hair" is an inference (unless you actually observed it or she told you).

A classroom experiment that is often used illustrates the point. The male professor enters the room, sits beside one of the attractive females in the class and whispers something in her ear. She promptly slaps him, at which point they begin yelling and the professor stalks out of the room. Afterwards, students are asked to report on what happened when another faculty member comes to investigate. The inevitable report is that the professor "got fresh" with the girl so she slapped him. Sometimes the story is embellished with tales about his previous flirtations with her, or her encouragements. Actually, the whole situation is staged, but it aptly convinces the sheepish students of their own reliance on inferences. Indeed, rumor mills would perish without the fodder of inferences.

In a group situation, the use of inferences can be especially critical because it is easier to accept them than to investigate them. The group member, eager to make his contribution, may offer inferences because he is "pretty sure they're true" or "he thinks that's what he heard." These inferences spawn additional inferences until reality is totally obscured. The effective group participant combats this problem by not only carefully scrutinizing his own "facts" but also insisting that others substantiate theirs. He questions and requests verification of potential inferences. If all group members participate in this normative behavior, faulty conclusions can be partially avoided.

Bypassing.   This story is told by a friend of the authors about an incident he had with his wife. It was late November and the weather was turning colder, so one morning before leaving for work the man asked his wife to stop at a gas station and put some antifreeze in the car. A few days later, the temperature dropped below zero overnight. In the morning the man went to start his car only to find that the engine block had cracked from the cold temperatures. Furious at the expense that would be involved, he yelled at his wife for failing to get the antifreeze. "But I did," she replied as she opened the back door. There on the floor of the back seat sat the cans of antifreeze.

This anecdote exemplifies the problem of bypassing. Bypassing occurs either when the same words have different meanings for the people using them, or different words have the same meaning. The example above illustrates words that are the same ("put antifreeze in the car") but have different meanings. The latter type of bypassing is evidenced by the extended group argument that terminates when the parties involved suddenly discover that they have been "saying the same thing," only they have been expressing it differently.

A corrective for bypassing is paraphrasing or repeating what the person has just said in your own words. If you can paraphrase what a person has just said to his satisfaction, you probably understand each other. This technique is particularly useful when tension rises, since stressful situations tend to foster misunderstandings. The effective group participant makes it a practice to ask "Is this what you mean?" after any ambiguous or opposing statement, so that any misconceptions can be immediately clarified through the process of paraphrasing. This is one of the most valuable discussion techniques that a group can use.

Stereotyping.   In discussions, we are frequently inclined to make broad generalizations. They often include stereotypes. We assign people and ideas to large categories then react to them as representatives of these categories, instead of as individuals. While our classifications may be accurate in many instances, we may unfairly infer attributes of individuals that are based solely on the stereotype. We are familiar with the stereotypes that all students are marijuana smokers, all blacks are athletic, or all blue collar workers are shot-gun-toting hippie-haters. None of these stereotypes is fair to the student, the black, or the blue collar worker. Although we may feel that we are personally not guilty of these blatant stereotypes, we are probably all vulnerable to more subtle forms of stereotyping. In a group situation, males may stereotype the females as irrational, while the females may stereotype the males as chauvinists. The person who presents one radical or one conservative argument may be categorized as a radical or a conservative. Then, not only will other contributions be reacted to within this perspective, but other characteristics, such as living habits, may also be attributed to the individual.

To counteract this problem, group members should engage in mental indexing; that is, they should recognize that Individual₁ is not the same as Individual₂ is not the same as Individual₃, or Idea₁ is not the same as Idea₂. Sensitivity to individual differences will mediate the harmful effects of false generalizations.

Failure to respond to time changes. This problem is similar to stereotyping in that we fail to recognize differences over an extended period of time. We can certainly tell that Johnny at age two is not the same person as Johnny at age fourteen. But we do not seem to make the same distinctions between communism in 1945 and communism in 1973, or our closest friend five years ago and the same person now. We tend to assume that people or concepts are invariant over a long period of time. This leads to erroneous judgments and rigid responses. It is unfair to respond to Germans today in the same manner as during World War II or to assume that a person's argument today is identical to the one he offered a month ago.

To reduce false assumptions because of the inability of our language to make these subtle distinctions, we should engage in mental dating. Statement$_{1963}$ is probably different from Statement$_{1973}$. Anger$_{morning}$ may not be identical to Anger$_{evening}$. Use of this technique adds accuracy to our communication.

Polarization. Another inadequacy of our language system is that it encourages dichotomous or polarized thinking. Word pairs like good-bad, black-white, high-low, and right-wrong discourage awareness of the middle ground or "gray" areas. In a group situation, if we are convinced that our solution is the "right" one, any alternatives become labeled "wrong." This creates polarization in discussions.

The effective small group participant attempts to overcome this problem by recognizing continuums rather than poles and avoids using language that expresses polarity. Where others use dichotomous, polarizing language, he draws attention to the middle ground.

Failure to delay responses. The final problem to be considered is the failure to delay responses. There are two ways that we can react to language: signally and symbolically. A signal response is immediate and automatic, like jumping at the word "snake" or crossing the street when the "walk" light flashes on. A symbolic response requires thinking or mental processing which makes it a slower, more deliberate, voluntary response. Too often, we respond to the suggestions of others as if they were signals rather than symbols: we react before we have thought about it. If you have ever responded angrily to someone, only to discover after you started that you actually agreed with what he said, you have been guilty of failing to delay your response.

To be effective in a group, we must not "jump to conclusions" or assume that we know what a person is going to say before he has said it. We will have much better discussions if we withhold judgments about others' suggestions until we have had adequate time to reflect upon them. One small group technique that recognizes the importance of delaying responses is brainstorming. In brainstorming, any and all ideas are freely expressed in random fashion with no evaluations made until all suggestions have been presented. Whether a group employs this specific technique or not, all members should learn to refrain from judging others' contributions until they have thought about them sufficiently.

These semantic problems and correctives by no means exhaust the possibilities, but they should sensitize the concerned group member to some potential barriers that should be sidestepped.

Communication Networks

Another factor of effective interaction in groups is the patterns or networks that develop. Networks indicate which channels are open or closed to communication between participants. They should not be

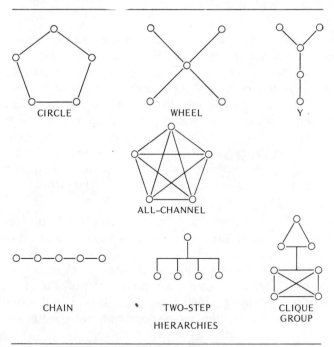

CIRCLE   WHEEL   Y

ALL–CHANNEL

CHAIN   TWO-STEP   CLIQUE
    HIERARCHIES   GROUP

confused with seating arrangement—a group may have any of the networks described below even though members are seated in a circle. The network simply tells you which channels are being used. The pattern that occurs in a group may be imposed externally or by a strong gatekeeper or leader, or it may develop voluntarily. The network that a group operates under influences efficiency, the quality of decisions, and member satisfaction. The most common networks are the circle, the wheel, the chain, the Y, the all-channel, and the two-step hierarchy. The lines represent open channels, i.e., who talks to whom.

A variety of research studies (Bavelas, 1950; Leavitt, 1951; Shaw, 1964) have drawn several conclusions about the effects of the various communication networks on information processing, decision making and member satisfaction. Their findings are:

1. Networks with centralized positions such as the wheel, Y, and chain, promote rapid, accurate communication, when simple problems are involved.
2. Decentralized networks, such as the circle and all-channel are faster and more accurate when complex problems are involved.
3. Member satisfaction is greater with more centralized positions.
4. Greater leadership control obtains with the wheel and two-step hierarchy, but morale may suffer.
5. Circle members send more information, give more answers, provide more feedback, and correct more errors.
6. The formation of cliques (subgroups) creates a hierarchical network, with most communication occurring within subgroups rather than between subgroups.

It should be clear that no single network should be advocated; it depends on the desired outcome. However, the most generally acceptable pattern is the all-channel because it combines the advantages of the wheel and the circle—it produces relatively high participation, satisfaction, and accuracy with the potential for adequate leadership control, since any position can become "central." We do advise avoidance of the hierarchical pattern because it hurts morale and, as pointed out in earlier chapters, may lead to conflict.

The effective group participant may not himself be able to determine the network that will prevail in a group; the network is dependent on all members. He should, however, be aware of their relative advantages and disadvantages and wherever possible, work to institute the most desirable pattern. A leader or gatekeeper can partially control the network employed. The concerned participant ought to attempt to open channels that should be used or close those that should not. If each member recognizes the importance of these networks, rational decisions can be made about the ones to adopt and the ones to overcome.

Feedback

The last element to be examined in the group process is feedback. In the opening chapter of the book, we talked about feedback links as one form of interconnection between elements or people in a group. In Chapter 2, feedback was introduced as an element in the model of communication. We considered in Chapter 3 the problems that result from ambiguity about the task, ideas, or relationships among members. The conclusion is that feedback is essential to a group. The effective participant gives feedback to other members about the nature of the task, their status, the accuracy of their information, his evaluations of their ideas, and his personal feelings about them. Moreover, he makes his feedback constructive. He provides criticisms that are helpful and praises or rewards whenever possible. By effectively utilizing feedback, a group can eliminate unnecessary, tension-producing ambiguity and can make corrections or improvements that are needed.

EVALUATING OUTCOMES

So far, we have talked about what the effective participant should bring to a group and which behaviors he or she should engage in during interaction. There is only one other aspect of participant behavior that needs attention—responses to the group's outcomes. We feel that there are three things the individual should do as follow-ups to the earlier recommendations.

First, each member should personally evaluate the outcomes to determine if they are consistent with his criteria for satisfaction and personal ethics. Second, if he decides that the outcomes meet his approval, he should reconfirm his commitment to implement solutions and support the group's continuation. Third, if he is unsatisfied with the group's outcomes, he should decide which actions he can take as an individual to improve the group and then take them. There is a basic point in these three recommendations; the individual should assume some responsibilties at the end of a group experience as well as at the beginning. If a group is functioning poorly, walking away from it or throwing blame on someone else won't help, but active concern and efforts to make improvements will. Similarly, at times when a group is functioning well, added reinforcement and commitment strengthen it. If small groups are to be viable social instruments, it is essential that people who benefit from them protect them from dissolution or abolish those that have become unreclaimable. Without this attitude of personal responsibility, group participation can degenerate into a quagmire like the one in the opening example in this chapter.

Given effective, responsible participation, groups can be vital, satisfying experiences.

SUMMARY

We began this chapter by contending that the relative value of group membership is dependent on the effective participation of each member. Accordingly, we recommended the inputs, interaction behaviors, and responses to outcomes that contribute to effective group processes.

As a prerequisite, we developed the notion of proper balance between effort and reward. When effort exceeds the individual's expectations or rewards fall short, group experiences are unsatisfactory. Through effective participation, however, the effort can be reduced while the reward is increased. Producing a high ratio of reward to effort should be one ultimate goal of a group.

To achieve this goal, participation can be improved by each member who brings to the group the orientations of responsibility, commitment, open-mindedness, flexibility, objectivity, cooperation, acceptance, and equality. These orientations foster constructive, nondefensive communication. Additionally, effective participation is enhanced if members clarify in advance their personal criteria for satisfaction, attitudes, beliefs, and values and bring adequate knowledge or information to the task.

During a group interaction more productive communication results if members perform task and maintenance roles, but avoid dysfunctional, self-centered roles. Sensitivity to language problems, the use of correctives and the adoption of the most appropriate communication network further improve small group communication. Additionally, adequate feedback on the accuracy of information, the requirements of the task, evaluations of contributions, and interpersonal relationships enhance small group communication and its outcomes.

Finally, member satisfaction, productivity, and group cohesiveness are heightened if members personally evaluate group outcomes and make decisions about their commitment or plan of action for improvement.

SUGGESTED READINGS

Barnlund, D. C. and **Haiman, F. S.** The Dynamics of Discussion. Boston: Houghton Mifflin Company, 1960.

Brilhart, J. K. Effective Group Discussion. Dubuque, Iowa: William C. Brown Company, Publishers, 1967.

Gulley, H. E. *Discussion, Conference and Group Process.* 2d ed. New York: Holt, Rinehart and Winston, Inc., 1968.

Phillips, G. M. *Communication and the Small Group.* 2d ed. Indianapolis: The Bobbs-Merrill Co., Inc., 1973.

Sattler, W. M. and **Miller, N. E.** *Discussion and Conference.* Englewood Cliffs, New Jersey: Prentice-Hall, Inc., 1954.

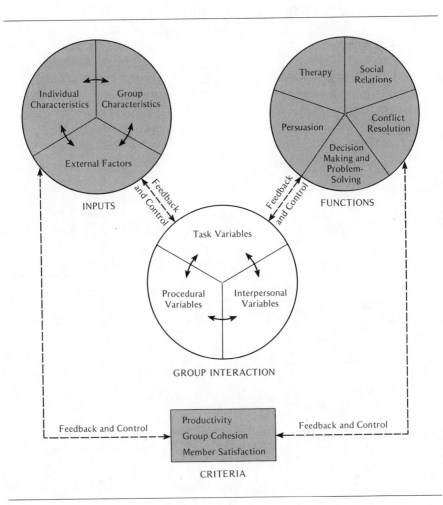

Appendix

METHODS OF UNDERSTANDING AND
EVALUATING INTERACTION IN THE SMALL GROUP

We have included this appendix so that the reader will be aware of many of the ways communication within small groups can be understood and evaluated. The first part of the appendix explains certain activities that allow groups to structure situations to experience some of the things we have discussed in the text. We hope that the activities in some way require using knowledge about all of the functions of small group communication discussed in this book. Simply reading about small group communication is not enough, one must participate in a broad range of experiences and observe one's behavior and that of others if one is truly to learn about groups. To that end we offer these explanations and descriptions.

Also included in this appendix are several instruments for observing and evaluating small group communication. It is our hope that you will use these instruments both in and out of class to determine what you think constitutes good communication. If these instruments are used in conjunction with each chapter and each exercise in class, you can begin to build profiles on what occurs when specific kinds of communication happen. This will do a great deal to contribute to understanding the things that affect communication and how communication affects desired outcomes.

SIMULATIONS, GAMES AND ROLE PLAYING

One way of attaining a greater understanding of groups is to participate in a directed or contrived group situation. This allows the experience to be structured in a manner that emphasizes certain principles or intensifies effects that might never evolve in a natural group interaction. Three popular techniques are simulations, games, and role playing.

Simulations are mock situations to which the individual must respond as if in real life. By acting out his reactions, the person learns what his behaviors would be under those circumstances and what the consequences would be. Then he can evaluate the appropriateness of his behaviors and the changes that he would make if confronted with the situation again. Through simulations, groups can learn the communication behaviors that are most effective, as well as how the various principles of group interaction operate.

Frequently, group simulations are based on case studies: groups are given a realistic story, problem, or task to tackle. For example, to illustrate some principles related to conflict resolution, two groups might be given instructions that create a conflict between them so that their subsequent behaviors could be observed. This can be accomplished by having each group separately rank-order a list of several items. (They can be anything amenable to ordering, as long as the ranking decision is difficult.) Then the two groups try to combine their lists. To the extent that the individual group rankings are ego-involving and difficult, conflict arises when the two groups try to integrate their lists. At the conclusion of the activity, the behaviors that emerge can be analyzed and evaluated. Another example of simulation is an information-processing exercise: each member of the group is given one or two bits of information on a problem, a few are irrelevant, but the rest must be combined to solve the problem; no member can solve it alone. The focus of the simulation is the way the group processes its information. Its procedures, communication patterns, and efficiency can be compared to other groups engaged in the same task.

Similar to simulations are games. The chief difference is that games involve the principle of winning and losing. These may be zero-sum games (where there is an absolute amount that can be won and each person can gain only at the expense of another) or nonzero-sum games (where the sum of the earnings of all the members need not equal zero, so all members can win). A popular game used to illustrate the effects of competition and cooperation in a group is the "Prisoner's Dilemma." Individuals or pairs of individuals within a group must make a series of decisions about whether to choose an X or a Y. The combined decisions of the group members determine each person's payoff. An example payoff matrix is shown.

4 X's :	Lose $1 each
3 X's : 1 Y	X's win $1 each Y loses $3
2 X's : 2 Y's	X's win $2 each Y's lose $2 each
1 X : 3 Y's	X wins $3 Y's lose $1 each
4 Y's :	Win $1 each

At several junctures, the group can discuss which choices they should make and try to persuade each other, but no one is actually bound by their professed choice. These discussions usually precede bonus rounds, during which payoffs are several times their usual value. The communication that occurs and the comparative outcomes successfully demonstrate principles of competition and cooperation. A variety of other bargaining, problem-solving, and decision-making games can be used.

Role playing is also similar to simulation except that people adopt the role or identity of someone else. They are required to project themselves into someone else's situation to gain insight into some aspect of group interaction. Members may be required to assume the roles of arbitrators negotiating a difficult case or doctors deciding the fate of twelve critically ill patients opting for the last three kidney machines. If case studies are used, they may become the characters involved in the action case. An example of the effectiveness of role playing as a therapeutic technique was given in Chapter 6. Regardless of the role adopted, the activity is structured to draw attention to some principle of group interaction, whether it is learning to empathize with opposing viewpoints, or gaining insight into some aspect of problem solving, or conflict resolution.

These three techniques—simulations, games, and role playing—provide the participants with experiences they might otherwise not have. They serve to focus attention on and intensify the significance of the elements of group interaction under consideration. It is presumed that by providing actual experiences, the principles of small group communication will become more meaningful and relevant. The personal involvement required should have more impact than the mere reading of books about group interaction or participation in a regular group. For these reasons, we strongly endorse extensive use of these techniques.

INTERACTION ANALYSIS

Another avenue to understanding small group communication is the use of interaction analysis techniques, which are methods of observing and analyzing interaction. Both students and instructors can benefit from their use. Many of these techniques have been designed specifically for classroom analysis of teacher-student interactions; others are specifically designed for or are readily adaptable to any kind of small group.

It would be impossible to survey all the available approaches. We have selected those that represent a range of alternatives and seem to be the most useful. They are the Reciprocal Category System, sociometric analysis, Bales' Interaction Process Analysis, and the Interaction Behavior Measure. We also briefly mention some nonverbal analysis systems.

The Reciprocal Category System

This system was developed primarily to measure teacher-student interaction, but it can easily be used for other small groups besides the classroom. It emphasizes verbal behaviors and their effects on the socioemotional climate of a group. There are ten categories of behavior that are numbered differently depending on whether the teacher or a student is talking. This situation can be modified for use in small groups by either substituting the

The Reciprocal Category System*

Category Number Assigned to Teacher Talk	Description of Verbal Behavior	Category Number Assigned to Student Talk
1	*"Warms" (informalizes) the climate:* Tends to open up and/or eliminate the tension of the situation; praises or encourages the action, behavior, comments, ideas, and/or contributions of another; jokes that release tension but not at the expense of others; accepts and clarifies the feeling tone of another in a friendly manner. (Feelings may be positive or negative; predicting or recalling the feelings of another are included.)	11
2	*Accepts:* Accepts the action, behavior, comments, ideas, and/or contributions of another; positive reinforcement of these.	12
3	*Amplifies the contributions of another:* Asks for clarification of, builds on, and/or develops the action, behavior, comments, ideas, and/or contributions of another.	13
4	*Elicits:* Asks a question or requests information about the content, subject, or procedure being considered with the intent that another should answer (respond).	14
5	*Responds:* Gives direct answer or response to questions or requests for information that are initiated by another; includes answers to one's own questions.	15
6	*Initiates:* Presents facts, information, and/or opinion concerning the content, subject, or procedures being considered that are self-initiated; expresses one's own ideas: lectures (includes rhetorical questions—not intended to be answered).	16
7	*Direct:* Gives directions, instructions, orders, and/or assignments to which another is expected to comply.	17
8	*Corrects:* Tells another that his answer or behavior is inappropriate or incorrect.	18
9	*"Cools" (formalizes) the climate:* Makes statements intended to modify the behavior of another from an inappropriate to an appropriate pattern; may tend to create a certain amount of tension (i.e., bawling out someone, exercising authority in order to gain or maintain control of the situation, rejecting or criticizing the opinion or judgment of another).	19
10	*Silence or confusion:* Pauses, short periods of silence, and periods of confusion in which communication cannot be understood by the observer.	10

* Reprinted from *Systematic Observation of Teaching* by R. L. Ober, E. L. Bentley, and E. Miller, Englewood Cliffs, N.J.: Prentice-Hall, Inc., © 1971, with permission from the publisher.

group's leader for the teacher, if you are interested in leadership, or ignoring the separate category numbers for teachers. If the group is small, it might even be possible to assign a range of numbers for each person.

To use this system, observers (who have memorized the categories and have practiced using the system) record in sequence the verbal behavior that occurs every three seconds. If a change in behavior occurs within the three second time period, he also records it. Observations usually last a maximum of twenty minutes, which means the observer makes a minimum of 400 tallies. These tallies are paired as follows:

$$
\begin{array}{l}
\text{second pair}\left\{\begin{array}{l} \left.\begin{array}{l} 10 \\ 7 \end{array}\right\}\text{first pair} \\ \left.\begin{array}{l} 8 \\ 2 \end{array}\right\}\text{third pair} \end{array}\right. \\
\text{fourth pair}\left\{\begin{array}{l} \\ 10 \end{array}\right. \\
\text{etc.}
\end{array}
$$

The pairs of tallies are placed in a matrix, with the first number of the pair determining the row of the matrix and the second number determining the column. Since each number is used twice, the matrix actually reflects the sequence of behaviors. For instance, if a teacher elicits (4) followed by a student response (15), a tally would be placed in the intersection of row 4 and column 15. If the student response were followed by a student correction (18), a tally would be placed in cell 15/18. A sample matrix is given below.

	1	2	3	4	5	6	7	8	9	10	11	12	13	14	15	16	17	18	19	TOTALS
1		///						/									/			5
2																		/		1
3			/						//					/						4
4					//												///			5
5				/								////						/		7
6										/								/		2
7		///	/													/				5
8						///														3
9															/					1
10			/		/					////			/				/			8
11												//								2
12				/	HHH												/			7
13														//		/		//		5
14								/							/		//			4
15									/				////		/	///		/		10
16			//								/			///			//	/		9
17				/									//		/	///				7
18			/			///				/				/		/				8
19														/		//	//	//		7
TOTALS	0	6	6	3	3	3	3	1	1	6	3	5	8	7	5	6	13	9	4	100

The totals for each column and row can be compared to the grand total to determine the percentage of each type of interaction behavior. Heavy buildups in the matrix indicate the most frequently occurring sequences of behavior. Thus, the matrix provides a picture of all the behaviors that have occurred as well as the most commonly emerging ones. The interaction can then be compared to the group's outcomes to evaluate their relationship to the interaction patterns. Specific instructions, problems, roles, and so forth can also be given the group; then, the resulting interaction pattern can be observed.

Actual use of the RCS is more involved than we have suggested. For complete instructions in its use, the reader should consult *Systematic Observations of Teaching* (Ober, Bentley and Miller, 1971). Our purpose has been simply to familiarize you with one possible technique.

Sociometric Analysis

Sociometric analysis is a very simple procedure for analyzing who talks to whom and how much. The names of group members are placed in a circle on a large piece of paper. Every time one person speaks to another, a line is drawn between their names. Sometimes an arrow is used to indicate direction. Also, lines or arrows may sometimes be drawn to the center if a comment is directed toward the group in general.

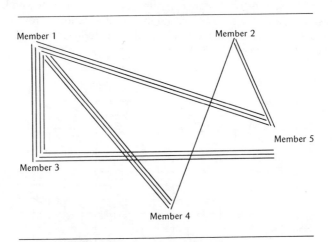

From this sample sociogram, it can be seen that member #1 is most often the center of conversation while member #2 is rarely involved. This type of analysis may also be used to map individual preferences for leaders, attraction networks, and so forth. It is very limited otherwise in the amount of information it reveals.

Bales' Interaction Process Analysis

The Bales system, originated in 1950, is specifically designed for small group use. Unlike the RCS, it may include both verbal and nonverbal behavior. Frequencies of each group member's contributions are placed in one of twelve mutually exclusive categories. Behaviors are generally classified as positive reactions, answers, questions, and negative reactions. Both socioemotional and task related behaviors are included. The categories follow.

Socioemotional Area: Positive Reactions
1. *Shows solidarity*, raises other's status, gives help, rewards.
2. *Shows tension release*, jokes, laughs, shows satisfaction.
3. *Agrees*, shows passive acceptance, understands, concurs, complies.

Task Area: Answers
4. *Gives suggestion*, direction, implying autonomy for others.
5. *Gives opinion*, evaluation, analysis, expresses feelings, wishes.
6. *Gives orientation*, information, repeats, clarifies, confirms.

Task Area: Questions
7. *Asks for orientation*, information, repetition, clarification, confirmation.
8. *Asks for opinion*, evaluation, analysis, expression of feeling.
9. *Asks for suggestion*, direction, possible ways of action.

Socioemotional Area: Negative Reactions
10. *Disagrees*, shows passive rejection, formality, withholds help.
11. *Shows tension*, asks for help, withdraws out of field.
12. *Shows antagonism*, deflates other's status, defends or asserts self.

Observation is similar to that of the RCS in that the observer needs to familiarize himself with the categories and to practice identifying behaviors. The observer need not memorize the categories because they appear on the tally sheet, along with columns for each participant's name. Rather than recording every three seconds, the observer determines how many separate acts each participation constitutes and places a tally in each of the appropriate categories. For example, if a discussant makes a statement that both demonstrates agreement and asks for an opinion, tallies are made under that person's name in categories 3 and 8. The resultant tally sheet provides both a breakdown of the frequencies of group behaviors and of individual behaviors.

This type of analysis can provide a considerable amount of information. Take the sample tally sheet as an example. What conclusions might be drawn, say, about leadership, or subgrouping, or balance? We might decide that member #3 is the socioemotional leader while member #4 is the task leader. We might notice that both members #2 and #5 give an overwhelming number of negative responses, which might lead us to expect them to form a clique. We might also discover that the group has a disproportionate amount of answers as compared to the number of questions. We would not be able to tell, however, the sequence of events. We could get a rough indication, though, by dividing observations into several time periods and comparing across them. Such an approach has been used to answer a variety of questions about groups. For instance, it can be used to illustrate the point that groups work through states of decision making: in the first stage, the emphasis is on orientation (categories 6 and 7); in the second stage, evaluation becomes more important (categories 5 and 8); in the third stage, emphasis shifts to control (categories 4 and 9). During these stages, both negative and positive responses increase.

We can also use IPA to check what happens when we give a group a simulation, game, roles, or other instructions, or it could be employed to evaluate which kinds of interaction lead to which kinds of outcomes. The IPA is, there-

11
Sample Tally Sheet

Time Period #1	Member #1	Member #2	Member #3	Member #4	Member #5	TOTALS
1. Shows solidarity	/		////			5
2. Shows tension release	///		₩		/	9
3. Agrees	/	/	////			6
4. Gives suggestion		///	//	//	/	8
5. Gives opinion	/	₩ /	///	₩ /	////	20
6. Gives orientation	/	///	////	₩ //		15
7. Asks for orientation	/		/	////		6
8. Asks for opinion	//		///	///		8
9. Asks for suggestion	///	/	///	//	////	9
10. Disagrees	/	₩	/	//	₩	13
11. Shows tension		///			₩ /	8
12. Shows antagonism		///				9
TOTALS	14	25	30	26	21	116

fore, a very useful method of learning about groups. We find it valuable both in evaluating other groups and in having our own groups analyzed.

Interaction Behavior Measure

The Interaction Behavior Measure (McCroskey and Wright, 1971) differs from the RCS and IPA in that it does not record every behavior. Rather, a panel of observers periodically rates each group member on a twelve-item semantic differential type of scale. The semantic differential has pairs of adjectives placed at opposite ends of a seven-interval continuum; marks are placed in whichever of the seven spaces best represents how closely one of the adjectives describes the observed behavior. The twelve items represent six dimensions of small group interaction (that is, six different considerations in evaluating a person's interaction behavior). They are: *relevance* (how relevant is the person's communication), *flexibility* (how flexible is the person), *tension* (how relaxed is the person), *orientation* (is the person more concerned with the task and ideas or with the socioemotional relationships), *interest* (how involved is the person), and *verbosity* (how talkative is the person).

With IBM, two or more practiced raters are used. In fact, a whole class may serve as raters (the more, the better). At specified intervals, such as three or five minutes, each observer rates each of the group members on all twelve items. For example, if a rater were observing a five-member group, he would fill out five complete IBMs each time a time period ended. If five observers

Interaction Behavior Measure

(Relevance) Relevant :____:____:____:____:____:____:____: Irrelevant
Related :____:____:____:____:____:____:____: Unrelated

(Flexibility) Flexible :____:____:____:____:____:____:____: Inflexible
Changeable :____:____:____:____:____:____:____: Unchangeable

(Tension) Bothered :____:____:____:____:____:____:____: Cool
Tense :____:____:____:____:____:____:____: Relaxed

(Orientation) Task Oriented :____:____:____:____:____:____:____: Socially Oriented
Ideational :____:____:____:____:____:____:____: Personal

(Interest) Interested :____:____:____:____:____:____:____: Apathetic
Involved :____:____:____:____:____:____:____: Withdrawn

(Verbosity) Wordy :____:____:____:____:____:____:____: Short
Brief :____:____:____:____:____:____:____: Lengthy

rated a five-man group three times, they would complete a combined total of 75 scales.

The resultant ratings can be analyzed in a variety of ways. The most common approach is to average each member's ratings on each dimension and compare the results to the other members. We could use this, for instance, to discover how relevant, flexible, involved, and verbose a high Machiavellian is in comparison to a low Machiavellian. If we are interested in individual changes over a period of time, we can average each person's ratings per dimension for each time period and compare them to one another. Thus, we might find that member #1 became increasingly withdrawn as the group progressed. This kind of analysis could tell us the effects of various problems or assignments on each member. Finally, we could combine all the members' scores on a given dimension to see the overall effects of some phenomenon on the group as a whole. We might find, for instance, that a therapy group becomes more socially oriented or more tense over an extended period of time. As with the RCS and IPA, we could also compare the nature of interaction to the quality of decisions, member satisfaction, or other group outputs. The IBM can be used effectively in a classroom to have one group observe another.

Nonverbal Analysis

One aspect of behavior that has been relatively ignored by small group people is nonverbal communication: facial and eye expressions, body movement, gestures, the use of the voice, touch, physical appearance, and the use of space and time—all of which carry messages in addition to the actual spoken word. It is our contention that nonverbal analysis must accompany verbal analysis if we are to gain full insight into the interactions in groups.

Many systems for recording nonverbal behavior have been developed, but their focus is on identifying and noting frequencies of all the nonverbal behaviors that occur rather than their effects on or their relationship to verbal communication. One system, for instance, has several notations for each of eight categories of nonverbal behavior: postural-sex identifiers, shoulder axis, distance, touch, visual contact, voice loudness, heat radiation, and odors. These deal with only one small area of nonverbal communication. Readers who are interested in pursuing methods of nonverbal analysis may wish to consult the nonverbal texts listed in the suggested reading at the end of the chapter.

For the purpose of understanding small groups, we feel a more useful approach to including nonverbal communication in our observations would be to incorporate it within some of the existing verbal interaction analysis systems. Both the IPA and IBM may include nonverbal communication. In fact, the IBM can be used exclusively for nonverbal communication. Other interaction analysis systems may also be adapted to cover nonverbal communication. By broadening our observations of groups to involve both the verbal and nonverbal aspects of interaction, we are convinced that we can achieve a better understanding of the group processes.

COMPUTER SIMULATION TECHNIQUES

A final, exciting new development in interaction analysis techniques is computer-assisted analysis. Programs have been devised that simulate groups and analyze which behaviors have which effects.

We will consider one of these techniques, PROANA 5 (Lashbrook and Bodaken, 1969), which does not look at verbal or nonverbal behavior per se, but at the lines of communication (channels) that are used and the frequencies of usage. During a specified time period, an observer records the number of times each channel is used. He also distinguishes between patterned and nonpatterned interaction. Patterned interactions are remarks directed to another individual that last forty-five seconds or less. Nonpatterned interactions are remarks that are directed toward the group in general, are not responded to, or exceed forty-five seconds (because anything beyond forty-five seconds changes the member's role from discussant to advocate). Remarks deemed by the observer to be irrelevant, i.e., not relating to the previous remarks, may also be classified as nonpatterned.

A sample tally sheet for a five-man group with members A, B, C, D, and E follows. There are ten possible lines of communication, each designated with a letter and a number. Tallies are recorded directly on the line for patterned interactions. Nonpatterned interactions are recorded next to a person's letter rather than on one of the lines of communication. Observations are made for three equal time periods (for example, twenty minutes each).

These tallies are all submitted for computer analysis, using the PROANA 5 program. Several elements of the interaction are analyzed. First, the results indicate the balance of participation by revealing how many group members participated and the number of interactive (patterned) and noninteractive communications by each person. Second, it considers channel usage: if any lines were not used, it takes note and determines if this constitutes isolation of any member by the group. (Isolation may also be cited if any member has reduced involvement and high nonpatterned interaction). Third, the output identifies clique-group formation, which is considered to exist when interaction between any two members exceeds their interaction with the rest of

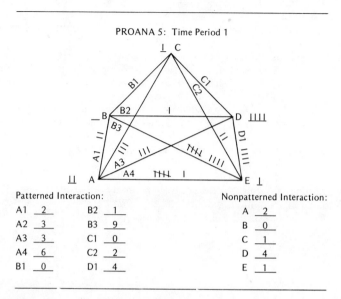

PROANA 5: Time Period 1

Patterned Interaction:

A1	2	B2	1
A2	3	B3	9
A3	3	C1	0
A4	6	C2	2
B1	0	D1	4

Nonpatterned Interaction:

A	2
B	0
C	1
D	4
E	1

the group. Fourth, based on patterns and frequencies of interactions, the program identifies the group's socioemotional and task leaders. Fifth, the program contains criteria for making judgments about who is dominating the group, whether the group is reasonably interactive or is bogging down, and whether conflict seems to be arising. Finally, it identifies stages in the group process and trends such as leadership changes. From these capabilities, it should be clear that PROANA5 can be used to test a variety of our hypotheses about small group interaction and to simulate various group phenomena. For schools with computer facilities, we recommend acquiring this or similar programs to experiment with various notions about small groups. Our personal experience is that students enjoy using PROANA 5 and we find that they learn much more about small groups by actually testing out their ideas.

SUMMARY

Our purpose in this appendix has been to present a variety of techniques for intensifying group experiences and engaging in systematic observations of groups. Through personal familiarity with group interaction variables and processes, the individual can better understand and improve small group communication. We conclude with the injunction of John Locke: "The only fence against the world is a thorough knowledge of it."

SUGGESTED READINGS

Amidon, E. J., and Hough, J. B. *Interaction Analysis: Theory Research and Application.* Reading, Mass.: Addison-Wesley Publishing Co., Inc., 1967.

Bales, R. *Interaction Process Analysis.* Reading, Mass.: Addison-Wesley Publishing Co., Inc., 1967.

Boocock, S., and **Schild, E. O.** *Simulation Games in Learning.* Beverly Hills, California: Sage Publications, Inc., 1968.

Krupar, K. *Communication Games.* New York: The Free Press, 1973.

McCroskey, J. C., and **Wright, D. W.** "The Development of an Instrument for Measuring Interaction Behavior in Small Groups." *Speech Monographs* 38(1971): 335–340.

Myers, G., and **Myers, M.** *The Dynamics of Human Communication: A Laboratory Approach.* New York: McGraw-Hill Book & Education Services Group, 1973.

Ober, R. L., Bentley, E. L., and **Miller, E.** *Systematic Observation of Teaching.* Englewood Cliffs, New Jersey: Prentice-Hall, Inc., 1971.

Pfeiffer, J. W., and **Jones, J. E.** *A Handbook of Experiences for Human Relations Training.* Volume II. Iowa City: University Associates Press, 1970.

Rosenfeld, L. B. *Human Interaction in the Small Group Setting.* Columbus, Ohio: Charles E. Merrill Publishing Company, 1973.

Bibliography

Adams, J. "Inequity in Social Exchange." In *Advances in Experimental and Social Psychology,* edited by L. Berkowitz. New York: Academic Press, Inc., 1965, 2:267–99.

Addington, D. "The Effect of Vocal Variations on Ratings of Source Credibility." *Speech Monographs* 38 (1971): 242–47.

————. "The Relationship of Selected Vocal Characteristics to Personality Perception." *Speech Monographs* 35 (1968): 492–503.

Adorno, T. W., Frenkel-Brunswik, E., Levinson, D., and Sandford, R. *The Authoritarian Personality.* New York: Harper & Row, Publishers, 1950.

Aiken, L. "Relationships of Dress to Selected Measures of Personality in Undergraduate Women." *Journal of Social Psychology* 59 (1963): 119–28.

Alland, A. *The Human Imperative.* New York: Columbia University, 1972.

Allyn, J., and Festinger, L. "The Effectiveness of Unanticipated Persuasive Communications." *Journal of Abnormal and Social Psychology* 62 (1961): 35–40.

Altman, I., and Haythorn, W. W. "The Ecology of Isolated Groups." *Behavioral Science* 12 (1967): 169–82.

Amidon, E. J., and Hough, J. B. *Interaction Analysis: Theory, Research, and Application.* Reading, Mass.: Addison-Wesley Publishing Co., Inc. 1967.

Anisfeld, M., Bogo, N., and Lambert, W. E. "Evaluational Reactions to Accented English Speech." *Journal of Abnormal and Social Psychology* 65 (1962): 223–31.

Ardrey, R. *The Social Contract.* New York: Atheneum Publishers, 1970.

————. *The Territorial Imperative.* New York: Atheneum Publishers, 1966.

Arnold, W. E., and McCroskey, J. C. "Experimental Studies of Perception Distortion and the Extensional Device of Dating." Paper presented at the Speech Association of America annual convention, December 1967.

Aronson, E., and Mills, J. "The Effect of Severity of Initiation on Liking for a Group." *Journal of Abnormal and Social Psychology* 59 (1959): 177–81.

Asch, S. E. "Effects of Group Pressure upon the Modification and Distortion of Judgments." In *Groups, Leadership and Men,* edited by H. Guetzkow. Pittsburgh: Carnegie Press, 1951, pp. 177–90.

Back, K. W. "The Group Can Comfort But It Can't Cure." *Psychology Today* 6, No. 7 (1973): 28–35.

————. Influence through Social Communication." *Journal of Abnormal and Social Psychology* 46 (1951): 9–23.

————. a letter to the editor in *Psychology Today* 6, No. 11 (1973): 101.

Backman, C., Secord, P., and **Peirce, J.** "Resistance to Change in the Self-Concept as a Function of Consensus among Significant Others." In *Problems in Social Psychology,* edited by Carl Backman and Paul Secord. New York: McGraw-Hill Book & Education Services Group, 1966, pp. 462–67.

Bales, R. F. "Adaptive and Integrative Changes as Sources of Strain in Social Systems." In *Small Groups: Studies in Social Interaction,* edited by A. P. Hare, E. F. Borgotta, and R. F. Bales. New York: Alfred A. Knopf, Inc., 1955, pp. 127–31.

————. "The Equilibrium Problem in Small Groups." In *Working Papers in the Theory of Action,* edited by T. Parsons, R. F. Bales, and E. A. Shils. New York: Free Press, 1953, pp. 111–61.

————. *Interaction Process Analysis: A Method for the Study of Small Groups.* Reading, Mass.: Addison-Wesley Publishing Co., Inc., 1950.

————. "Task Roles and Social Roles in Problem Solving Groups." In *Readings in Social Psychology,* edited by E. E. Maccoby, T. M. Newcomb, and F. L. Hartley, 3rd ed. New York: Holt, Rinehart and Winston, Inc., 1958, pp. 196–413.

————. "Task Status and Likeability as a Function of Talking and Listening in Decision-Making Groups." In *The State of the Social Sciences,* edited by L. D. White. Chicago: University of Chicago Press, 1956, pp. 148–61.

————, and **Slater, P. E.** "Role Differentiation in Small Decision-Making Groups." In *The Family, Socialization, and Interaction Process,* edited by T. Parson, R. F. Bales, et al., New York: The Free Press, 1955, pp. 259–306.

————, and **Strodtbeck, F. L.** "Phases in Group Problem Solving." *Journal of Abnormal and Social Psychology* 46 (1951): 485–95.

Bandura, A., Ross, D., and **Ross, S.** "Transmission of Aggression through Imitation of Aggression Models." *Journal of Abnormal and Social Psychology* 63 (1961): 575–82.

Bardeen, J. P. "Interpersonal Perception through the Tactile, Verbal, and Visual Modes." Paper presented at the International Communication Association annual convention, April 1971.

Barker, L. L., and **Kibler, R. J.** *Speech Communication Behavior—Perspectives and Principles.* Englewood Cliffs, New Jersey: Prentice-Hall, Inc., 1971.

Barnlund, D. C. "A Comparative Study of Individual, Majority, and Group Judgment." *Journal of Abnormal and Social Psychology* 58 (1959): 55–60.

————. "Consistency of Emergent Leadership in Groups with Changing Tasks and Members." *Speech Monographs* 29 (1962): 45–52.

————. "Experiments in Leadership Training for Decision-Making Groups." *Speech Monographs* 22 (1955): 1–14.

————, ed. *Interpersonal Communication: Survey and Studies.* Boston: Houghton Mifflin Company, 1968.

————, and **Haiman, F. S.** *The Dynamics of Discussion.* Boston: Houghton Mifflin Company, 1960.

Bass, B. M. "An Analysis of the Leaderless Group Discussion." *Journal of Applied Psychology* 33 (1949): 527–33.

————. "Conformity, Deviation, and a General Theory of Interpersonal Behavior." In *Conformity and Deviation*, edited by I. Berg and B. M. Bass. New York: Harper & Row, Publishers, 1961, pp. 38–100.

————. "The Leaderless Group Discussion." *Psychology Bulletin* 51 (1954): 465–492.

————. *Leadership, Psychology and Organizational Behavior.* New York: Harper & Row, Publishers, 1960.

————, and **Dunteman, G.** "Biases in the Evaluation of One's Own Group, Its Allies and Opponents." *Journal of Conflict Resolution* 7 (1963): 16–20.

————, and **McGeehee, C. R., Hawkins, W. C., Young, P. C.,** and **Gebel, A. S.** "Personality Variables Related to Leaderless Group Discussion Behavior." *Journal of Abnormal and Social Psychology* 48 (1953): 120–28.

Bavelas, A. "Communication Patterns in Task-oriented Groups." *Journal of the Acoustical Society of America* 22 (1950): 725–30.

————. "Leadership: Man and Function." *Administrative Science Quarterly* 4 (1960): 491–98.

————. "A Mathematical Model for Group Structure." *Applied Anthropology* 7 (1948): 16–30.

Begum, B. O., and **Lehr, D. J.** "Effects of Authoritarianism on Vigilance Performance." *Journal of Applied Psychology* 47 (1963): 75–77.

Benne, K., and **Sheats, P.** "Functional Roles of Group Members." *Journal of Social Issues* 4 (1948): 41–49.

Bennis, W. G., and **Shepard, H. A.** "A Theory of Group Development." *Human Relations* 9 (1956): 415–37.

Berenda, R. W. *The Influence of the Group on Judgments of Children.* New York: King's Crown Press, 1950.

Berkowitz, L. *Aggression: A Social Psychological Analysis.* New York: McGraw-Hill Book & Education Services Group, 1962.

————. "Aggressive Cues in Aggressive Behavior and Hostility Catharsis." *Psychological Review* 71 (1964): 104–22.

————. "Some Factors Affecting the Reduction of Overt Hostility." *Journal of Abnormal and Social Psychology* 60 (1960): 14–22.

Berlo, D. K. *The Process of Communication.* New York: Holt, Rinehart, and Winston, Inc., 1960.

Berscheid, E., and **Walster, E. H.** *Interpersonal Attraction.* Reading, Mass.: Addison-Wesley Publishing Co., Inc., 1969.

Bettinghaus, E. P. *Message Preparation: The Nature of Proof.* Indianapolis: The Bobbs-Merrill Co., Inc., 1966.

————. *Persuasive Communication.* New York: Holt, Rinehart and Winston, Inc., 1968.

————. *Persuasive Communication.* 2d ed. New York: Holt, Rinehart, and Winston, Inc., 1973.

Bible, B. L., and **McComas, J. D.** "Role Consensus and Teacher Effectiveness." *Social Forces* 42 (1963): 225–33.

Bion, W. R. "Experiences in Groups: I." *Human Relations* 1 (1948): 314–20.

──. Experiences in Groups: II." *Human Relations* 1 (1948): 487–96.

──. *Experiences in Groups.* New York: Basic Books, Inc., Publishers, 1961.

Bird, C. *Social Psychology.* New York: Appleton-Century-Crofts, 1940.

Birdwhistell, R. *Kinesics and Context. Essays on Body Motion Communication.* Philadelphia: University of Pennsylvania Press, 1970.

Blake, R. R., and **Mouton, J. S.** "Competition, Communication, and Conformity." In *Conformity and Deviation,* edited by I. Berg and B. M. Bass. New York: Harper & Row, Publishers, 1961b, pp. 199–229.

──. "Conformity, Resistance and Conversion." In *Conformity and Deviation,* edited by I. Berg and B. M. Bass. New York: Harper & Row, Publishers, 1961a, pp. 1–37.

Bliese, N. W. "The Effect of Communication Vs. No Communication in Two Types of Games of Strategy." Paper presented at the Speech Communication Association annual convention, December 1971.

Bochner, A. P., and **Tucker, R. K.** "A Multivariate Investigation of Machiavellianism and Task Structure in Four-man Groups." Paper presented at the Speech Communication Association annual convention, December 1971.

Bodaken, E. M., Lashbrook, W. B., and **Champagne, M.** "PROANA 5: A Computerized Technique for the Analysis of Small Group Interaction," *Western Speech* 35 (1971): 112–15.

Bogardus, E. as quoted in *Studies in Leadership: Leadership and Democratic Action,* edited by A. W. Gouldner. New York: Harper & Row, Publishers, Inc., 1950.

Boocock, S., and **Schild, E. O.** *Simulation Games in Learning.* Beverly Hills: Sage Publications, Inc., 1968.

Borden, G. A., Gregg, R. B., and **Grove, T. G.** *Speech Behavior and Human Interaction.* Englewood Cliffs, New Jersey: Prentice-Hall, Inc., 1969.

Borgotta, E. F. "A Diagnostic Note on the Construction of Sociograms and Action Diagrams." *Group Psychotherapy* 3 (1951): 300–08.

──. "Analysis of Social Interaction and Sociometric Perception." *Sociometry* 17 (1954): 7–32.

──. "Role and Reference Group Theory." In *Social Science Theory and Social Work Research,* edited by L. Logan. New York: National Association of Social Workers, 1960, pp. 16–25.

Borgotta, E. F., and **Bales, R. F.** "Sociometric Status Patterns and Characteristics of Interaction." *Journal of Social Psychology* 43 (1956): 289–97.

Bowers, D. G., and **Seashore, S. E.** "Peer Leadership within Work Groups." *Personnel Administration* 30 (1967): 45–50.

Bowers, J. W. "The Influence of Delivery on Attitudes Towards Concepts and Speakers." *Speech Monographs* 32 (1965): 154–58.

──. "Some Correlates of Language Intensity." *Quarterly Journal of Speech* 50 (1964): 340–50.

Braden, W. W., and **Brandenburg, E.** *Oral Decision-Making.* New York: Harper & Row, Publishers, 1955.

Bradford, L. P., Gibb, J. R. and **Benne, K. D.** *T-Group Theory and Laboratory Method: Innovation in Re-education.* New York: John Wiley & Sons, Inc., 1964.

Brewer, R. E. "Attitude Change, Interpersonal Attraction, and Communication in a Dyadic Situation." *Journal of Social Psychology* 75 (1968): 127–34.

Brilhart, J. K. *Effective Group Discussion.* Dubuque, Iowa: Wm. C. Brown Company, Publishers, 1967.

Brown, R. *Social Psychology.* New York: The Free Press, 1965.

Budd, R. W. "Encounter Groups: An Approach to Human Communication." In *Approaches to Human Communication,* edited by R. W. Budd and B. D. Ruben. New York: Spartan Books, 1972, pp. 75–96.

Budner, S. "Intolerance of Ambiguity as a Personality Variable." *Journal of Personality* 30 (1962): 24–51.

Burgess, R. L. Communication Networks: An Experimental Re-evaluation." *Journal of Experimental Social Psychology* 4 (1968a): 324–37.

———. "An Experimental and Mathematical Analysis of Group Behavior within Restricted Networks." *Journal of Experimental Social Psychology* 4 (1968b): 338–49.

Burgoon, M. "Amount of Conflicting Information in a Group Discussion and Tolerance for Ambiguity as Predictors of Task Attractiveness." *Speech Monographs* 28 (1971b): 121–24.

———. *Approaching Speech/Communication.* New York: Holt, Rinehart and Winston, Inc., 1974.

———. "The Relationship Between Willingness to Manipulate Others and Success in Two Different Types of Basic Speech Communication Course." *The Speech Teacher* 20 (1971a): 178–83.

Buss, A. H. *The Psychology of Aggression.* New York: John Wiley and Sons Inc., 1961.

———. "Physical Aggression in Relation to Different Frustrations." *Journal of Abnormal and Social Psychology* 67 (1963): 1–7.

Byrne, D., and **Griffit, W.** "Similarity Versus Liking: A Classification." *Psychonomic Science* 6 (1966): 295–96.

Campbell, D. T. "Common Fate, Similarity, and Other Indices of the Status of Aggregates of Persons as Social Entities." *Behavioral Science* 3 (1958): 14–25.

Cannon, W. B. " 'Voodoo' Death." *American Anthropologist* 44 (1942): 169–81.

Cantril, H. "The Invasion from Mars." In *Readings in Social Psychology,* edited by E. E. Maccoby and T. M. Newcomb. New York: Holt, Rinehart and Winston, Inc., 1958, pp. 291–99.

Carter, L. "On Defining Leadership." In *Group Relations at the Crossroads,* edited by M. Sherif and M. O. Wilson. New York: Harper & Row, Publishers, 1953, pp. 262–65.

Carter, L., Haythorn, W., Shriver, B., and **Lanzetta, J.** "The Behavior of Leaders and Other Group Members." *Journal of Abnormal and Social Psychology* 46 (1950): 589–95.

Cathcart, R. S., and **Samovar, L. A.** *Small Group Communication: A Reader.* Dubuque, Iowa: Wm. C. Brown Company, Publishers, 1970.

Cartwright, D., and **Zander, A.** "Leadership and Group Performance: Introduction." In *Group Dynamics,* edited by D. Cartwright and A. Zander. 2d. ed. New York: Row, Peterson, 1960, pp. 487–510.

Cartwright, D., and Zander, A., eds. *Group Dynamics: Research and Theory.* New York: Harper & Row, Publishers, 1968.

Cattell, R. B. "New Concepts for Measuring Leadership, in Terms of Group Syntality." *Human Relations* 4 (1951): 161–84.

Cattell, R. B., and Stice, G. F. "Four Formulae for Selecting Leaders on the Basis of Personality." *Human Relations* 7 (1954): 493–507.

Chesebro, J., Cragan, J., and McCullough, P. "The Small Group Technique of the Radical-Revolutionary: A Synthetic Study of Consciousness Raising." Paper presented at the Speech Communication Association annual convention, December 1971.

Christie, R., and Geis, F. L. *Studies in Machiavellianism.* New York: Academic Press, Inc., 1970.

Clinard, M. B. *Anomie and Deviant Behavior: A Discussion and Critique.* New York: The Free Press, 1964.

Cline, M. G. "The Influence of Social Context on the Perception of Faces." *Journal of Personality* 25 (1956): 142–58.

Coe, W. C., and Sarbin, T. R. "An Experimental Demonstration of Hypnosis as Role Enactment." *Journal of Abnormal Psychology* 71 (1966): 400–06.

Cohen, A. M. "Changing Small Group Communication Networks." *Journal of Communication* 11 (1961): 116–24.

Cohen, A. R. "Need for Cognition and Order of Communication as Determinants of Opinion Change." *The Order of Presentation in Persuasion,* edited by C. I. Hovland. New Haven, Conn.: Yale University Press, 1957, pp. 102–120.

Collins, B. E., and Guetzkow, H. *A Social Psychology of Group Process for Decision Making.* New York: John Wiley & Sons, Inc., 1964.

Combs, A., and Snygg, D. *Individual Behavior.* New York: Harper & Row, Publishers, 1959.

Coser, L. *The Functions of Social Conflict.* New York: The Free Press, 1968.

Costley, D. L., and Miller, G. R. "A Study in the Relationships Between Selected Factors in Interpersonal Communication and Group Attraction." Unpublished paper. Michigan State University, 1964.

Coutu, W. "Role-Playing Vs. Role-Taking: An Appeal for Clarification." *American Sociological Review* 16 (1951): 180–87.

Cronkhite, G. *Persuasion—Speech and Behavioral Change.* Indianapolis: Bobbs-Merrill, 1969.

Crowell, L., and Scheidel, T. M. "Categories for Analysis of Idea Development in Discussion Groups." *The Journal of Social Psychology* 54 (1961): 155–68.

Crutchfield, R. S. "Conformity and Character." *American Psychologist* 10 (1955): 191–98.

Daniels, V. "Communication, Incentive and Structural Variables in Interpersonal Exchange and Negotiation." *Journal of Experimental Social Psychology* 3 (1967): 47–74.

Davis, J. H., and Hornseth, J. "Discussion Patterns and Word Problems." *Sociometry* 30 (1967): 91–103.

Davitz, J. R., and Davitz, L. J. "Nonverbal Vocal Communication of Feeling." *Journal of Communication* 11 (1961): 81–86.

Dean, D. G. "Alienation: Its Meaning and Measurement." *American Sociological Review* 26 (1961): 753–58.

DeLong, A. J. "Dominance—Territorial Relations in a Small Group." *Environment and Behavior* 2 (1970): 170–91.

Deutsch, M. "Conflicts: Productive and Destructive." *Journal of Social Issues* 25 (1969a): 7–42.

———. "An Experimental Study of the Effects of Cooperation and Competition upon Group Process." *Human Relations* 2 (1949): 199–232.

———. "The Face of Bargaining." *Operations Research* 9 (1961): 886–98.

———. "Socially Relevant Science: Reflections on Some Studies of Interpersonal Conflict." *American Psychologist* 24 (1969b): 1076–92.

———. "Some Factors Affecting Membership Motivation and Achievement Motivation." *Human Relations* 12 (1959): 81–95.

———. "Studies of Interpersonal Bargaining." *Journal of Conflict Resolution* 6 (1962): 52–76.

———. "A Theory of Cooperation and Competition." *Human Relations* 2 (1949): 129–52.

———, and **Collins, M. E.** *Interracial Housing: A Psychological Evaluation of a Social Experiment.* Minneapolis: University of Minnesota Press, 1951.

———, **Epstein, Y., Canavan, D.,** and **Gumpert, P.** "Strategies of Inducing Cooperation: An Experimental Study." *Journal of Conflict Resolution* 11 (1967): 345–60.

———, and **Gerard, H.** "A Study of Normative and Informational Social Influences on Individual Judgment." *Journal of Abnormal and Social Psychology* 51 (1955): 629–36.

———, and **Krauss, R. M.** "The Effect of Threat on Interpersonal Bargaining." *Journal of Abnormal and Social Psychology* 61 (1960): 181–89.

Dewey, J. *How We Think.* Lexington, Mass.: D. C. Heath and Company, 1933.

———. *The Public and Its Problems.* New York: Henry Holt and Company, 1927.

Dickens, M., and **Heffernan, M.** "Experimental Research in Group Discussion." *Quarterly Journal of Speech* 35 (1949): 23–29.

Doll, H. "The Closer We Come the Further We Get: Some Thoughts on Empathic and Psychic Distance." Paper presented at the Speech Communication Association annual convention, December 1971.

Dollard, J., Doob, L., Miller, N., Mowrer, O., and **Sears, R.** *Frustration and Aggression.* New Haven, Conn.: Yale University Press, 1939.

Dosey, M., and **Meisels, M.** "Personal Space and Self Protection." *Journal of Personality and Social Psychology* 11 (1969): 93–97.

Drake, R. M. "A Study of Leadership." *Character and Personality* 12 (1944): 285–89.

Ehrlich, H. J., and **Rinehart, J. W.** "The Study of Role Conflict: Explorations in Methodology." *Sociometry* 25 (1962): 85–97.

Eisenson, J., Sourther, S., and **Fisher, J.** "The Affective Value of English Speech Sounds." *Quarterly Journal of Speech* 26 (1940): 589–94.

Ekman, P. "Communication through Nonverbal Behavior: A Source of Information about an Interpersonal Relationship." In *Affect, Cognition, and Personality: Empirical Studies,* edited by S. S. Tomkins and C. E. Izzard, New York: Springer Publishing Co., Inc., 1965, pp. 390–442.

Ekman, P., and **Friesen, W.** "Nonverbal Behavior in Psychotherapy Research." In *Research in Psychotherapy,* edited by J. Shlien. Washington, D. C.: American Psychological Association, 1968, pp. 179–216.

Ellis, D. S. "Speech and Social Status in America." *Social Forces* 14 (1967): 431–37.

Emery, D. A. "Leadership through Motivation by Objectives." *Personnel Psychology* 12 (1959): 65–79.

Ewbank, E., and **Auer, J. J.** *Handbook for Discussion Leaders.* New York: Appleton-Century-Crofts, 1954.

Faust, W. "Group Versus Individual Problem Solving." *Journal of Abnormal and Social Psychology* 59 (1959): 68–72.

Fay, P., and **Middleton, W.** "The Ability to Judge Truth-Telling or Lying from the Voice as Transmitted over a Public Address System." *Journal of General Psychology* 24 (1941): 211–15.

Fearnside, W. W., and **Holther, W. B.** *Fallacy: The Counterfeit of Argument.* Englewood Cliffs, N. J.: Prentice-Hall Inc., 1959.

Feshback, S. "The Stimulating Versus Cathartic Effects of a Vicarious Aggressive Activity." *Journal of Abnormal and Social Psychology* 63 (1961): 381–85.

Festinger, L. *The Theory of Cognitive Dissonance.* New York: Harper & Row Publishers, 1957.

Festinger, L., Schachter, S., and **Back, K.** *Social Pressures in Informal Groups: A Study of Human Factors in Housing.* New York: Harper & Row, Publishers, 1950.

Fiedler, F. E. "Assumed Similarity Measures as Predictors of Team Effectiveness." *Journal of Abnormal and Social Psychology* 49 (1954): 381–88.

————. "A Contingency Model of Leadership Effectiveness." In *Advances in Experimental Social Psychology,* edited by L. Berkowitz. New York: Academic Press, Inc., 1964, 1: 146–90.

————. "The Contingency Model: A Theory of Leadership Effectiveness." In *Basic Studies in Social Psychology,* edited by H. Proshansky and B. Seidenberg, New York: Holt, Rinehart and Winston, Inc., 1965; pp. 538–551.

————. "The Influence of Leader-Keyman Relations on Combat Crew Effectiveness." *Journal of Abnormal and Social Psychology* 51 (1955): 227–35.

————. *A Theory of Leadership Effectiveness.* New York: McGraw-Hill Book & Education Services Group, 1967.

Filley, A. C., and **Jesse, F. C.** "Training Leadership Styles: A Survey of Research." *Personnel Administration* 28 (1965): 14–21.

Fisher, B. A. "Decision Emergence: Phases in Group Decision-Making." *Speech Monographs* 37 (1970): 53–66.

Fisher, S. *Body Experience in Fantasy and Behavior.* New York: Appleton-Century-Crofts, 1970.

————, and **Cleveland, S. E.** *Body Image and Personality.* New York: Dover Publications Inc., 1968.

Fleishman, E. A. "The Measurement of Leadership Attitudes in Industry." *Personnel Psychology* 6 (1953): 153–58.

————, and **Peters, D. P.** "Interpersonal Values, Leadership Attitudes, and Managerial Success." *Personnel Psychology* 15 (1962): 127–43.

Fontana, A. F. "The Effects of Acceptance and Rejection by Desired Membership Groups on Self-evaluation." University of Michigan, 1964. *Dissertation Abstracts* 25 (1964): 3675.

Forston, R. F., and **Larson, C.** "The Dynamics of Space: An Experimental Study in Proxemic Behavior among Latin Americans and North Americans." *Journal of Communication* 18 (1968): 109–16.

Foulkes, S. H. *Therapeutic Group Analysis.* New York: International Universities Press, 1965.

Freedman, J. L., Wallington, S. A., and **Bless, E.** "Compliance without Pressure: The Effect of Guilt." *Journal of Personality and Social Psychology* 7 (1967): 117–24.

French, J. R. P. "The Bases of Social Power." In *Studies in Social Power,* edited by D. Cartwright. Ann Arbor: University of Michigan Press, 1959, pp. 150–67.

——, **Morrison, H.,** and **Levinger, G.** "Coercive Power and Forces Affecting Conformity." *Journal of Abnormal and Social Psychology* 61 (1960): 93–101.

——, and **Raven, B. N.** "Legitimate Power, Coercive Power and Observability in Social Influence." *Sociometry* 21 (1958): 83–97.

Friedenberg, E. *The Vanishing Adolescent.* Boston: Beacon Press, 1959.

Galton, F. *Hereditary Genius.* London: Rinehart and Company, 1941.

Geier, J. "A Trait Approach to the Study of Leadership." *Journal of Communication* 17 (1967): 316–23.

Gerard, H. B. "Deviation, Conformity, and Commitment." In *Current Studies in Social Psychology,* edited by I. D. Steiner and M. Fishbein. New York: Holt, Rinehart and Winston, Inc., 1965, pp. 263–76.

——. "Some Effects of Status Role Clarity and Group Goal Clarity upon the Individual's Relations to Group Process." *Journal of Personality* 25 (1957): 475–88.

Gerlach, L. P., and **Hine, V. H.** *People, Power, Change—Movements of Social Transformation.* Indianapolis: Bobbs-Merrill Co. Inc., 1970.

Gibb, C. A. "The Emergence of Leadership in Small Temporary Groups of Men." Publication Number 1392, University of Michigan Microfilms, 1949a.

——. "The Principles and Traits of Leadership." *Journal of Abnormal and Social Psychology* 42 (1947): 267–84.

——. "The Sociometry of Leadership in Temporary Groups." *Sociometry* 13 (1950): 226–43.

——. "Some Tentative Comments Concerning Group Rorschach Pointers to the Personality Traits of Leaders." *Journal of Social Psychology* 30 (1949b): 251–63.

Gibb, J. R. "Climate for Trust Formation." In *T-Group Theory and Laboratory Method: Innovation in Re-education,* edited by L. P. Bradford, J. R. Gibb, and K. D. Benne, New York: John Wiley & Sons, 1964, pp. 279–309.

——. "Leadership" *Handbook of Social Psychology* Vol. IV, edited by G. Lindzey and E. Aronson. Reading, Mass.: Addison-Wesley Publishing Co. Inc., 1969, pp. 205–82.

Giffin, K. "Interpersonal Trust in Small Group Communication." *Quarterly Journal of Speech* 53 (1967): 224–34.

——. "Social Alienation by Communication Denial." Research Report, University of Kansas, 1970.

———, and **Patton, B. R.** *Fundamentals of Interpersonal Communication.* New York: Harper & Row, Publishers, 1971.

Gilchrist, J. C., Shaw, M. E., and **Walker, L. C.** "Some Effects of Unequal Distribution of Information in a Wheel Group Structure." *Journal of Abnormal and Social Psychology* 49 (1954): 554–56.

Gilkinson, H., Paulson, S. F., and **Sikkink, D. E.** "Conditions Affecting the Communication of Controversial Statements in Connected Discourse; Forms of Presentation and the Political Frame of Reference of the Listener." *Speech Monographs* 20 (1955): 253–60.

Glanzer, M., and **Glaser, R.** "Techniques for the Study of Group Structure and Behavior: II. Empirical Studies of the Effects of Structure in Small Groups." *Psychological Bulletin* 58 (1961): 1–27.

Gobel, A. S. "Self-perception and Leaderless Group Discussion." *Journal of Social Psychology* 40 (1954): 309–18.

Goffman, E. *Asylums.* Chicago: Aldine Publishing Co., 1961a.

———. *Behavior in Public Places.* New York: The Free Press, 1963.

———. *Encounters: Two Studies in the Sociology of Interaction.* Indianapolis: The Bobbs-Merrill Co. Inc., 1961b.

———. *The Presentation of Self in Everyday Life.* Garden City, New York: Doubleday & Company, Inc., 1959.

Goldberg, S. C. "Influence and Leadership as a Function of Group Structure." *Journal of Abnormal and Social Psychology* 51 (1955): 119–22.

Golembiewski, R. T. *The Small Group: An Analysis of Research Concepts and Operations.* Chicago: University of Chicago Press, 1962.

———. "Three Styles of Leadership and Their Uses." *Personnel* 38 (1961): 34–45.

Gowin, E. B. *The Executive and His Control of Men.* New York: Macmillan Inc., 1915.

Greenberg, B. S., and **Miller, G. R.** "The Effects of Low-Credible Sources on Message Acceptance." *Speech Monographs,* 33 (1966): 127–36.

Griffit, W. B. "Anticipated Reinforcement and Attraction." *Psychonomic Science,* 11 (1968): 355.

———. "Interpersonal Attraction as a Function of Self-concept and Personality Similarity-Dissimilarity." *Journal of Personality and Social Psychology* 5 (1966): 581–84.

———. "Personality Similarity Self-concept, and Positiveness of Personality Description, as Determinants of Interpersonal Attraction." University of Texas, 1967. *Dissertation Abstracts* 5 (1967): 1900–1901.

Gross, N., Mason, W. L., and **McEachern, A. W.** *Explorations in Role Analysis.* New York: John Wiley & Sons, Inc., 1958.

Grove, T. G. "Attitude Convergence in Small Groups." *Journal of Communication* 15 (1965): 226–38.

Guetzkow, H., and **Dill, W. R.** "Factors in the Organizational Development of Task-oriented Groups." *Sociometry* 20 (1957): 175–204.

Guetzkow, H., and **Simon, H. A.** "The Impact of Certain Communication Nets upon Organization and Performance in Task-oriented Groups." *Management Science* 1 (1955): 233–50.

Gulley, H. E. *Discussion, Conference and Group Process.* 2nd ed., New York: Holt, Rinehart and Winston, Inc., 1968.

Haiman, F. "An Experimental Study of the Effects of Ethos in Public Speaking." *Speech Monographs* 16 (1949): 190–202.

———. *Group Leadership and Democratic Action.* Boston: Houghton Mifflin Company, 1950.

———. "A Measurement of Authoritarian Attitudes Toward Discussion and Leadership." *Quarterly Journal of Speech* 41 (1955): 140–44.

Hall, E. T. *The Silent Language.* Greenwich, Connecticut: Fawcett World Library: Crest, Gold Medal & Premier Books, 1959.

———. *The Hidden Dimension.* Garden City, New York: Doubleday & Company, Inc., 1966.

———. "A System for the Notations of Proxemic Behavior." *American Anthropologist* 65 (1963): 1003–26.

Hall, J. "Decisions, Decisions, Decisions." *Psychology Today* 5 (1971): 51–54, 86, 88.

Halpin, A. W. "Evaluation Through the Study of the Leader's Behavior." *Educational Leadership* 14 (1956): 172–76.

———. "The Leader Behavior and Effectiveness of Airplane Commanders." In *Leader Behavior: Its Description and Measurement,* edited by R. M. Stogdill and A. E. Coons. Columbus: Ohio State University Press, 1957, pp. 52–64.

———. "The Leader Behavior and Leadership Ideology of Educational Administrators and Aircraft Commanders." *Harvard Educational Review* 25 (1955): 18–32.

———. "The Leadership Behavior and Combat Performance of Airplane Commanders." *Journal of Abnormal and Social Psychology* 49 (1954): 19–22.

———, and **Winer, B. J.** *The Leadership Behavior of the Airplane Commander.* Columbus: Ohio State University Research Foundation, 1952.

Hamblin, R. L. "Leadership and Crisis." *Sociometry* 21 (1958): 322–35.

Haney, R. D. "The Role of Encoding and Decoding Aggressive Messages on Subsequent Hostility." Paper presented at the Speech Communication Association annual convention, December 1971.

Hardy, K. "Determinants of Conformity and Attitude Change." *Journal of Abnormal and Social Psychology* 54 (1957): 289–94.

Hare, A., and Bales, R. F. "Seating Position and Small Group Interaction." *Sociometry* 26 (1963): 480–86.

———, **Borgotta, E., and Bales, R. F.** *Small Groups: Studies in Social Interaction.* New York: Alfred A. Knopf, Inc., 1966.

Harold, G. B. "Self-evaluation and the Evaluation of Choice Alternatives." *Journal of Personality* 32 (1964): 395–410.

Harmon, S. J. "Crisis: Group Response to Emergency." *Journal of Communication* 21 (1971): 266–72.

Harms, L. S. "Listener Judgments of Status Cues in Content Free Speech." *Quarterly Journal of Speech* 47 (1961): 164–68.

Harnack, R. V. "A Study of the Effect of an Organized Minority upon a Discussion Group." *Journal of Communication* 13 (1963): 12–24.

———, and **Fest, T. B.** *Group Discussion Theory and Technique.* New York: Appleton-Century-Crofts, 1964.

Harrison, R. "Nonverbal Communication: Explorations into Time, Space, Action, and Object." In *Dimensions in Communication,* edited by J. Campbell and H. Hepler. Belmont, California: Wadsworth Publishing Co. Inc., 1965. 158–74.

————. "Nonverbal Approaches." In *Communications Handbook,* edited by I. deSola Pool, W. Schramm, N. Maccoby, and E. Parker. Chicago: Rand McNally Company, 1972.

Harsanyi, J. C. "Bargaining in Ignorance of the Opponent's Utility Function." *Journal of Conflict Resolution* 6 (1962): 29–38.

Harvey, O. J., and **Consalvi, C.** "Status and Conformity to Pressure in Informal Groups." *Journal of Abnormal and Social Psychology* 60 (1960): 182–87.

Hass, H., and **Maehr, M.** "Two Experiments on the Concept of Self and the Reaction of Others." *Journal of Personality and Social Psychology* 1 (1965): 100–105.

Haythorn, W. W., Couch, A., Heafner, D., Langham, P., and **Carter, L. F.** "The Behavior of Authoritarian and Equalitarian Personalities in Groups." *Human Relations* 9 (1956): 57–74.

Hearne, G. "The Process of Group Development." *Autonomous Groups Bulletin* 13 (1957): 1–7.

Hechmaum, G. M. "The Relation between Group Members' Self-confidence and Their Reaction to Group Pressure to Uniformity." *American Sociological Review* 19 (1954): 678–87.

Heider, F. "Attitudes and Cognitive Organization." *Journal of Psychology,* 21 (1946): 107–12.

————. *The Psychology of Interpersonal Relations.* New York: John Wiley & Sons, Inc. 1958.

————. "Social Perception and Phenomenal Causality." *Psychological Review* 51 (1944): 358–74.

Heimstra, N. W., and **Ellingstad, V. S.** *Human Behavior: A Systems Approach.* Belmont, California: Brooks/Cole, 1972.

Heise, G. A., and **Miller G. A.** "Problem Solving by Small Groups Using Various Communication Nets." *Journal of Abnormal and Social Psychology* 46 (1951): 327–35.

Hemphill, J. K. *Leader Behavior Description.* Columbus: Ohio State University Personnel Research Board, 1950a.

————. "Relations Between the Size of the Group and the Behavior of Superior Leaders." *Journal of Social Psychology* 32 (1950b): 11–22.

————. *Situational Factors in Leadership.* Columbus: Ohio State University Personnel Research Board, 1949.

————. "Why People Attempt to Lead." In *Leadership and Interpersonal Behavior,* edited by L. Petrullo and B. M. Bass. New York: Holt, Rinehart and Winston, Inc., 1961, pp. 201–215.

Hess, E. H. "Attitude and Pupil Size." *Scientific American* 212 (1965): 46–54.

Heston, J. K. "Effects of Personal Space Invasion and Anomia on Anxiety, Nonperson Orientation and Source Credibility." Paper presented at the Speech Communication Association annual convention, December 1972.

————. "Ideal Source Credibility: A Re-examination of the Semantic Differential." a Paper presented at the International Communication Association annual convention, April 1973.

————, and **Andersen, P.** "Anomia-Alienation and Restrained Communication Among High School Students." Contributed paper, Western States Speech Communication Association annual convention, December 1972.

Hirota, K. "Group Problem Solving and Communication." *Japanese Journal of Psychology* 24 (1953): 176–77.

Hoffman, L. R. "Homogeneity of Membership Personality and Its Effect on Group Problem Solving." *Journal of Abnormal and Social Psychology* 58 (1959): 27–32.

Hollander, E. P. "Authoritarianism and Leadership Choice in a Military Setting." *Journal of Abnormal and Social Psychology* 49 (1954): 365–70.

————. "Conformity, Status and Idiosyncrasy Credit." *Psychological Review* 65 (1958): 117–127.

————. "Emergent Leadership and Social Influence." In *Leadership and Interpersonal Behavior,* edited by L. Petrullo and B. M. Bass. New York: Holt, Rinehart and Winston, Inc., 1961, pp. 30–47.

————, and **Webb, W. B.** "Leadership, Followership, and Friendship: An Analysis of Peer Nominations." *Journal of Abnormal and Social Psychology* 50 (1955): 163–67.

————, and **Willis, R. H.** "Some Current Issues in the Psychology of Conformity and Nonconformity." *Psychological Bulletin* 68 (1967): 62–76.

Holtzman, W. H. "Adjustment and Leadership." *Journal of Social Psychology* 36 (1952): 179–89.

Homans, G. C. *The Human Group.* New York: Harcourt Brace Jovanovich, Inc., 1950.

————. "Social Behavior as Exchange." *American Journal of Sociology* 63 (1958): 597–506.

————. *Social Behavior: Its Elementary Forms.* New York: Harcourt Brace Jovanovich, Inc., 1961.

Hope, L. H., and **Kerly, S. A.** "The Relationship between Self-concept and Academic Aptitude of Entering Male Freshmen." *Psychology, a Journal of Human Behavior* 8 (1971): 43–47.

Horney, K. *Our Inner Conflicts.* New York: W. W. Norton and Company Inc., 1945.

House, R. J. "Leadership Training: Some Dysfunctional Consequences." *Administrative Science Quarterly* 12 (1968): 556–71.

Hovland, C., Janis, I., and **Kelley, H.** *Communication and Persuasion.* New Haven: Yale University Press, 1953.

Hovland, C. S., Lumsdaine, A. A., and **Sheffield, F. D.** "Experiments on Mass Communication," vol. 3 of *Studies in Social Psychology in World War II.* Princeton: Princeton University Press, 1949, pp. 201–27.

Hunt, R., and **Kau Lin, T.** "Accuracy and Judgments of Personal Attributes from Speech." *Journal of Personality and Social Psychology* 6 (1967): 450–53.

Hymes, D. "The Anthropology of Communication." In *Human Communication Theory—Original Essays,* edited by F. E. X. Dance. New York: Holt, Rinehart and Winston, Inc., 1967.

Inglis, R. "The Effects of Personality Similarity on Empathy and Interpersonal Attraction." Dissertation, Duke University, Durham, North Carolina, 1965.

Jackson, J., and **Saltzstein, H. D.** "The Effect of Person-Group Relations on Conformity Processes." *Journal of Abnormal and Social Psychology* 57 (1958): 17–24.

Jacobson, W. D. *Power and Interpersonal Relationships.* Belmont, California: Wadsworth Publishing Co. Inc., 1972.

Jandt, F. E., ed. *Conflict Resolution Through Communication.* New York: Harper & Row, Publishers, 1973.

Janis, I. L., and **Mann, L.** "Effectiveness of Emotional Role Playing in Modifying Smoking Habits and Attitudes." *Journal of Experimental Research in Personality* 1 (1965): 84–90.

Jennings, H. H. "Individual Differences in the Social Atom." *Sociometry* 4 (1941): 269–70.

————. *Leadership and Isolation.* New York: Longmans, Green, 1950.

————. "Leadership and Sociometric Choice." *Sociometry* 10 (1947): 32–49.

————. "Sociometric Structure in Personality and Group Formation." In *Group Relations at the Crossroads,* edited by M. Sherif and M. Wilson. New York: Harper & Row, Publishers, 1953, pp. 332–65.

Jersild, A. T. *In Search of Self.* New York: Columbia University Teachers College, 1969.

Johnson, W. *People in Quandaries.* New York: Harper & Row, Publishers, 1946.

Jones, S. C. "Some Determinants of Interpersonal Evaluating Behavior." *Journal of Personality and Social Psychology* 3 (1966): 397–403.

————, and **Ratner, C.** "Commitment to Self-appraisal and Interpersonal Evaluations." *Journal of Personality and Social Psychology* 6 (1967): 442–47.

Jones, S. E. "A Comparative Proxemics Analysis of Dyadic Interaction in Selected Subcultures of New York City." *Journal of Social Psychology* 84 (1971): 35–44.

Jourard, S. M. *The Transparent Self.* New York: D. Van Nostrand Company, 1964.

————, and **Remy, R.** "Perceived Parental Attitudes, the Self and Security." *Journal of Consulting Psychology* 19 (1955): 364–66.

Justice, M. T. *Field Dependency, Intimacy of Topic and Interaction Distance.* Dissertation, University of Florida, Gainesville, 1969.

Kelley, H. H. "Two Functions of Reference Groups." In *Readings in Social Psychology,* edited by G. E. Swanson, T. M. Newcomb, and E. L. Hartley. 2d ed. New York: Holt, Rinehart and Winston, Inc., 1952, pp. 410–14.

Kelman, H. C. "Compliance, Identification, and Internalization." *Journal of Conflict Resolution* 2 (1958): 51–60.

Kerr, C. "Industrial Conflict and Its Mediation." *American Journal of Sociology* 60 (1954): 230.

Kidd, J. S., and **Campbell, D. T.** "Conformity to Groups as a Function of Group Success." *Journal of Abnormal and Social Psychology* 51 (1955): 390–93.

Kiesler, C. A., Collins, B. E., and **Miller, N.** *Attitude Change—A Critical Analysis of Theoretical Approaches.* New York: John Wiley & Sons, Inc., 1969.

Kiesler, C. A., and **Kiesler, S. B.** *Conformity.* Reading, Mass.: Addison-Wesley Publishing Co., Inc., 1969.

Kirscht, J. P., Lodahl, T. M., and Haire, M. "Some Factors in the Selection of Leaders by Members of Small Groups." *Journal of Abnormal and Social Psychology* 58 (1959): 406–08.

Knapp, M. L. *Nonverbal Communication in Human Interaction.* New York: Holt Rinehart and Winston, Inc., 1972.

Korzybski, A. *Science and Sanity.* Lancaster, Pa.: Science Press, 1951.

Kramer, E. "Judgment of Personal Characteristics and Emotions from Nonverbal Properties of Speech." *Psychological Bulletin* 60 (1963): 408–20.

————. "Personality Stereotypes in Voice: A Reconsideration of the Data." *Journal of Social Psychology* 62 (1964): 247–51.

Krauss, R. M., and Deutsch, M. "Communication in Interpersonal Bargaining." *Journal of Personality and Social Psychology* 4 (1966): 572–77.

Krieger, L. H. "Individual or Group Success or Failure and Its Influence on the Evaluation of Self and Group," Rutgers University, 1966. *Dissertation Abstracts* 27 (1966): 1928.

Krupar, K. R. *Communication Games.* New York: The Free Press, 1973.

Kwal, T., and Fleshler, H. "Self Concept and Leadership Behavior." Paper presented at the Speech Communication Association annual convention, December 1971.

Laing, R. D. *Knots.* New York: Pantheon Books, Inc., 1970.

————, **Phillipson, H., and Lee, A. R.** *Interpersonal Perception: A Theory and a Method of Research.* New York: Springer Publishing Co., Inc., 1966.

Laird, D., and Laird, E. *The New Psychology for Leadership.* New York: McGraw-Hill Book & Education Services Group, 1956.

Landy, D., and Aronson, E. "Liking for an Evaluator as a Function of His Discernment." *Journal of Personality and Social Psychology* 9 (1968): 133–41.

Lane, I. M., and Messe, L. A. "Differential Inputs as a Determinant in the Selection of a Distributor of Rewards." *Psychonomic Science* 22 (1971): 228–29.

Lane, L. L. "Communicative Behavior and Biological Rhythms." *Speech Teacher* 20 (1971): 16–20.

Lashbrook, W. B. "PROANA 5: A Computerized Technique for the Analysis of Small Group Interaction." Report 3–67, Speech Communication Research Laboratory, Michigan State University, 1967.

————, and **Bodaken, E. M.** "PROANA 5: A Venture in Computer Assisted Instruction in Small Group Communication." *Computer Studies in the Humanities and Verbal Behavior* 2 (1969): 98–101.

Lawson, E. D. "Change in Communication Nets, Performance, and Morale." *Human Relations* 18 (1965): 139–47.

League, B. J., and Jackson, D. N. "Conformity, Veridicality, and Self-esteem." *Journal of Personality and Social Psychology* 68 (1964): 113–15.

Leathers, D. A. "Process Disruption and Measurement in Small Group Communication." *Quarterly Journal of Speech* 55 (1969): 287–300.

Leavitt, H. J. "Some Effects of Certain Communication Patterns on Group Performance." *Journal of Abnormal and Social Psychology* 46 (1951): 38–50.

Lefkowitz, M., Blake, R., and Mouton, J. "Status Factors in Pedestrian Violation of Traffic Signals." *Journal of Abnormal and Social Psychology* 51 (1955): 704–6.

Leventhal, H., and **Sharp, E.** "Facial Expressions as Indicators of Distress." In *Affect, Cognition, and Personality: Empirical Studies,* edited by S. S. Tomkins and C. E. Izzard. New York: Springer Publishing Co., Inc., 1965, pp. 296–318.

Levine, J. M., and **Murphy, G.** "The Learning and Forgetting of Controversial Material." *Journal of Abnormal and Social Psychology* 49 (1954): 23–28.

Levine, S. "An Approach to Constructive Leadership." *Journal of Social Issues* 5 (1949): 46–53.

Levinger, G. "Kurt Lewin's Approach to Conflict and Its Resolution." *Journal of Conflict Resolution* 1 (1957): 329–40.

Levinger, G., and **Schneider, D. J.** "Test of the 'Risk Is A Value' Hypothesis." *Journal of Personality and Social Psychology* 11 (1969): 165–69.

Lewin, K., Lippitt, R., and **White, R. K.** "Patterns of Aggressive Behavior in Experimentally Created 'Social Climates'." *Journal of Social Psychology* 10 (1939): 271–99.

Lipman, A. "Building Design and Social Interaction." *The Architects Journal* 147 (1968): 23–30.

Lippitt, R., and **White, R. K.** "The 'Social Climate' of Children's Groups." In *Child Behavior and Development,* edited by R. G. Barker, J. Kounin, and H. Wright. New York: McGraw-Hill Book & Education Services Group, 1943, pp. 485–508.

Little, K. B. "Personal Space." *Journal of Experimental Social Psychology* 1 (1965): 237–47.

Loomis, J. L. "Communication, the Development of Trust and Cooperative Behavior." *Human Relations* 12 (1959): 305–15.

Luce, G. B. "Understanding Body Time in the Twenty-four Hour City." *New York,* November 15, 1971, pp. 38–43.

Luft, J. "On Nonverbal Interaction." *Journal of Psychology* 63 (1966): 261–68.

Lundberg, G. A., and **Style, M.** "Social Attraction Patterns in a Village." *Sociometry* 1 (1938): 375–419.

Mabel, S., and **Rosenfeld, H. M.** "Relationship of Self-concept to the Experience of Imbalance in P-O-X Situations." *Human Relations* 19 (1966): 381–89.

Macbride, P. D., and **Tuddenham, R. D.** "The Influence of Self-confidence upon Resistance of Perceptual Judgments to Group Pressures." *Journal of Psychology* 60 (1965): 9–23.

McCroskey, J. C. *An Introduction to Rhetorical Communication.* Englewood Cliffs, New Jersey: Prentice-Hall, Inc., 1968.

———. "Measures of Communication-Bound Anxiety." *Speech Monographs* 37 (1970): 269–277.

———. "A Summary of Experimental Research on the Effects of Evidence in Persuasive Communication." *Quarterly Journal of Speech* 55 (1969): 169–176.

———, **Jensen, T.,** and **Valencia, C.** "Measurement of the Credibility of Peers and Spouses." Paper presented at the International Communication Association annual convention, April 1973.

———, **Larson, C. E.,** and **Knapp, M. L.** *An Introduction to Interpersonal Communication.* Englewood Cliffs, New Jersey: Prentice-Hall, Inc., 1971.

————, and **McCain, T. A.** "The Measurement of Interpersonal Attraction." Paper presented at Western Speech Communication Association annual convention, November 1972.

————, and **Mehrley, R. S.** "The Effects of Disorganization and Nonfluency on Attitude Change and Source Credibility." *Speech Monographs,* 36 (1969): 13–21.

————, and **Wright, D. W.** "The Development of an Instrument for Measuring Interaction Behavior in Small Groups." *Speech Monographs* 38 (1971): 335–40.

McEwen, W. J., and **Greenberg, B. S.** "The Effects of Message Intensity on Receiver Evaluations of Source, Message, and Topic." *Journal of Communication* 20 (1970): 340–350.

McGrath, J. E., and **Altman, I.** *Small Group Research: A Synthesis and Critique of the Field.* New York: Holt, Rinehart and Winston, Inc. 1966.

McGuire, W. J. "Inducing Resistance to Persuasion: Some Contemporary Approaches." *Advances in Experimental Social Psychology,* edited by L. Berkowitz. New York: Academic Press, Inc., 1964, I:191–229.

————. "The Nature of Attitudes and Attitude Change." in *Handbook of Social Psychology,* Vol. III, edited by G. Lindzey and E. Aronson. Reading, Mass.: Addison-Wesley Publishing Co., Inc., 1969, pp. 136–314.

Mack, R. W., and **Snyder, R. C.** "The Analysis of Social Conflict—Toward an Overview and Synthesis." *Journal of Conflict Resolution* 1 (1957): 212–48.

McKeachie, W. "Lipstick as a Determiner of First Impressions of Personality: An Experiment for the General Psychology Course." *Journal of Social Psychology* 36 (1952): 241–44.

Malamud, D. I., and **Machover, S.** "The Workshop in Self Understanding Group Techniques in Self-confrontation." In *Group Therapy Today,* edited by H. M. Ruitenpeek. New York: Lieber-Atheton Incorporated, 1969, pp. 245–55.

Mann, R. D. "A Review of the Relationships between Personality and Performance in Small Groups." *Psychological Bulletin* 56 (1959): 241–70.

Manneheim, B. F. "Reference Groups, Membership Groups, and the Self-image." *Sociometry* 29 (1966): 265–79.

Marquis, D. G. "Individual Responsibility and Group Decision Involving Risk." *Industrial Management Review* 3 (1962): 8–23.

Martin, E. A., and **Hill, W. F.** "Toward a Theory of Group Development: Six Phases of Therapy Group Development." *International Journal of Group Psychotherapy* 7 (1957): 20–30.

Maslow, A. H. "A Comparative Approach to the Problem of Destructiveness." In *Man and International Relations,* edited by J. K. Zawodny. San Francisco: Chandler, 1966a, pp. 156–61.

————. Conflict, Frustration, and the Theory of Threat." In *Man and International Relations,* edited by J. K. Zawodny. San Francisco: Chandler, 1966b, pp. 166–69.

May, R. *Love and Will.* New York: W. W. Norton & Company, Inc., 1969.

Mead, G. H. *Mind, Self, and Society.* Chicago: University of Chicago Press, 1934.

Mehrabian, A. "Communication without Words." *Psychology Today* 2 (1968): 53–55.

————. "Orientation Behaviors and Nonverbal Attitude Communication." *Journal of Communication* 17 (1967): 324–32.

————. *Silent Messages.* Belmont, California: Wadsworth Publishing Co., Inc., 1972.

————, and **Friar, J. T.** "Encoding of Attitudes by a Seated Communicator via Posture and Positional Cues." *Journal of Consulting and Clinical Psychology* 33 (1969): 330–36.

Mehrley, R. S., and **McCroskey, J. C.** "Opinionated Statements and Attitude Intensity as Predictors of Attitude Change and Source Credibility." *Speech Monographs* 37 (1970): 47–52.

Michalos, A. C. *Improving Your Reasoning.* Englewood Cliffs, New Jersey: Prentice-Hall, Inc., 1970.

Miles, M. B. "Human Relations Training: How a Group Grows." *Teachers College Record* 55 (1953): 90–96.

Milgram, S. "Liberating Effects of Group Pressure." *Journal of Personality and Social Psychology* 1 (1965): 127–34.

————. "Some Conditions of Obedience and Disobedience to Authority." In *Current Studies in Social Psychology,* edited by I. D. Steiner and M. Fishbein. New York: Holt, Rinehart and Winston, Inc., 1965: 243–62.

Miller, G. R., "Studies on the Use of Fear Apeals: A Summary and Analysis." *Central States Speech Journal* 14 (1963): 117–125.

Miller, G. R., and **Burgoon, M.** *New Techniques of Persuasion.* New York: Harper & Row, Publishers, 1973.

————, and **Hewgill, M.** "The Effect of Variations in Non-fluency on Audience Ratings of Source Credibility." *Quarterly Journal of Speech* 50 (1964): 36–41.

————, and **Lobe, J.** "Opinionated Language, Open- and Closed-Mindedness and Responses to Persuasive Communications." *Journal of Communication* 17 (1967): 333–41.

Miller, N. and **Campbell, D. T.** "Recency and Primacy in Persuasion as a Function of the Timing of Speeches and Measurements." *Journal of Abnormal Social Psychology* 59 (1959): 1–9.

Miller, N. E. "The Frustration-Aggression Hypotheis." *Psychological Review* 48 (1941): 337–42.

Miltman, S. "The Relationship Between Anxiety, Learning and Opinion Change." Dissertation, Columbia University, New York, 1965.

Mills, J., and **Aronson, E.** "Opinion Change as a Function of the Communicator's Attractiveness and Desire to Influence." *Journal of Personality and Social Psychology* 1 (1965): 173–177.

Mills, J., Aronson, E., and **Robinson, H.** "Selectivity in Exposure to Information." *Journal of Abnormal and Social Psychology* 59 (1959): 250–53.

Mills, T. M. *The Sociology of Small Groups.* Englewood Cliffs, New Jersey: Prentice-Hall, Inc., 1967.

Milton, G. A. "The Effects of Sex-Role Identification upon Problem Solving Skill." *Journal of Abnormal and Social Psychology* 55 (1957): 219–44.

————. "Sex Differences in Problem Solving as a Function of Role Appropriateness of the Problem Content." *Psychological Reports* 5 (1959): 705–8.

Mintz, N. L. "Effects of Esthetic Surroundings: II. Prolonged and Repeated Experience in a 'Beautiful' and an 'Ugly' Room." *The Journal of Psychology* 41 (1956): 459–66.

Moreno, J. L. "Foundations of Sociometry, an Introduction." *Sociometry* 4 (1941): 15–35.

——. "The Psychodrama." In *Personal Problems and Psychological Frontiers,* edited by J. E. Fairchild. New York: Sheridan House, 1957.

——. "Sociometry and Cultural Order." *Sociometry* 6 (1943): 299–344.

——. *Who Shall Survive?* New York: Beacon House, 1953.

——, and **Kipper, D. A.** "Group Psychodrama and Community Centered Counseling," *Basic Approaches to Group Psychotherapy and Group Counseling,* edited by G. M. Gazda. Springfield, Illinois: Charles C Thomas, Publisher, 1968, pp. 27–79.

Morse, N. C., and Reimer, E. "The Experimental Change of a Major Organizational Variable." *Journal of Abnormal and Social Psychology* 52 (1956): 120–29.

Moult, R. "Experimental Measurement of Clothing as a Factor in the Social Ratings of Selected American Males." *American Sociological Review* 19 (1954): 324–28.

Mowrer, O. H. *The New Group Therapy.* New York: D. Van Nostrand Company, 1964.

Mulder, M. "Communication Structure, Decision Structure and Group Performance." *Sociometry* 23 (1960): 1–14.

Murry, R. I. "A Comparison of Interaction Process Analysis and the Interaction Behavior Measure." Paper presented at the International Communication Association annual convention, April 1972.

Nash, J. F. "The Bargaining Problem." *Econometrica* 18 (1950): 155–62.

Nerbonne, G. P. *The Identification of Speaker Characteristics on the Basis of Aural Cues.* Doctoral Dissertation, Michigan State University, 1967.

Newcomb, T. M. "Attitude Development as a Function of Reference Groups; The Bennington Study." In *Readings in Social Psychology,* edited by E. E. Maccoby, T. M. Newcomb, and E. L. Hartley. New York: Holt, Rinehart and Winston, Inc., 1958, pp. 265–75.

Newman, W. H. *Administrative Action.* Englewood Cliffs, New Jersey: Prentice-Hall, Inc. 1963.

Newport, G. "Study of Attitudes and Leadership Behavior." *Personnel Administration* 25 (1962): 42–46.

North, R. C., Koch, H. E., and Zinnes, D. A. "The Integrative Functions of Conflict." *Journal of Conflict Resolution* 4 (1960): 355–74.

Nye, R. D. *Conflict Among Humans.* New York: Springer Publishing Co., Inc., 1973.

Ober, R. L., Bentley, E. L., and Miller, E. *Systematic Observation of Teaching.* Englewood Cliffs, New Jersey: Prentice-Hall, Inc., 1971.

Olmsted, M. S. "Orientation and Role in the Small Group." *American Sociological Review* 19 (1959): 741–51.

——. *The Small Group.* New York: Random House, Inc., 1959.

Osgood, C. E., and Tannenbaum, P. H. "The Principle of Congruity in the Prediction of Attitude Change." *Psychology Review* 62 (1955): 42–55.

Oskamp, S., and **Perlman, D.** "Factors Affecting Cooperation in the Prisoner's Dilemma Game." *Journal of Conflict Resolution* 9 (1965): 359–74.

———. "The Effect of Vocal Cues on Credibility and Attitude Change." *Western Speech* 34 (1971): 176–84.

Pearce, W. B., and **Conklin, R.** "Nonverbal Vocalic Communication and Perceptions of a Speaker." *Speech Monographs* 38 (1971): 235–41.

Pepinsky, P., Hemphill, J. K., and **Shevitz, R. N.** "Attempts to Lead, Group Productivity, and Morale under Conditions of Acceptance and Rejection." *Journal of Abnormal and Social Psychology* 57 (1958): 47–54.

Pepitone, A., and **Reichling, G.** "Group Cohesiveness and the Expression of Hostility." *Human Relations* 3 (1955): 327–37.

Petrullo, L., and **Bass, B. M.,** eds. *Leadership and Interpersonal Behavior.* New York: Holt, Rinehart and Winston, Inc., 1961.

Pfuetze, P. E. *The Social Self.* New York: Twayne Publishers, Inc., 1954.

Pfeiffer, J. W., and **Jones, J. E.** *A Handbook of Experiences for Human Relations Training,* Vol. II. Iowa City: University Associates Press, 1970.

Phillips, G. M. *Communication and the Small Group.* Indianapolis: The Bobbs-Merrill Co., Inc., 1973.

———. "Reticence: Pathology of the Normal Speaker." *Speech Monographs* 35 (1968): 39–49.

———, and **Erickson, E. C.** *Interpersonal Dynamics in the Small Group.* New York: Random House, Inc., 1970.

Philip, H., and **Dumphy, D.** "Developmental Trends in Small Groups." *Sociometry* 22 (1969): 162–74.

Powers, W. B., and **Wright, D. W.** "Individual Confidence Levels as a Function of Group Size, Task Complexity, and Correctness of Decision." Paper presented at the International Communication Association annual convention, April 1971.

Preston, M. C., and **Heintz, R. K.** "Effects of Participatory Vs. Supervisory Leadership on Group Judgment." *Journal of Abnormal and Social Psychology* 44 (1949): 345–55.

Randall, E. V. "Motivation through Leadership Action." *Personnel Journal* 40 (1968): 104–8.

Rapoport, A. *Two-Person Game Theory.* Ann Arbor: University of Michigan, 1966.

———, and **Chammah, A. M.** *Prisoner's Dilemma: A Study in Conflict and Cooperation.* Ann Arbor: University of Michigan Press, 1965.

Raven, B., and **Kruglanski, A.** "Conflict and Power." In *The Structure of Conflict,* edited by P. Swingle. New York: Academic Press, Inc., 1970, pp. 69–110.

Reusch, J. "The Role of Communication in Therapeutic Transactions." *Journal of Communication* 13 (1963): 131–39.

Robinson, R. D., and **Spaights, E.** "A Study of Attitude Change through Lecture/Discussion Workshops." *Adult Education Journal* 19 (1969): 163–71.

Rokeach, M. "Authority, Authoritarianism, and Conformity." In *Conformity and Deviation,* edited by I. Berg and B. M. Bass. New York: Harper & Row, Publishers, 1961, pp. 230–57.

————. *The Open and Closed Mind*. New York: Basic Books, Inc., Publishers, 1960.

Rogers, C. "Communication: Its Blocking and Its Facilitation." *Etc.: A Review of General Semantics* 9 (1953): 83–88.

————. *On Becoming a Person*. Boston: Houghton Mifflin Company, 1961.

————. *On Encounter Groups*. New York: Harper & Row, Publishers, 1970.

Rogers, D. L. "Correlates of Membership Attraction in Voluntary Associations," Dissertation, University of Wisconsin, 1968,

Rogers, E. M., and **Shoemaker, F. F.** *Communication of Innovations: A Cross-Cultural Approach*. New York: The Free Press, 1971.

Rosegrant, T. "The Effects of Race and Sex on Proxemic Behavior in an Interview Setting." Paper presented at the International Communication Association annual convention, April 1973.

Rosenfeld, L. B. *Human Interaction in the Small Group Setting*. Columbus, Ohio: Charles E. Merrill Publishing Company, 1973.

Sargent, J. F., and **Miller, G. R.** "Some Differences in Certain Communication Behaviors of Autocratic and Democratic Leaders." *Journal of Communication* 21 (1971): 233–52.

Sattler, W. M., and **Miller, N. E.** *Discussion and Conference*. Englewood Cliffs, New Jersey: Prentice-Hall, Inc., 1954.

Schachter, S. "Deviation, Rejection, and Communication." *Journal of Abnormal and Social Psychology* 46 (1951): 190–207.

Scheff, T. J. "A Theory of Social Coordination: Application to Mixed-Motive Games." *Sociometry* 30 (1967): 215–34.

Scheflen, A. E. "Quasi-courtship Behavior in Psychotherapy." *Psychiatry* 28 (1965): 245–57.

————. "The Significance of Posture in Communication Systems." *Psychiatry* 27 (1964): 316–31.

Scheidel, T. M., and **Crowell, L.** "Idea Development in Small Groups." *Quarterly Journal of Speech* 50 (1964): 140–45.

Schein, E. H. "The Development of Organization in Small Problem-solving Groups." Final Report, Sloan Project No. 134, Massachusetts Institute of Technology, 1958.

Schellenberg, J. A. "Group Size as a Factor in Success of Academic Discussion Groups." *Journal of Educational Psychology* 33 (1959): 73–79.

Schultz, W. C. *FIRO: A Three Dimensional Theory of Interpersonal Behavior*. New York: Holt, Rinehart, 1958.

————. "The Interpersonal Underworld." *Harvard Business Review* 36 (1958): 123–35.

————. "What Makes Groups Productive?" *Human Relations* 8 (1955): 429.

Secord, P. "Facial Features and Inference Processes in Interpersonal Perception." In *Person Perception and Interpersonal Behavior*, edited by R. Tagiuri and L. Petrullo. Berkeley: University of California Press, 1958, pp. 300–16.

————, **Bevan, W.,** and **Katz, B.** "The Negro Stereotype and Perceptual Accentuation." *Journal of Abnormal and Social Psychology* 53 (1956): 78–83.

Selvin, H. C. *The Effects of Leadership*. New York: The Free Press, 1960.

Sereno, K., and **Hawkins, G.** "The Effects of Variations in Speaking Nonfluency upon Audience Ratings of Attitude toward the Speech Topic and Speakers' Credibility." *Speech Monographs* 34 (1967): 58–64.

Shapiro, J. G. "Responsibility to Facial and Linguistic Cues." *Journal of Communication* 18 (1968): 11–17.

Shapiro, J. G., Foster, C. P., and **Powell, T.** "Facial and Bodily Cues of Genuineness, Empathy, and Warmth." *Journal of Clinical Psychology* 24 (1968): 233–36.

Shaw, M. E., "Communication Networks." In *Advances in Experimental Social Psychology,* edited by L. Berkowitz. New York: Academic Press, 1964, 1: 111–47.

———. "A Comparison of Individuals and Small Groups in the Rational Solution of Complex Problems." *American Journal of Psychology* 44 (1932): 491–504.

———. "A Comparison of Two Types of Leadership in Various Communication Nets." *Journal of Abnormal and Social Psychology* 50 (1955): 127–34.

———. "Some Effects of Unequal Distribution of Information upon Group Performance in Various Communication Nets." *Journal of Abnormal and Social Psychology* 49 (1954): 547–53.

———, and **Reitan, H. T.** "Attribution of Responsibility as a Basis for Sanctioning Behavior." *British Journal of Social and Clinical Psychology* 8 (1969): 217–26.

———, and **Rothchild, G. H.** "Some Effects of Prolonged Experience in Communication Nets." *Journal of Applied Psychology* 40 (1956): 281–86.

Sherif, M., and **Sherif, C. W.** *An Outline of Social Psychology.* New York: Harper & Row, Publishers, 1956.

———, **Sherif, C.,** and **Nebergall, R.** *Attitude and Attitude Change.* Philadelphia: W. B. Saunders Company, 1965.

Sherwood, J. J. "Self-identity and Referent Others." *Sociometry* 28 (1965): 66–81.

Shontz, F. C. *Perceptual and Cognitive Aspects of Body Experience.* New York: Academic Press, Inc., 1969.

Shore, M. F., and **Massimo, J. L.** "The Alienated Adolescent: A Challenge to the Mental Health Professional." *Adolescence* 4 (1969): 19–34.

Showell, M. "Interpersonal Knowledge and Related Leader Potential." *Journal of Abnormal and Social Psychology* 61 (1960): 87–92.

Simpson, R. H. "Attitudinal Effects of Small Group Discussion: Shifts on Certainty-Uncertainty and Agreement-Disagreement Continua." *Quarterly Journal of Speech* 46 (1960): 415–18.

———. "The Effect of Discussion on Intra-Group Divergencies of Judgment." *Quarterly Journal of Speech* 25 (1939): 546–52.

Slater, P. E. "Role Differentiation in Small Groups." *American Sociological Review* 20 (1955): 300–310.

Smith, A. J. "A Developmental Study of Group Processes." *Journal of Genetic Psychology* 97 (1960): 29–39.

Smith, M. "Social Situation, Social Behavior, Social Group." *Psychological Review* 52 (1945): 224–29.

Sommer, R. "The Distance for Comfortable Conversation: A Further Study." *Sociometry* 25 (1962): 111–16.

――――. *Personal Space*. Englewood Cliffs, New Jersey: Prentice-Hall, Inc. 1969.

――――. "Small Group Ecology." *Psychological Bulletin* 67 (1967): 145–58.

――――. "Studies in Personal Space." *Sociometry* 22 (1959): 274–60.

Stagner, R. *Psychology of Personality*. New York: McGraw-Hill Book & Education Services Group, 1961.

Starkweather, J. "Vocal Communication of Personality and Human Feelings." *Journal of Communication* 11 (1961): 63–72.

Steiner, I. D., and **Field, W. G.** "Role Assignment and Interpersonal Influence." *Journal of Abnormal and Social Psychology* 61 (1960): 239–45.

Steinfatt, T. M., and **Miller, G. R.** "Suggested Paradigms for Research in Conflict Resolution." Paper presented at the Speech Communication Association annual convention, December 1971.

Steinzor, B. "The Spacial Factor in Face to Face Discussion Groups." *Journal of Abnormal and Social Psychology* 45 (1950): 552–55.

Stock, D., and **Thelen, H.** *Emotional Dynamics and Group Culture*. New York: New York University Press, 1958.

Stogdill, R. M. "Personal Factors Associated with Leadership: A Survey of the Literature." *Journal of Psychology* 25 (1948): 35–71.

Stogdill, R. M., and **Koehler, K.** *Measures of Leadership Structure and Organization Change*. Columbus: Ohio State University Research Foundation, 1952.

Stoner, J. A. F. "Risky and Cautious Shifts in Group Decisions: The Influence of Widely Held Values." *Journal of Experimental Social Psychology* 4 (1968): 442–59.

Storey, A. W. "Responsibility Sharing Vs. Strong Procedural Leadership." *Central States Speech Journal* 15 (1964): 285–89.

Sullivan, H. S. *The Interpersonal Theory of Psychiatry*. New York: W. W. Norton & Company Inc., 1953.

Super, J. "Self and Other Semantic Concepts in Relation to Choice of a Vocation." *Journal of Applied Psychology* 51 (1967): 242–46.

Tagiuri, R. "Relational Analysis: An Extension of Sociometric Method with Emphasis upon Social Perception." *Sociometry* 15 (1952); 91–104.

Tannenbaum, R., Weshler, I. R., and **Massarik, F.** *Leadership and Organization: A Behavioral Science Approach*. New York: McGraw-Hill Book & Education Services Group, 1961.

Tead, O. *The Art of Leadership*. New York: McGraw-Hill Book & Education Services Group, 1935.

Thayer, L. O. *Administrative Communication*. Homewood, Illinois: Richard D. Irwin, Inc., 1961.

Thelen, H., and **Dickerman, W.** "Stereotypes and the Growth of Groups." *Educational Leadership* 6 (1949): 309–16.

Theodorson, G. A. "Elements in the Progressive Development of Small Groups." *Social Forces* 31 (1953): 311–20.

Thibaut, J. W., and **Coules, J.** "The Role of Communication in the Reduction of Interpersonal Hostility." *Journal of Abnormal and Social Psychology* 47 (1952): 770–77.

Thibaut, J. W., and **Kelley, H. H.** *The Social Psychology of Groups*. New York: John Wiley & Sons, Inc., 1959.

Thorndike, E. "Euphony and Cacophony of the English Words and Sounds." *Quarterly Journal of Speech* 30 (1944): 201–7.

Toby, J. "Some Variables in Role Conflict Analysis." *Social Forces* 30 (1952): 323–37.

Tokuda, K., and **Jensen, G. D.** "The Leader's Role in Controlling Aggressive Behavior in a Monkey Group." *Primate* 9 (1968): 319–22.

Toulmin, S. *The Uses of Argument.* Cambridge: Cambridge University Press, 1959.

Travis, L. E. "The Effect of a Small Audience upon Eye-Hand Coordination." *Journal of Abnormal and Social Psychology* 20 (1925): 142–46.

Triplett, N. "The Dynamogenic Factors in Pacemaking and Competition." *American Journal of Psychology* 9 (1897): 507–33.

Tuckman, B. W. "Development Sequence in Small Groups." *Psychological Bulletin* 63 (1965): 384–99.

Utterback, W. E. "The Influence of Conference on Opinion." *Quarterly Journal of Speech* 36 (1950): 365–70.

———. "Majority Influence and Cogency of Argument in Discussion." *Quarterly Journal of Speech* 48 (1962): 412–14.

———. "Measuring the Outcome of an Intercollegiate Discussion Conference." *Journal of Communication* 6 (1956): 33–37.

Verba, S. "Leadership: Affective and Instrumental." In *Small Groups and Political Behavior: A Study of Leadership.* Princeton, N. J.: Princeton University Press, 1961, pp. 161–84.

Vinacke, W. E. "Variables in Experimental Games: Toward a Field Theory." *Psychological Bulletin* 71 (1969): 293–318.

———, and **Arkoff, A.** "An Experimental Study of Coalitions in the Triad." *American Sociological Review* 22 (1957): 406–14.

Vroom, V. H., and **Mann, F. C.** "Leader Authoritarianism and Employee Attitudes." *Personnel Psychology* 13 (1960): 125–40.

Wallach, M. A., and **Kogan, N.** "The Roles of Information, Discussion, and Consensus in Group Risk Taking." *Journal of Experimental Social Psychology* 1 (1965): 1–19.

Wallach, M. A., Kogan, N., and **Bem, D. J.** "Diffusion of Responsibility and Level of Risk Taking in Groups." *Journal of Abnormal and Social Psychology* 68 (1964): 263–74.

———. "Group Influence on Individual Risk Taking." *Journal of Abnormal and Social Psychology* 65 (1962): 75–86.

Wallach, M. A., Kogan, N., and **Burt, R. B.** "Can Group Members Recognize the Effect of Group Discussion upon Risk Taking?" *Journal of Experimental Social Psychology* 1 (1965): 379–95.

Walster, E., and **Festinger, L.** "The Effectiveness of 'Overheard' Persuasive Communications." *Journal of Abnormal and Social Psychology,* 65 (1962): 395–402.

Wapner, S., and **Werner, H.,** eds. *The Body Percept.* New York: Random House, Inc., 1965.

Watzlawick, P., Beavin, J. H., and **Jackson, D.** *Pragmatics of Human Communication.* New York: W. W. Norton & Company, Inc., 1967.

Weaver, J. F. "The Effects of Verbal Cueing and Initial Ethos upon Perceived Organization, Retention, Attitude Change, and Terminal Ethos." Dissertation, Michigan State University, 1969.

Wechsler, D. "Conformity and the Idea of Being Well Born." In *Conformity and Deviation,* edited by I. Berg and B. M. Bass. New York: Harper & Row, Publishers, 1961, pp. 412–23.

Weiss, W., and **Fine, B. J.** "The Effect of Induced Aggressiveness on Opinion Change." *Journal of Abnormal and Social Psychology* 52 (1956): 109–14.

———. "Opinion Change as a Function of Some Intra-Personal Attributes of the Communicatees." *Journal of Abnormal and Social Psychology* 51 (1955): 246–53.

Wenburg, J. R., and **Wilmot, W. W.** *The Personal Communication Process.* New York: John Wiley & Sons, Inc., 1973.

Weston, J. R. "Argumentative Message Structure and Prior Familiarity as Predictors of Source Credibility and Attitude Change." Dissertation, Michigan State University, 1967.

Wherry, R. J., and **Fryer, D. H.** "Buddy Ratings: Popularity Contestor Leadership Criteria." *Personnel Psychology* 2 (1949): 147–159.

White, A. "The Patient Sits Down." *Psychosomatic Medicine* 15 (1953): 256–57

White, J. E. "Theory and Method for Research in Community Leadership." *American Sociological Review* 15 (1950): 50–60.

White, R., and **Lippitt, R.** "Leader Behavior and Member Reaction in Three 'Social Climates'." *Group Dynamics.* 3rd ed., edited by D. Cartwright and A. Zander, New York: Harper & Row, Publishers, 1968, pp. 318–35.

Whyte, W. F. *Street Corner Society: The Social Structure of an Italian Slum.* Chicago: University of Chicago Press, 1943.

———. "The Social Structure of the Restaurant." *American Journal of Sociology* 54 (1949): 302–8.

Whyte, W. J., Jr. *The Organization Man.* Garden City, New York: Doubleday & Company Inc., 1957.

Widgery, R. N., and **Webster, B.** "The Effects of Physical Attractiveness Upon Perceived Initial Credibility." *Michigan Speech Association Journal* 4 (1969): 9–19.

Williamson, E. G., and **Hoyt, D.** "Measured Personality Characteristics of Student Leaders." *Educational Psychology Measurement* 12 (1952): 65–78.

Willis, F. N. "Initial Speaking Distance as a Function of the Speaker's Relationship." *Psychonomic Science* 5 (1966): 221–22.

Wischmeier, R. R. "Group-Centered and Leader-Centered Leadership: An Experimental Study." *Speech Monographs* 22 (1955): 43–48.

Wright, J. M., and **Harvey, O. J.** "Attitude Change As a Function of Authoritarianism and Positiveness." *Journal of Personality and Social Psychology* 1 (1965): 177–81.

Wrightsman, L. W., Jr., and **Cook, S. W.** "Factor Analysis and Attitude Change." *Peabody Papers in Human Development* 3 (1965): No. 2.

Zdep, S. M., and **Oakes, W. I.** "Reinforcement of Leadership Behavior in Group Discussion." *Journal of Experimental Social Psychology* 3 (1967): 310–20.

Zelko, H. P. The Business Conference: Leadership and Participation. New York: McGraw-Hill Book & Education Services Group, 1969.

Ziller, R. C. "Four Techniques of Group Decision Making under Uncertainty." Journal of Applied Psychology 4 (1957): 384–88.

Znaniecki, F. "Social Groups as Products of Participating Individuals." American Journal of Sociology 44 (1939): 799–811.

Index